INDIGENOUS IDENTITY AND RESISTANCE

INDIGENOUS
IDENTITY AND RESISTANCE
RESEARCHING THE DIVERSITY OF KNOWLEDGE

EDITED by Brendan HOKOWHITU, Nathalie KERMOAL,
Chris ANDERSEN, Michael REILLY, Anna PETERSEN,
Isabel ALTAMIRANO-JIMÉNEZ and Poia REWI

Published by Otago University Press
PO Box 56 / Level 1, 398 Cumberland Street
Dunedin, New Zealand
Fax: 64 3 479 8385
Email: university.press@otago.ac.nz

First published 2010, Revised (ch. 6) 2011
Volume copyright © Brendan Hokowhitu, Nathalie Kermoal, Chris Andersen,
Michael Reilly, Anna Petersen, Isabel Altamirano-Jiménez and Poia Rewi 2010
Individual chapters copyright © individual authors as listed in contents list 2010

ISBN 978 1 877372 83 4

Publisher: Wendy Harrex
Editor: Georgina McWhirter
Designed and typeset by Christine Buess
Maps p. 91–2: Allan Kynaston
Front cover: J. Allen, 'Prolongation of Rattray Street Jetty',
The Hocken Collections Uare Taoka o Hakena,
University of Otago, Dunedin, album 10, p. 26.

Back cover: *Tipi* outside Faculty of Native Studies,
University of Alberta, Edmonton, 2007.

LIST OF CONTENTS

Acknowledgements 7

Introduction   Indigenous Studies: Research, Identity and Resistance
Brendan Hokowhitu 9

IDENTITY

CHAPTER 1   Mixed Ancestry or Métis?
Chris Andersen 23

CHAPTER 2   'My Poetry is a Fire'
Alice Te Punga Somerville. 37

CHAPTER 3   Culture: Compromise or Perish!
Poia Rewi 55

CHAPTER 4   *piko ka-sôhki-nitohtaman ka-nisitohtaman nêhiyawêwin*
You Must Listen Very Hard to Understand the Cree Language
Naomi McIlwraith. 75

CHAPTER 5   Resisting Language Death: A Personal Exploration
Hana O'Regan. 89

CHAPTER 6   Towards a Model for Indigenous Research
Jim Williams. 107

CHAPTER 7   Rediscovering the Hidden Heritage from Ancient Mangaia
Michael P.J. Reilly 125

RESISTANCE

CHAPTER 8   Indigenous Political Representation and Comparative Research
Janine Hayward. 139

CHAPTER 9   Urban Indigenous Governance Practices
Shalene Jobin Vandervelde 151

CHAPTER 10	The Nationalist Gaze of an Aboriginal Artist *Nathalie Kermoal*	*169*
CHAPTER 12	The Fiction of Post-Colonial Pacific Writers *Sina Vaai*	*179*
CHAPTER 12	Neoliberalism, Racialised Gender and Indigeneity *Isabel Altamirano-Jiménez*	*193*
CHAPTER 13	A Genealogy of Indigenous Resistance *Brendan Hokowhitu*	*207*

Notes *227*

Glossary of Māori Words. *249*

List of Contributors *253*

ACKNOWLEDGEMENTS

University of Alberta

We would like to thank the Provost of the University of Alberta, Carl Amrhein, for all his support, financial and otherwise, for the original Te Tumu initiative in Dunedin, New Zealand (which he and his team took the time to attend with us). As well, we thank Ellen Bielawski (Dean of the Faculty of Native Studies at the University of Alberta) for her leadership and support in the initiative in all its phases; Elder Florida Thunder for her wisdom and advice on cultural protocols while in New Zealand; our colleagues at the Faculty of Native Studies for taking up the slack while we were away in Aotearoa/New Zealand but also for their assistance during the 'Research as Resistance: Exploring the Diversity of Indigenous Studies Approaches' conference in Edmonton that produced many of the papers published in this volume. Likewise, we thank the various academic units on campus at the University of Alberta for their financial support of this conference. Finally, we would like to thank Emily Snyder for her administrative assistance in helping us with the Edmonton conference; her work was crucial to its success and we thank her for her efforts.

University of Otago

We would especially like to thank Alistair Fox, former Pro-Vice-Chancellor, Division of Humanities, and Acting Dean, Te Tumu. He provided financial support for 'Turoua ngā Whetū: Celebrating Indigenous Knowledge', the 2006 colloquium of Indigenous scholars held here in Dunedin, the Te Tumu staff who travelled to Edmonton, and, most importantly, ensured this volume's future at a time when its viability seemed in doubt. Our thanks to all those who made the 2006 colloquium such an exciting gathering of Indigenous scholars. Thanks, too, to everyone who helped with Te Tumu's visits to the University of Alberta, and those who contributed at various times to the development of this volume. Janine Hayward wishes to acknowledge the support of the Law Faculty, University of British Columbia, for their support with this research. The editors thank all the contributors for their passion and commitment. Our thanks also to archaeologist Atholl Anderson, whose commentary helped in the revision of parts of Chapter 5 in 2011. Finally, particular thanks to all those scholars who silently contributed to the quality of this volume by acting as anonymous readers.

> *Turoua koutou katoa, ngā Manawa-taki-hā.*
> *Patuki tahi he ngaru tai tawhiti, he ngaru tai tata.*
> *He rōma mātauranga te māpuna i nuku.*

INTRODUCTION

Indigenous Studies: Research, Identity and Resistance

Brendan Hokowhitu

This collection of essays stems from papers presented at two international colloquia devoted to transcultural understandings of Indigenous Studies, with a particular emphasis on Indigenous identity and resistance. The first was held in New Zealand in 2006, hosted by Te Tumu School of Māori, Pacific and Indigenous Studies at the University of Otago, Dunedin. The second, held in Canada in 2007, was hosted by the Faculty of Native Studies, University of Alberta, Edmonton. Both colloquia concentrated on bringing together Indigenous Studies academics working in Canada, New Zealand and the broader Pacific, in the hope of sharing, comparing and creating research conversations that transcended the imperial boundaries of the colonial 'nations' in which we are located. The colloquia aimed at facilitating a consciousness and space that would foster and enable discussion on what a transcultural 'Indigenous Studies' discipline might resemble.

In this edited collection we hope to draw the reader's attention to the multifaceted nature of Indigenous Studies by specifically questioning in what ways local Indigenous contexts relate to each other. First and foremost, however, it is important to recognise that as a canonical field Indigenous Studies does not exist. Its genesis has been *ad hoc* (yet organic) in the sense that the amorphous concept of Indigenous Studies has arisen out of pre-established local departments, such as Māori Studies in New Zealand and Native or First Nations Studies in Canada. Such departments remain the strongholds in the various local contexts, while Indigenous Studies *per se* is a very recent auxiliary to localised core curricula. Typically, local departments have developed as subdivisions of larger faculties that have their own established canons, such as Anthropology. Indigenous Studies thus lacks any semblance of a coherent genealogy from which it can build, in large part because it has borrowed multilaterally from various disciplines, while trying to account for a diverse range of Indigenous contexts. This is not to say that local departments necessarily lack a coherent genealogy within their own distinct context. However the broader genealogical incongruence and orphan-like history suggests that the genesis of a universal Indigenous Studies is at best embryonic.

Although the timing of this collection reflects a growing interest in the conceptualisation of Indigenous Studies as a discipline, the will to move beyond local Māori, Aboriginal or Native Studies departments to develop the canons of Indigenous Studies remains ambiguous. A handful of Indigenous scholars have attempted to conceive the underpinning tenets of a 'universal' Indigenous Studies, while others have conducted comparative work across colonial contexts, theorised at a global level and/or examined the impact of world events upon Indigenous people. Indeed, the inevitable impulse to produce internationally recognised scholarship within Western academia has compelled many Indigenous writers to theorise their local context via dialogues understandable across colonial contexts. As pointed out by Linda Tuhiwai Smith, 'the movement has developed a shared international language or discourse which enables Indigenous activists to talk to each other across their cultural differences'.[1] Yet such discourses are often epistemologically limited because of the ontological importance of local contexts, languages and cultures. Moreover, as an unfortunate consequence of the need to share through 'international languages', often Indigenous Studies scholars find themselves in the unenviable position of unearthing common-ground (i.e., 'Indigenous Studies') within the ontological violence of colonialism and, indeed, in the languages of the coloniser. In this catch-22 dilemma, inevitably loss occurs. As Naomi McIlwraith outlines in this volume, 'A common struggle is to translate a concept from one language to another: some essential quality in the original language escapes the colonial language's ability to express it'.

In this collection, as with the nebulous concept of Indigenous Studies in general, 'truth' is situated locally. Truth becomes a lived concept beyond and in resistance to the more detached scientific use of the term; beyond and in resistance to the impersonal structures of research as a tool for 'discovery'. It is the subjective indigenisation of what has typically been conceived of as objective, whether that be time, history or space, that will challenge the notion of one monolithic knowledge. Indigenous truth here is not accidental or objective, it does not come at the conclusion of an argument; it is a requisite of Indigenous subjectivity. Ironically, the acceptance that truth is amorphous must be an underpinning canon of the developing discipline of Indigenous Studies (discipline, in this sense, meaning an ambiguous space where certain knowledges are tacit and taken for granted, whilst other knowledges are to be challenged, honed and produced).

Epistemic resistance and transcultural Indigenous Studies

This volume reflects the tacit and ambiguous space of comparative Indigenous Studies. One often unspoken tenet of Indigenous Studies is the epistemic challenge to Western academe that Indigenous knowledges bring to bear. Indeed, some have constructed the aim of post-colonial Indigenous thought as the liberation of universal thought and, whilst Indigenous Studies remains irresolutely grounded in the shifting soil of Western academe, the transcendence required for such lofty objectives is truly paradigmatic and metaphysical. No mean feat, yet such are the stakes if Indigenous Studies is to move beyond tokenism. Gandhi no less,

> ... implicitly defined his ultimate goal as the liberation of the British from the history and psychology of British colonialism .. the battle he was fighting for the minds of men was actually a universal battle to discover the softer side of human nature, the so-called non-masculine self of man relegated to the forgotten zones of the Western concept.[2]

Many of the authors in this collection likewise put forth challenges to universalising notions of truth. Sina Vaai, for instance, discusses the work of Epeli Hau'ofa, who passed away in January 2009. In the theoretical essay 'Our Sea of Islands', Vaai writes, 'Hau'ofa called for a liberation of the mind, especially amongst Pacific Islanders, in the way that Pacific island nations and their inhabitants were seen and represented' and in particular 'the vastness and richness of the Oceanian "pasts", in which Islanders interacted in large exchange communities across this great "sea of islands"'. Hau'ofa's work reverberates in the words of the poet Vernice Wineera, as analysed by Alice Te Punga Somerville, where 'the ocean itself is a place that both manifests and produces history'. Te Punga Somerville also contends the poetry of Robert Sullivan 'refuses that the history of voyaging to Aotearoa is a one-way process'. Similarly operating at the epistemic level, Isabel Altamirano-Jiménez resists the neo-liberal construction of the global economy where the world is inhabited by individuals 'who increasingly relate to each other only as consumers'. Such neo-liberal governance is read in particular reference to human rights discourses 'which often champions the freedom of individual action' leaving Indigenous peoples' resistance struggles 'limited to the local construction of human rights' "universals" ignoring other place-situated ways of resolving conflict and conferring social responsibilities'.

Epistemic challenges do not merely migrate West, however. As authors in this collection point out, it is not only the confrontation of colonial knowledges that needs to take place. For a healthy Indigenous Studies to develop, Indigenous peoples and cultures must also endure criticism and self-reflection. As Poia Rewi writes, '*kia ora te tikanga, me takahi te tikanga*. That is, in order for culture to survive, culture must be transgressed'. Chris Andersen's use of Bourdieu to describe the tacit imposition of 'truth', which enables the *order of things*, challenges Indigenous peoples to question their own paradigmatic assumptions. Andersen argues that 'the perseverance of the legitimacy of race in Aboriginal communities rests on the fact that those of us who imbue race with symbolic capital … remain unaware that we are doing so and thus, fail to perceive anything illegitimate about its use'. Altamirano-Jiménez argues for a more complex understanding of inequity, pointing out that 'gender discrimination within Indigenous communities while real … is constructed as an anomaly inherent to Aboriginal cultures'. My own chapter describes dominant conceptualisations of Indigenous resistance as reactionary in the face of colonial and neocolonial oppression leading to the internalisation of colonisation's psychology and, subsequently, the commonly heard idiom on the Indigenous academic circuit, 'decolonising the mind'. Such analyses may be alluring within a mentality of guilt, however the assertion of Indigenous self-determination in constant referral to the colonising Other merely serves to re-establish the power structures themselves.

With these provocations, this collection thus promotes the tenet of 'epistemic challenge' as a key pillar for the development of the currently ambiguous discipline of Indigenous Studies. Such challenges will confront how the world has been constructed within universalising discourses and under the colonial gaze. These challenges cannot be directed merely outward, but must also create a space where Indigenous peoples can be self-critical about the construction of their own realities.

The second key pillar of Indigenous Studies this collection puts forth is the notion of 'transcultural Indigenous dialogue'. Put simply, this is the production of a transcultural space where locally indigenised truths are tabled for analyses that go beyond 'discovery' or 'conclusion' to an imaginative realm that recognises the multiplicity of Indigenous subjectivities. This is not necessarily aimed at forming an 'oppositional collective identity' focused on contesting the social inequalities of colonisation or to breaking down the binary of the Indigenous Other and Western Self. Rather, it is towards a collective determined by issues of Indigenous existentialism, where Indigenous situatedness is emphasised, including embodied notions of place and culture that dismiss attempts to locate Indigenous people in the exotic other. Any transcultural Indigenous collective thus needs to be based on difference and contradiction. This situated fluidity in what it means to be

'Indigenous' should underpin Indigenous Studies as a discipline above all else.

The space imagined here therefore needs necessarily to be a place of relativity, multiplicity of truth and ambiguity, as opposed to a location that promotes singularity of truth and conclusion. Here the Celtic Indigenous formation of 'The Fifth Province' and other Indigenous spaces such as *marae* (courtyard) for Māori and other Pacific peoples and the sweatlodge for First Nations peoples can be imagined as physical metaphors for intellectual domains. The Fifth Province, in particular, was an imagined space 'where one could detach from provincial conflicts, divisions and contradictions in order to imagine new solutions. It was an imagined domain where oppositions could co-exist. It was a domain which celebrated ambivalence and difference rather than clarity and uniformity'.[3]

Identity

This book is divided into two sections, awkwardly named 'Identity' and 'Resistance', following the themes of the two colloquia. The first colloquium focused on identity, with the sub-themes of 'land', 'language' and 'lore'. The second was named 'Research as Resistance'. While acknowledging that 'Identity' is etymologically cumbersome given that it can mean everything and nothing, in this collection identity is defined as a 'problematic', that is, as the problematics of Indigenous identity construction. Identity is not referred to in the monolithic sense where, for instance, 'Māori identity' is associated with singularity of meaning. In contrast, 'Māori identity' in this collection refers to the inherent ambiguity of such coinage, which thus produces the problematic to be *re*searched, probed and *re*constructed.

As the Indigenous interpretations of 'identity' in this collection demonstrate, how Indigenous peoples come to define themselves, represent markers of their indigeneity and govern themselves within the often contradictory situatedness of their existence, points to a process of intellectual interrogation that removes the Indigenous subject from the colonial binary. As such, a central question of an Indigenous Studies discipline will be 'are people born Indigenous or do we become Indigenous?' In effect, to what extent has and does social construction and Indigenous facticity (the situation colonised Indigenous peoples face) determine how Indigenous peoples have been (mis)represented and how Indigenous people choose to represent themselves? Does Indigenous existence precede Indigenous essence? How do Indigenous peoples interpret authenticity and, further, what are the inauthentic identities Indigenous peoples have tethered themselves to in the unsteady waters since colonisation? And so the problematic of Indigenous identity gains the limelight.

In the first chapter of this section, entitled 'Mixed Ancestry or Métis?', Andersen describes the power of Canada's colonial nation-state, specifically its juridical system, in constituting 'Métis' as a category of indigeneity. Here Andersen's argument centres on the unrealisability of power's ubiquitousness in 'that nothing Indigenous exists "outside" them … the fundamental power of modernity/colonialism is not that as Indigenous people we live in *it*, but rather, that it lives in *us*'. In particular, Andersen points out the internalisation of the *symbolic violence* of race, including Canadian constitutional categories like 'Indian', 'Inuit' and 'Métis', and bemoans 'the absurdity of attempting to box such diverse nations of peoples into three neat categories'. Te Punga Somerville in her chapter '"My Poetry is a Fire": Wineera and Sullivan Writing Fire from Hawai'i' continues on the theme of self-definition particularly in relation to physical occupation of place. Through the writings of the Māori poets Robert Sullivan and Vernice Wineera, Te Punga Somerville argues that telling, singing and writing are forms of maintaining *ahi kā* (concept of maintaining cooking fires on land to maintain possession through continuous physical habitation). She challenges, 'If language is a form of assertion, a form of *fire*, then the massive number of Māori who do not reside on their traditional homelands are not necessarily cut out of the equation of asserting an active relationship with place … emphasising the possibility of imaginative occupation through telling stories'. Like Andersen, Te Punga Somerville challenges us to think about the unspoken frames through which both Indigenous peoples and non-Indigenous peoples have come to construct indigeneity: 'Sullivan centres a claim that Māori are ocean people: voyagers, navigators, travellers; deeply embedded in specific land because of, not despite, previous migrations'.

Questions surrounding markers of indigeneity continue in the third chapter by Rewi, 'Culture: Compromise or Perish!' Central to Rewi's deliberations is the question of whether cultural transformation is inevitable to ensure the survival of Indigenous cultures exposed to 'the elements' of the colonial context. 'Living in a multicultural society', Rewi points out, 'raises difficult questions over the processes and practices that are required to protect those cultural observances that have been passed down through the generations of Indigenous peoples'. Rewi's chapter focuses on *whaikōrero*, the art of Māori oratory that, prior to colonisation, 'was the primary medium of expressing opinion and of presenting topics for discussion'. Rewi brings to the forefront a number of topical issues in relation to *whaikōrero*, such as gender, time constraints, the use of English within *whaikōrero* and the propagation of *whaikōrero* in the modern workplace.

Like Rewi, McIlwraith examines the impact of colonisation on a key Indigenous identity marker. Her chapter '*piko ka-sôhki-nitohtaman ka-nisitohtaman nêhiyawêwin*: You Must Listen Very Hard to Understand the Cree Language', centralises the importance of language to Indigenous identity. McIlwraith argues that language loss is a 'fracturing process for Indigenous peoples', however she concludes optimistically, providing an example of Indigenous language production. To enable transcultural analysis, McIlwraith's chapter is followed by Hana O'Regan's piece, 'Resisting Language Death – A Personal Exploration'. Like McIlwraith, O'Regan focuses on a programme of Indigenous language revitalisation and regeneration initiated and propagated by members of Kāi Tahu, her own *iwi* (people, nation). The programme named '*Kotahi Mano Kāika, Kotahi Mano Wawata* – A Thousand Homes, A Thousand Dreams' envisaged 1000 homes speaking the Māori language by 2025. O'Regan personalises this Indigenous language revival programme through a reflective account of her own experiences as a second language learner.

In the next chapter, 'Towards a Model for Indigenous Research', Jim Williams discusses the concerns that arise when researchers interpret Indigenous knowledge. Williams focuses on specific published examples, highlighting the incongruity between 'etic' and 'emic' approaches. For researchers, Williams prescribes incorporation of both approaches, terming such a method an 'etmic' study entailing 'a familiarity with the strengths and shortcomings of both perspectives, arriving at a point where the researcher can see both the wood and the trees'. Following on from this, in the final chapter of this section, Michael Reilly *re*interprets Indigenous cultural understanding in 'Rediscovering the Hidden Heritage from Ancient Mangaia'. Reilly follows the intellectual relationship between an Indigenous Mangaian, Mamae, and a missionary, Gill, through a particular story that Mamae wrote, which Gill later translated and published in 1876. In looking at both the Mangaian and English texts in unison, Reilly expounds on the importance of subjectivity and context in relation to interpreting historical Indigenous material. Reilly argues, as 'part of a larger body of ethnographic writing, the dominance of Gill's own version reflects the hegemony being assumed by Europe' and, in particular, Gill's translation 'speaks to the aspirations of mission societies as well as European colonies, such as New Zealand, to found their own versions of empire in the islands of the Pacific'. For Indigenous Studies, such *re*search has become a foundational component, breathing Indigenous life and voice into the misrepresentations of Indigenous identities, uncovering, in Sidney Moko Mead's words, 'Te Wahi Ngaro (The Lost Portion of the Heritage)'. At the same time, Reilly also acknowledges the complexity of the colonial condition in arguing that a more intricate interplay between the two texts was occurring that reflected the two writers' personal collaborations as church ministers.

Resistance

'After colonisation', Vaai articulates in this collection, 'comes the desire to be liberated, to write out the resilience of Pacific peoples and their ability to survive the impact of imperial domination'. For Reilly, the *re*interpretation of Mamae's vernacular text in the archives 'evokes the resistance of Indigenous languages which continue to be heard in spite of the dominance of colonising languages such as English'. To paraphrase Foucault then, given colonisation's coercive force, do you really think Indigenous people would *not* resist it? Like Andersen above, Foucault argues that people cannot resist power structures because they fail to perceive them in their ubiquitous guises. Foucault's critics argue that such positioning disables agency and therefore denies the possibility of resistance. The point is possibly moot in the colonial context given the visibility of colonial atrocities: the violent coercive arm of colonialism and the cultural wreckage it entailed was hardly invisible. Taking stock, however, in the neocolonial context means that Indigenous Studies needs to again reassess the power structures that *live in us*. The markers of resistance that Indigenous self-determination movements have been anchored to, such as land, language and culture, have been laid out so clearly along the colonial binary of coloniser/colonised, that resistance through these key concepts has to some extent conventionalised Indigenous Studies. As Te Punga Somerville imaginatively argues, it is perhaps how we currently frame Indigenous resistance strategies that speaks to how colonial power *lives within us*. In contemporary dominant discourses, Somerville argues, there is a 'focus on Māori in terms of "Indigeneity"... and connection to land rather than in terms of migration and connection to water'.

The chapters in the identity section thus all include elements of resistance that, through colonisation, have come to be constitutive of Indigenous identities. As Linda Tuhiwai Smith outlines, 'The strength of the movement is to be found in the examples of how communities have mobilised locally, the grassroots development. It is at the local level that indigenous cultures and the cultures of resistance have been born and nurtured over generations'.[4] Many Indigenous communities, therefore, have become communities of resistance and thus resistance has come to frame the individual and community identities. As shown in Andersen's chapter, for example, '[b]eing Métis moved from a statement of ancestry to an assumed corporate identity around which to mobilise and fight'. Likewise, as Nathalie Kermoal points out, 'During the rise of Aboriginal nationalism in the 1960s in Canada, an artist like Alex Janvier would sign his work using only his treaty number. For him, this was an expression of identity, of his difference and was, in fact, an act of resistance'.

Analyses in Janine Hayward's chapter look at how Indigenous identity has, in part, been determined by the historical modes of political representation chosen or forced upon Indigenous peoples. Hayward outlines activist and author Gerald Taiaiake Alfred's view, for instance, of an impasse between Aboriginal nation citizenry and being a citizen of the Canadian nation. Thus, for Indigenous peoples, the interface between self-governance and citizenship within the colonial nation predicates a political identity that determines how Indigenous people both represent themselves and are represented by others, politically and symbolically.

As the authors in this section demonstrate, one of the primary facets of Indigenous Studies has been the study of the political and symbolic terrain of colonial societies, including the scoping of methods of resistance appropriate to various genealogies of subjugation and the understanding of resistance teleologically. Kermoal argues via Emma Larocque: 'to appreciate Native resistance we need to understand their "long walk" as they have experienced it and as they have told it and now as they are recording it'. In the first chapter of this section, 'Indigenous Representation and the Value of Comparative Research', Hayward foregrounds much of what follows by historicising Indigenous political representation in both Canada and New Zealand. Since the late 1860s, Māori have made use of legislated representation through the guaranteed Māori seats, whilst First Nations have negotiated at the federal level on a case-by-case basis. Hayward deliberates that the variant colonial histories, specifically Indigenous engagement with and exclusion from the escalating nation-state and the degree the indigene became inculcated as a 'British subject', foretold the contemporary political contexts. She moves to explore the mutual exclusivity of self-government and guaranteed representation for First Nations in Canada and Māori in New Zealand, asking 'whether, in principle, it is problematic for First Nations to have guaranteed representation as Māori do and for Māori to exercise some "law-making" capacity through self-government as do some First Nations?' From the macro-historical view of Indigenous governance, Shalene Jobin Vandervelde's chapter, 'Urban Indigenous Governance Practices', moves to a situationally specific example of Indigenous community governance, discussed via a non-profit urban-based Indigenous agency, the Bent Arrow Traditional Healing Society. For Jobin Vandervelde, 'one of the distinguishing factors for Aboriginal peoples living in the city is not having access to their own land base'. With the increasing numbers of Indigenous peoples in urban environments, communities such as Bent Arrow are organically forming to build on 'the strengths of Aboriginal children, youth and their families to enable them to develop spiritually, emotionally, physically and mentally so they can walk proudly in both Aboriginal and non-Aboriginal communities'.

In Kermoal's chapter, 'The Nationalist Gaze of an Aboriginal Artist', the theme of *re*search touched on by Reilly is expanded upon, contesting that 'women's contemporary Aboriginal art is part of a movement to re-write history, born from the desire to correct misrepresentation and stereotypes and the necessity to re-establish an aboriginal female knowledge'. Kermoal positions Indigenous women's art, specifically the Mi'kmaq artist Teresa Marshall's *Elitekey*, in terms of social voice: 'the displaced and dormant voices ... the female voice, one that has been muffled first by the colonial history of Canada and then by the androcentric discourses of political leaders ... contesting Canadian history's meta-narrative'. In her chapter entitled 'The Fiction of Post-Colonial Pacific Writers', Vaai reflects the challenges to colonial meta-history confronted by Kermoal, but via the medium of fiction and in relation to the Pacific. Through the telling of 'our own' Indigenous stories, Vaai argues that an Indigenous sense of self erased through colonisation is reaffirmed: 'In the contemporary era of post-colonialism', Vaai writes, 'Empire and its consequences have not only been addressed but also aggressively assaulted in the fiction emanating from this region ... a literature of resistance, reassertion and reclaiming is the quest for identity, often connected to and grounded in the land or place'. To situate her analysis, Vaai discusses the notion of 'turning the inside out' through Sudesh Mishra's play *Ferringhi* and Sia Figiel's performance poem *The Centre*, calling upon the 'need to celebrate' the multi-faceted, multi-voiced and fluid nature of the Pacific self, leading to a process of healing and forgiveness.

In the penultimate chapter, 'Neoliberalism, Racialised Gender and Indigeneity', Altamirano-Jiménez argues that, combined, *neo-liberal* ideology and the discourse of human rights 'perpetuate a hierarchy and a global codification of peoples and places that are within and outside of global progress'. Violence and gender discrimination against Aboriginal women, for example, are typically demarcated as 'a cultural problem ... that only happens in certain places and in certain cultures'. In depicting a different subjugatory reality, Altamirano-Jiménez describes a terminus of social, economic and political power relations where 'systematic gender differences, uneven access to property rights, resources and the legal system' disqualify Aboriginal women as subjects. The construction of 'Indigenous problems' as beyond neocolonial power structures invites state intervention 'to rectify such anomalies', while concealing the power structures that actually produce them. As a clear example, Altamirano-Jiménez argues that 'while the Human Rights Act is envisioned to enable Aboriginal women to challenge Aboriginal governments', in actuality, the system 'prevents these same women from challenging federal government legislation and policies'. The final chapter of this collection, 'A Genealogy of Indigenous Resistance', problematises the common discourses underpinning Indigenous resistance and, therefore, the basic tenets by which Indigenous identity has come to be marked. Employing an existentialist lens, a genealogy of Indigenous resistance specific to New Zealand is traced.

Conclusion

This collection of essays reasserts the right of Indigenous peoples to theorise and to think with reference to the facticity of colonisation, but grounded in the will to be culturally self-reflective. Rewi asks to what extent the authenticity of Indigenous cultures has become compromised by the realities of colonisation, while Kermoal points out the inauthentic quest for authenticity located in the gaze upon the works of contemporary Aboriginal artists, where often art is not deemed 'Indian' enough. According to Altamirano-Jiménez, the neocolonial free market and human rights discourses 'work together to codify people and places that are within and outside of a modernist notion of progress'. In essence then, this collection helps claim back the moral space disenfranchised through colonisation, where Indigenous peoples were constituted as lying beyond the moral reason of modernity. In claiming the epistemic complexity to determine, put on the table and debate what notions like identity, resistance, research and authenticity mean to Indigenous peoples, the writers in this collection reassert an Indigenous moral space.

At the heart of the intellectual cultural exchanges that provided the impetus for this book was the determination to bring together academics focused on local Indigenous meanings within the broader context. Whilst these transcultural exchanges implicitly de-legitimate colonial notions such as 'the nation' and encourage discussions about indigeneity that move beyond imperial boundaries, it is extremely important that 'Indigenous Studies' as a discipline does not become reductive, lest we follow the universalising footsteps of European modernism. And here I am mindful of Robert Young's critique of the best (and worst) part of postcolonial theory that, 'despite its espousal of subaltern resistance, scarcely values subaltern resistance that does not operate according to its own secular terms'.[5] Such inattention to the epistemologies of local Indigenous cultures inherently devalues the very concept of indigeneity because of its localised tethering to place, identity and language. Thus, the epistemic autonomy of Māori Studies, Native Studies and Pacific Studies, for instance, must remain, with, perhaps, the adjunct of 'Indigenous Studies'. It is a time, therefore, not to dislocate local knowledges in favour of universalising discourses, but rather for Indigenous peoples to theorise their existence both locally and through the tacit and ambiguous space of Indigenous Studies – a space where the complexity of the 'glocal' Indigenous positioning demands and will determine the development of a more coherent transcultural Indigenous Studies discipline.

IDENTITY

CHAPTER ONE

Mixed Ancestry or Métis?

Chris Andersen

In September 2003, the first court case on the constitutional boundaries of Métis rights (*R.* vs. *Powley*) came before the Supreme Court of Canada. The case attracted attention from diverse members of Canada's legal community, including the federal and provincial governments, Aboriginal organisations and various hunting, fishing and conservation organisations. The question before the *Powley* court was a narrowly technical one about the right of 'Métis' to hunt for food in the Great Lakes region of Northern Ontario, but the decision was more broadly positioned as a test case for defining the boundaries of Métis identity[1] and thus setting the boundaries of who could be accorded Métis constitutional protections. The eventual decision was applauded and widely viewed as a 'slam dunk' for Métis litigants and, potentially, for Métis everywhere (who precisely this refers to, however, is the subject of this chapter). If the victory was one viewed as clear-cut however, the actual definition of 'Métis' was more ambiguous: 'given the vast territory of what is now Canada, we should not be surprised to find that different groups of Métis exhibit their own distinctive traits and traditions. This diversity among groups of Métis may enable us to speak of Métis "peoples"...'.[2]

This chapter examines the power of a colonial nation-state generally, and the courts specifically, in shaping the contemporary constitution of 'Métis' as a category of indigeneity. My argument is based on the notion that colonial nation-states are so elementally powerful that nothing Indigenous exists 'outside' them. Our indigeneity (as Aboriginals, Māori, Hawaiians, Sāmoans, etc.) is thus constitutively shaped by the power within which our Indigenous societies remain embedded. This argument is deliberately provocative although not disrespectfully so – its intellectual impulse is grounded in the observation that the fundamental power of modernity/colonialism is not that as Indigenous people we live in *it*, but rather, that it lives in *us*.[3] Two of the ways it lives in us, I argue here, include our internalisation of the *symbolic violence* of race upon which the 'colonial divide'

: 23

between Europeans and Indigenous peoples rests; and our internalisation of Canadian constitutional categories like 'Indian', 'Inuit' and 'Métis' in common parlance. This latter internalisation is, I will also argue, exacerbated by the power of Canadian law in shaping more broadly the taxonomies we use to think and talk about indigeneity in Canadian society.

Perched on the analytical points of these two internalisations, this chapter is presented in four parts. The first explores the policies of the British imperial and Canadian nation-state governments that removed Indigenous people from the traditional communities and territories claimed by the Mi'kmaq in the Maritime provinces of (what has become) Eastern Canada (specifically Nova Scotia and New Brunswick). Exploring this history is necessary not least because Mi'kmaq ancestry constitutes a central pillar of contemporary claims of Maritime 'Métis'. Such state policies have, as numerous scholars point out, exerted horrendous impacts on Indigenous communities and play a large role in the inability of those recently self-identifying as 'Métis' to gain political voice (or more pragmatically, social programmes and benefits) as First Nations/'Indians'.

The second part explores Indigenous internalisations of the symbolic violence of race to show how a term used to identify a nationalist constituency – Métis – is so easily conflated with mere mixed Aboriginal/non-Aboriginal ancestry. The third part demonstrates the power of this symbolic violence in the specific empirical context of the Maritimes. The final part discusses the ways in which the symbolic power of Canadian law exacerbates and worse, seemingly legitimises this conflation. My intention is not simply to delegitimise their political struggles or critique their self-identification choices. This chapter seeks more fundamentally to understand the conditions – both material and discursive – under which Maritime Indigenous collectivities have begun to perceive and employ 'Métis' as a self-descriptor of their mixed Indigenous/European ancestry. It is to the issue of colonialism in the Maritimes that we now turn.

Colonialism in the Maritimes of Eastern Canada

The area of geographical focus for this chapter, the Maritimes, encompasses much of the southern coastline of Eastern Canada and includes the provinces of Prince Edward Island, New Brunswick and Nova Scotia. This region was home to (among other Indigenous peoples) the Mi'kmaq and the Maliseet. Wicken argues that evidence on early Mi'kmaq society is scant, largely due to the fact that the Mi'kmaq had little sustained interaction (other than trade) with European intruders during the period prior to the eighteenth century.[4] The Mi'kmaq's pre-existing marine-

Map of Canada relating to the Métis population. Nuno Luzio

based seasonal economies were well-positioned to fill a niche in the economic desires of European fishermen and whalers[5] – indeed, Mi'kmaq territories were considered strategic by European imperialists at least partly because of their adjacency to the rich Atlantic fish stocks.[6]

Upon the signing of the Treaty of Utrecht in 1713,[7] the British made clear that they viewed their own claims to Maritime territory as superior to pre-existing Indigenous claims. Wicken argues that the Treaty of Utrecht exerted a profound impact on the social world of the Mi'kmaq and their allies in that it marked the beginning of more formal British attempts to assert political control over Indigenous territories.[8] British intrusions led to armed conflicts by the Mi'kmaq and their Wabanaki allies and, in so doing, changed the very nature of warfare itself: '... the defeat of the French in Acadia in 1710 and the advent of English settlement had put another cast entirely on the conflict ... [Mi'kmaq] and Malecite were now fighting for their land and for their very survival as a people'.[9]

Several features of seventeenth-century French colonial policy make this geographical region relevant for studying the conflation of Métis with mixed

Indigenous/non-Indigenous ancestry and will be expanded upon in part three. For our purposes, however, the impact of British and later Canadian forms of colonialism on the formation of Indigenous collectivities in the region is particularly important. Tobias argued famously that Canada's 'Indian Policy' was based on a three-pronged, teleological approach of protection,[10] civilisation and assimilation. Canadian Indian policy was rooted in pre-confederation policies carried over from the exigencies of the eighteenth-century imperial rivalries between France and Britain that shaped much of the political character of the region.[11] Milloy argues, however, that it was not until the mid-nineteenth century that the predecessor of the Canadian government gained formal control. Prior to then, 'Indian tribes were de facto, self-governing. They had exclusive control over their population, land and finances'.[12] More cynically, the Royal Commission on Aboriginal Peoples suggests a different take:

> Former enemies of the victorious British, the Mi'kmaq and Maliseet, were simply ignored, left to find their own way in the rapidly changing world. Dispossessed of much of their land, separated from resources and impoverished, they were also ravaged by disease and in the early 1800s they seemed to be on the road to virtual extinction.[13]

Tobias argues that by the beginning of the nineteenth century – coterminous with the end of their inter-empire rivalries with France and the United States and the waning need for Indigenous assistance, British colonial governors began to perceive and position Indigenous communities as 'impediments to progress'. Part of their attempts to 'civilise' those they designated as Indians included a reliance on Christianisation (a tactic already long-used in Eastern Canadian Indigenous communities) as well as the establishment of Indian reserves as a means of turning them into farmers. Tobias suggests that these efforts were made in an attempt to 'help' Native communities withstand the onslaught of European civilisation. These attempts at civilisation soon turned to full-blown attempts to assimilate, the foremost avenue of which was the 1876 Indian Act and the previous legislative enactments it consolidated.[14]

Canadian policies like the Indian Act exacerbated the historical movement of formerly status Indian individuals (usually women) and their families out of the reserve Indian 'bands' created under the auspices of the Indian Act. One cause of this was the enfranchisement[15] (voluntary or otherwise) of those categorised as status Indians, which in turn required their removal from their reserve. Enfranchisement in fact served as a key plank for Canadian state assimilation policies and was 'bestowed' upon those who gained a professional degree, served in the armed forces or left their reserves for more than five years.[16] Moreover, by the twentieth century, status Indians could be removed by the Indian Agent without their consent and, by the middle part of the twentieth century, thousands of First Nations people had been stripped of their status and required to move off their reserves and away from their families.

These policies constituted a direct manifestation of the gender discrimination inherent in the Indian Act provisions, well-documented elsewhere,[17] which essentially came in three forms: matrimonial property, community membership and political representation.[18] The legal movement of Indigenous individuals and their families between categories also necessitated a geographical move. The main cause of this movement was the gender discrimination that applied to status and band membership for non-status Indian women. Status Indian women who married non-status men (whether Métis, Inuit or non-Aboriginal altogether) automatically lost their status under the Indian Act and, with it, various privileges (meagre though they were). Conversely, males categorised as status Indians faced no penalties upon their marriage to a non-status woman (whether 'white' or otherwise). Indeed, Jamieson notes, they 'may marry whom they please without penalty and indeed by so doing confer on their non-Indian spouses and children full Indian rights and status'.[19]

Banishment from Indian reserves resulted in women moving into off-reserve communities. Over subsequent generations, thousands of 'non-status' Indians in Eastern Canada left or were forced out of their communities. More recently, the descendants of these families have banded together to pursue political objectives. Though many 'detribalised' individuals and collectivities[20] would rather be using the First Nation to which they were historically attached, this option is no longer available to them, since after 1985 Indian bands' right to control their community membership was recognised through Bill C-31.[21]

As elsewhere, the enactment of Indian Act legislation in the Maritimes created a situation in which, generations later, numerous individuals continue to possess familial and kinship ties to relatives living in reserve band communities but lack any formal legal relationship. As such, they are denied not only the benefits that accrue from band membership but must bear the indignity of being defined as something other than what they are (and, as I argue in the conclusion, as something other than what they might be). Turpel writes poignantly,

> [a] First Nations woman cannot necessarily look to her mother, grandmother or older aunties to help her because she may have been forced to leave the community through discrimination. Moreover, she may now have trouble

reconnecting because of her experiences in a foreign culture, because poverty has led her to equate being a First Nations person with being worthless and because of lost self-esteem due to racism commonly experienced outside the community. She may also be excluded because her Indian Act-elected government will not let her return.[22]

Though not the focus of this chapter, Turpel and others[23] explore powerfully the ways in which a patriarchal value system synonymous with British colonialism devalued the status of women and marginalised their political power. As I explore further in the next section, the symbolic power of patriarchy is not the only discourse to invest itself in Indigenous communities and in the associated formation of contemporary Indigenous subjectivities, there is also that of race. It is to that issue that I now turn.

'Mētis' and the symbolic violence of race

The term 'Métis' is often (though for reasons I go into below, not just) associated with the Métis Nation. Although historians have traced the roots of Métis to eighteenth-century intermarriage between fur traders and Indigenous women in the Great Lakes region,[24] 'Métis Nation' Métis tend to emphasise instead the birth of 'la nation métisse' in Red River, an area comprising the plains of what is now called Southern Manitoba. The Métis built a niche for themselves in the sub-arctic fur trade as wage labourers, transporters and suppliers[25] and lived according to a mixed economy including fur trading, farming and buffalo hunting.

The term 'Métis' is, in this context, associated with a distinctive collective history, culture, language, land tenure and political institutions, derived, as is much nationalism, 'from increasingly problematic relations with other interest groups coupled with rapidly changing social and economic situations'.[26] In this context, '[b]eing Métis moved from a statement of ancestry to an assumed corporate identity around which to mobilize and fight'[27] against the encroachment of Anglo-colonialism, particularly following the inception of the Canadian state in 1867. Today Métis claim a homeland including Northwestern Ontario, Manitoba, Saskatchewan, Alberta and (though to a lesser extent) Eastern British Columbia, the North West Territories and the upper parts of North Dakota and Montana. Métis living within this geographical space would, the Métis National Council tells us,[28] have referred to themselves historically as Métis, as their descendants do today.

The same colonialism that led to the demise of Métis political power on the prairies, through their defeat in the so-called 'North West Rebellion' in 1885, has produced the current conundrum about the meaning and boundaries of the term 'Métis'. This has coalesced into a debate between, as Peterson and Brown generously term it, 'small-m' metis (denoting simple mixed Indigenous and non-Indigenous ancestry) and 'large-M' Métis (denoting a national constituency).[29] 'Small-m' metis designations are by far the more common ones, a taxonomy the courts have also been caught up in. I argue that such categorisations both underpin and rely on a configuration of *symbolic violence* and power that characterises the Canadian nation-state.

Although ample evidence exists that the Canadian state engages in economic and physical violence when necessary, it also expends significant resources in maintaining control over the production of *symbolic* violence. Borrowing from the French sociologist Pierre Bourdieu, I use the term to mean the power through which elements of social reality come to be seen as real or true, despite their socially constructed and thus arbitrary character. Symbolic violence attains its power by virtue of the fact that we do not see it as an act of violence, oppression or power at all but rather, as 'just the way things are'. As Bourdieu puts it: 'being born of a social world, we accept a whole range of postulates, axioms, which go without saying and which require no incalculating. … Of all forms of "hidden persuasion", the most implacable is the one exerted, quite simply, by the *order of things*'.[30]

In Canada, as in much of the world, *race* is one such dominant discourse that has played an elementally powerful role in how Indigenous people are positioned not only vis-à-vis the nation-state but within our own nations and communities. That is to say, once race is perceived as 'real', it gets unproblematically positioned as a valid means of differentiating humanity by both whitestream Canadians and Indigenous peoples alike. In a context where such logic is prevalent, the category 'Indian' is positioned as pure, while the category 'Métis' is positioned as a derivative of 'Indians'. That is, to say, whatever the distinctiveness of cultural characteristics, the 'core' or essence of Métis social selves is 'mixedness', marked through Indigenous/non-Indigenous ancestry and post-contact origins. My point in emphasising this is, of course, not to suggest that 'Métis' are not of mixed Indigenous and non-Indigenous ancestry, but merely to question why, given that all Indigenous people are, it remains such a remarkable feature of the category.

Yet Aboriginal people are apparently no more transcendental of the colonialism we live in than non-Aboriginals. Even though many of us have been raised in communities that demonstrate the patent absurdity of simplified or abstracted notions of racial 'mixedness', we seem unable to shake off their persistent power. The perseverance of the legitimacy of race in Aboriginal communities rests on the fact that those of us who imbue race with symbolic capital (i.e., treat and thus use race as though it was real) usually remain unaware that we are doing so and thus fail to perceive anything illegitimate about its use. It is in this important sense that Bourdieu positions one's habitus as 'pre-reflective'. The legitimacy of discourses like race is possible 'only through the complicity of those who do not want to know that they are subject to it or even that they themselves exercise it'.[31]

In Canada, although race plays an important role in shaping how Indigenous identities are negotiated in different administrative contexts, its baldness as a discourse is somewhat blunted by virtue of the bureaucratic doublespeak produced through the legislative discourses of the Indian Act. For example, even though the Indian Act works largely through a racial purity requirement, we talk instead about being a 6(1) or 6(2),[32] a discourse that masks its visibility (though importantly, not its effects). Moreover, the legitimacy of race and racial purity remains a reality for many Indian Act bands where part of their community membership is based on a modified blood quantum test. All of this is to say that, despite ourselves, blood purity – a marker of Indianness – remains an important legitimating symbol (and thus, a boundary) in Native communities. Some First Nations, like Kahnawake Mohawk Nation, have pushed this even further to argue a requisite 50 per cent blood quantum rule to assure membership.[33]

This section discussed how Indigenous people internalise colonial discourses, paying particular attention to the symbolic violence of race that conflates Métis with mixed ancestry. As I discuss in the next section, the conflation of Métis with 'mixed ancestry' has produced a drastic increase of Indigenous peoples in Eastern Canada self-identifying as Métis, despite the lack of any historical Métis communities.

'Métis' come(s) to the Maritimes

The lack of a historically distinctive and self-identifying Métis presence in the Maritimes has not stopped the recent rise in those self-identifying as Métis. In the last decade, Nova Scotia, for example, experienced an 830 per cent increase and New Brunswick, the province directly east, a 350 per cent increase.[34] This is part of a 91 per cent rise in Canada's total Métis population, a near doubling of numbers from just over 200,000 in 1996 to almost 400,000 in 2006. Statistics Canada argues that this increase has not been demographically 'natural' (i.e., simply the result of birth and mortality rates) but rather happened as a result of 'ethnic mobility': the process by which individuals who have not done so before come to self-identify as Métis.[35]

This increase in self-identification as Métis is interesting since the historical record is clear that Indigenous communities in Nova Scotia and New Brunswick hold historical legacies of intermixing between European traders and Indigenous peoples. Jaenen argues that, at least among the French, intermixing with 'Amerindians' was widespread.[36] Dickason argues more forcefully that 'it is doubtful that there was any more mixing of the races, in the biological sense, in [Western Canada] than there was in the East or on the West Coast. In fact, the reverse may well be true, at least as far as the East is concerned …'.[37] The French in particular used racial intermixing as a component of their empire building,[38] a practice so formalised as to be included as an article of incorporation for the Charter of the Company of New France.[39]

The 'Confederation of Nova Scotia Métis'[40] argues that '[t]he joining of European and Native cultures created distinct and unique cultures, separate from both parent cultures. Regardless of what name was applied to this new breed of individual, they were and their descendants are, Métis'.[41] However Jaenan and Dickason make it clear that the offspring of these unions were nearly always reabsorbed into the mother's Indigenous community and culture.[42] Thus, for all intents and purposes, the children of unions between Frenchmen and Mi'kmaq women were raised, were thought of *and thought of themselves* as Mi'kmaq.

More complexly, the 'Confederation of Nova Scotia Métis' historical narrative additionally affiliates them with the historical Acadian community of the region. Acadia represented France's first permanent settlement in the Maritimes region. It included parts of what we now call Nova Scotia, New Brunswick and Prince Edward Island[43] and various historians have pointed out that many Acadians possess(ed) Mi'kmaq ancestry. For example, Dickason uses a priest's letter from 1755 to argue that Acadians were perceived as 'a mixed breed, that is to say, most of them proceeded from marriages or concubinage of the savage woman with the first settlers, who were of various nations, but chiefly French'.[44] She goes on to say that, according to one local priest of the era, 'he did not expect more than fifty years to elapse before the French colonists were so mixed with the Mi'kmaq and Maliseet that it would be impossible to distinguish them'.[45] Francis et al. go even further, arguing the presence of a 'Métis community' (albeit one lacking a precise definition) on the Southeast coast of Nova Scotia.[46] However, in her monumental volume on Acadian history, Griffiths argues that regardless of their ancestral multi-raciality, by the beginning of the eighteenth century, Acadians 'were a people … who considered themselves to be first and foremost Acadians rather than members of any other group'.[47]

The preceding discussion should make it clear that the issue here is not one of individuals 'choosing' an Indigenous identity when in actuality they are not – clearly they are Indigenous (or what in Canada we would refer to as 'Native' or 'Aboriginal'). Rather, the question is why they are (choosing to identify as) 'Métis' when, by the most generous interpretation, their ancestors would have self-identified as part of one of the Indigenous nations which owned and lived on those territories or alternatively, as Acadians, like those mentioned by Dickason in her discussion of the priest's letter.[48] More fundamentally, what are the conditions of possibility which allow Paul Ross, spokesperson for the 'Confederation of Nova Scotia Métis', to confidently state '[e]verybody in this area is Métis ... We just want to be recognized as Métis here in Nova Scotia'?[49]

In further attempting to anchor their legitimacy as 'Métis', the Confederacy of Nova Scotia Métis mimics cultural traditions long taken for granted as constitutive of 'Métis Nation' Métis culture, such as fiddling, jigging, square dancing and sash wearing:

> Métis culture in Nova Scotia is a combination of both [*sic*] French, English and Mi'kmaq. Fiddling, step and square-dancing and aspects of traditional Mi'kmaq beliefs abound in each and every community of Métis people in Nova Scotia. The Sash, recognized as the symbol of the Métis Nation and people in Western Canada, has long been part of Métis culture here in the Maritimes.[50]

This narrative is curious not (just) for its falsity but rather, given the recent vintage of their organisation, its 'piggybacking' on pre-existing Métis Nation constructions of distinctive Métis culture. In other words, many First Nations communities possess(ed) the above characteristics, particularly those in long contact with adjacent Métis communities but this does not make them Métis nor does their ancestral communities' possession of these characteristics make *their ancestors* Métis. I am not challenging their statement that these cultural icons were present in Eastern communities. Rather, I suggest that their presence does not make the communities 'Métis' any more than the presence of American popular culture (TV, books, magazines, etc.) in Canada makes Canadians, Americans.

Concomitant with this denaturalisation and *post hoc* pilfering of Métis Nation symbols, the Confederacy's construction of 'Métis' is clearly indebted to their internalisation of racial purity/blood quantum discourses. For these Indigenous people, Métis is synonymous with 'mixed': 'In this day and age, Métis people are all of those with both Native and non-Native bloodlines'.[51] Likewise, the *we'kopekwitk* Métis Council (until recently an affiliate of the Confederacy of Nova Scotia Métis) states their membership as comprising 'the common bond of being Métis, a person of mixed Native and non-Native heritage. People with Mi'kmaq,

Wendat, Kanien'keha:ka, Eyou, Inuit, Dakota and other Native heritage. And, of course, mixed with French, English, Irish, Scottish, African and more'.[52] Further, they state:

> Our members come from all walks of life and heritage. Most are Indigenous Métis, whose Native heritage is Mi'kmaq, while others are Western Métis whose Native heritage may be Cree, Ojibwa, Blackfoot, Sioux or any other. Our commonalities: our inability to walk in either Indian or white worlds comfortably, our non-acceptance within either world and our wish to simply be who we are.[53]

Such an obvious internalisation of the symbolic power of race is not surprising. Nor is it surprising, despite their proclamations to the contrary, that Nova Scotia Indigenous peoples have begun to call themselves 'Métis' in greater numbers over the past several years. In the next and final section I detail the symbolic violence produced by the Canadian courts through the ambiguity of their wording in the *Powley* decision, which encourages the conflation of 'Métis' with 'mixed'.

'Métis' and the symbolic violence of law

In his discussion of law's symbolic power in modern nation-states, Bourdieu argues that law has, in modern Western societies, achieved an unparalleled power to *name*:

> Law is the quintessential form of the symbolic power of naming that creates the things named and creates social groups in particular. It confers upon the reality which arises from its classificatory operations the maximum permanence that any social entity has the power to confer upon another, the permanence which we attribute to objects.[54]

Law gains this power, he argues, through its standardisation, formalisation and claims to universality.[55] More specifically McCann argues

> the activity of courts in 'policing' official legal meanings and practices contributes to the legal construction of shared cultural understandings about how society is organized ... and the public status accorded to various citizen subjects – in short, to the very foundations of authoritative knowledge that inform our politics and public life.[56]

Thus, the real power of law is in the extent to which we, as citizens, view the rulings of decisions like that of the *Powley* court as legitimate and binding. We do so, McCann argues, because we understand and pre-reflectively agree with the particular ways of 'knowing the world' and of settling disputes that courts operate on and in.

Certainly, the most commonsensical ways of categorising indigeneity by the contemporary Canada public are legal, particularly those rooted in Section 35 of the Constitution Act, 1982. This Section 'recognizes and affirms' the Aboriginal rights of three distinct 'groups': Indians (now called First Nations); Inuit (formerly called 'Eskimos') and Métis. The absurdity of attempting to box such diverse nations of peoples into three neat categories notwithstanding, 'Indians', 'Inuit' and 'Métis' have come to enjoy a naturalised and largely unchallenged place in public parlance. They constitute the government administrative categories *de jure* and, indeed, these taxonomies' legitimacy stretches into the most powerful technologies of governance in the nation-state, Census Canada, who uses these categories to obtain data on 'Aboriginal people'.

The constitution is a central part of the Canadian legal system and has, since its patriation in 1982, proved a valuable tool for Aboriginal litigants. Unlike First Nations and Inuit, however, prior to the *Powley* decision, the Métis had never appeared before the courts in a Section 35 case. As such, the *Powley* case was momentous and eagerly anticipated by the many organisations that intervened, not to mention Métis more generally. Legal commentators had noted the term's juridical vagueness prior to *Powley* and as such, the *Powley* case represented the first opportunity to sharpen the term's boundaries. The decision itself was not particularly lengthy (a mere 55 paragraphs) but the court dealt squarely with the issue of Métis identity early on:

> The term "Métis" in s. 35 does not encompass all individuals with mixed Indian and European heritage; rather, it refers to distinctive peoples who, in addition to their mixed ancestry, developed their own customs, way of life and recognizable group identity separate from their Indian or Inuit and European forebears. Métis communities evolved and flourished prior to the entrenchment of European control, when the influence of European settlers and political institutions became pre-eminent.[57]

Two features of this definition are worth noting for the extent to which they presuppose and reproduce the symbolic violence of race. First, the court argues that, whatever the other features of identity which make them distinctive, Métis are first and foremost 'mixed'. Second, the court also suggests that this mixedness-cum-distinctiveness is a necessary but insufficient element to receive constitutional protection as 'Métis'. Additionally, this mixedness must also be anchored in pre-colonial communities. This latter element, in particular, is interesting because it at once constructs and delimits authentic Métisness: following on the heels of *physical* and *technological* whiteness is fine (i.e., pre-colonial) but *political* whiteness (i.e., colonialism) is not.

In any event, this definition clearly included Métis Nation Métis. However, who else might it include? Might it include so-called 'Maritime Métis'? In expanding the logic of their definition, the *Powley* states that '… given the vast territory of what is now Canada, we should not be surprised to find that different groups of Métis exhibit their own distinctive traits and traditions. This diversity among groups of Métis may enable us to speak of Métis "peoples"….'.[58] Thus, in putting meat on the bones of the term, the *Powley* court potentially left the door ajar for any groups: first of mixed European/Indigenous ancestry and, second, part of a pre-colonial community, to self-identify as Métis. A (perhaps) unintended consequence of the *Powley* decision in Eastern Canada is captured by a newspaper article headline from the *Halifax Daily News*: 'Métis definition fits Acadians: Wording could allow them special hunting rights: Nova Scotia's Acadian community appears to fit neatly within Ottawa's definition of Métis and could qualify for special hunting rights protected under the Constitution'.[59] Ultimately, it appears that rather than any contemporary *and* historical self-identification as Métis, their 'mixedness' and the extent to which they were or are seen as such, conspire to produce their construction as Métis. And, in doing so, it legitimates and perpetuates the ethnocidal policies that separated these individuals from their historical nations, communities and territories in the first place.

Conclusion

This chapter has sought to examine the ways in which colonialism's symbolic violence has impacted and constituted identification and Canadian categories for recognising indigeneity. I have argued that the power of contemporary nation-states within which Indigenous societies (necessarily) remain embedded has constitutively shaped the taxonomies we use to make sense of ourselves and the world around us. In such a context, the prevalence and currency of discourses of race and racial purity have assumed a dominant and thus largely unquestioned legitimacy in contemporary Canadian society. Race, in other words, operates as a form of power imbued with a symbolic capital matched by few other discourses.[60]

Given that contemporary indigeneity constitutes both the resistance to and the reproduction of such colonial discourses, it is reasonable to assume that we have internalised the same kinds of racial discourses as non-Aboriginal Canadians.

In the end, there may well be no way out of this colonially induced quagmire. The signals sent out to broader society by the Canadian Census and the Supreme Court of Canada are (pardon the term) mixed at best and short of changing their current term for self-identification, Métis Nation Métis (are forced to) live an unhappy coexistence with Indigenous peoples in Eastern Canada who have begun to refer to themselves as Métis. This is not so big a problem, as eastern 'Métis' have little or no contact with Métis in Western Canada. As well, the Métis National Council's factum, presented before the *Powley* decision discussed above, argued that whether or not the term may legitimately be used by others, 'Métis' must at the very least include Métis Nation constituents.[61] That some of the Indigenous people of Eastern Canada are banding together to collectively pursue their goals and objectives is a specific example of a larger phenomenon of contemporary Aboriginal–Canadian state relations. That they do so under the banner of 'Métis' is an effect of both their internalisation of racial purity discourses and the conditions of possibility left open to them by current Canadian law and policy.

CHAPTER TWO

'My Poetry is a Fire'

Alice Te Punga Somerville

Writing fire. In the last section of Robert Sullivan's 2005 volume, *Voice Carried My Family*, a poem entitled 'Ahi Kā – the House of Ngā Puhi' begins:

> We light the poem and breathe out
>   the growing flames. Ahi kā. This
>   is our home – our fire.[1]

The poem moves through a series of fire-y images: Māui and the sun, *hāngi* (earth oven to cook food). Fire-y words are repeated: flames, fires, rays, burnt, char, firing, embers, molten and *ahi* (fire). Although *ahi kā*, the concept by which land boundaries and resource-use rights are maintained through continual physical habitation – 'keep[ing] the home fires burning', is about physical occupation of space, in this poem Sullivan extends the mode of occupation into the spoken, the rhetorical, the poetic. He starts, after all, with an act of 'light[ing] the poem'. Rather than merely transferring the concept of *ahi kā* from the practical world of land into the abstract world of oratory and literature, the poem brings those two worlds together. The close connection between the physical realm and the utterance of language is repeated throughout the poem: 'light the poem and breathe out/the growing flames', 'turn words to steam', 'Shadows shrink in our hand's quiver/as we speak', 'sing fire/scoop embers'. This is telling, singing, writing as a form of maintaining *ahi kā*. By itself, this claim is an enormously productive – and perhaps provocative – mobilisation of the concept of *ahi kā* in relation to poetry. If language is a form of assertion, a form of *fire*, then the massive number of Māori who do not reside on their traditional homelands are not necessarily cut out of the equation of asserting an active relationship with place. Further, where land is not under the control of physical occupation, Sullivan emphasises the possibility of imaginative occupation through telling stories: 'ahi kā, carried by our tribe's forever-story/firing every lullaby'. This is fabulous stuff and produces a timely and staunch intervention that has potential implications for our thinking about the relationship between people and land.

More fire. In the same section, immediately following 'Ahi Kā', Sullivan includes a two-line poem titled in lower-case, 'the crackling page':

> my poetry is a fire –
> if I close my mouth I will die[2]

Again, poetry is related to fire: the difference between the poem about Ngā Puhi (an *iwi*) and this one about poetry is the positioning of the writer in the space between the linguistic and physical realms. Not only does the maintenance of *ahi kā* demand the fire of poetry, but the poet himself is compelled to speak it. The stakes of poetry, for the speaker of the poem, are high: to *not* speak has implications for the ability of the *iwi* to continue to assert *ahi kā* but it also has rather dire implications for the individual poet. This is about urgency, compulsion, survival.

Even more fire. There's another fire-y place in Sullivan's collection: Hawai'i. In an earlier section entitled 'For the Ocean of Kiwa', the poem 'Ocean Birth' journeys around – and centres – the various originary stories of Oceania. It starts, appropriately enough, in Aotearoa (New Zealand, 'Land of the Long White Cloud') and the speaker retraces the steps to Hawaiki (ancient homeland from where Māori migrated) alongside those who journey there after their lives in this physical world have ended:

> With the leaping spirits we threw
>   our voices past Three Kings to sea –
>   eyes wide open with ancestors.[3]

Thus for the 'babies' of the Pacific (these were the most recently settled islands according to archaeological and genealogical evidence),[4] a journey into the Pacific is simultaneously a journey home and a journey back in time along the routes of the navigators who brought Māori to Aotearoa first. Or, as Peter Adds might put it, the journey brought Pacific people to Aotearoa to become Māori. In this sense, the 'sea', the 'Ocean of Kiwa', is full of 'ancestors': those who have journeyed there after passing away here, and those people who come from earlier bloodlines and continue to inhabit the islands from which we departed. So what about this fire? 'Ocean Birth' names the originary stories of Rapanui, Tahiti, Hawai'i, Aotearoa, Sāmoa, Tonga and beyond to the Lapita[5] people. The origin of Hawai'i is described this way:

> Hawai'i called from liquid
> fire: the goddess Pele churning
>
> land from sea: born as mountains[6]

Fire, then, is central to Sullivan's articulation of connection with Ngā Puhi land and people and to the specific form of poetry, but it is also central to his understanding of Hawai'i. It is, perhaps, no accident that these three form a triangulated relationship: Sullivan wrote *Voice Carried My Family* in Hawai'i, where he resides.

Wineera and Sullivan: Departing and returning

Vernice Wineera of Toa Rangatira and Ngāti Raukawa *iwi* and Robert Sullivan of Ngā Puhi and Kāi Tahu *iwi* are two of the most significant Māori writers who produce poetry in English but, more than this, they are both 'writing fire' in Hawai'i. In very different ways these two poets negotiate their ongoing membership both of Māori and *iwi* communities while they live in Hawai'i and in particular they negotiate the relationships of their identifications as 'Māori' with the ideas of being 'Indigenous' and 'Pacific'. Their identification as Indigenous is underpinned by real engagement with other Indigenous communities in the Pacific and, in particular, Indigenous Hawaiians. Indeed, rather than suggesting that an 'Indigenous' identity is diluted in Pacific waters or that distance from Aotearoa necessarily produces a distance from continued and deep consideration of what it is to be Indigenous, Wineera and Sullivan both demonstrate the tensions between their identifications as Indigenous and Pacific as a crucial driver in their articulation of what it is to be Māori. Wineera and Sullivan are two very different writers: one older, one younger; one woman, one man; one from lower North Island *iwi*, one from Northern and Southern *iwi*; one with longstanding residence in Hawai'i, whose link to Aotearoa derives its strength from emotional connection, and one who has been there for a comparatively short time, with a view to an eventual physical return home. Exacerbating, perhaps, these differences is my decision to focus on Wineera's first collection (1978) and Sullivan's most recent (2005).

Although relatively few texts and even fewer critical discussions articulate Aotearoa as part of the Pacific, the Pacific has been a part of Māori writing in English from the get-go. Most intriguing (and weirdly quiet) are the formidable and impressive offerings of the first two Māori women who published collections of poetry: Vernice Wineera Pere, whose *Mahanga* was published in 1978 in La'ie,

Hawai'i, by the Institute for Polynesian Studies at Brigham Young University-Hawai'i (BYU-H) in cooperation with the Polynesian Cultural Centre,[7] and Evelyn Patuawa-Nathan, a Sydney-based teacher, who was the only Māori writer published through the Suva-based University of the South Pacific's Pacific Writers Series when her *Opening Doors* came out in 1979.[8] Later, in 1987, Ihimaera's *The Whale Rider*, which unlike the later film of the same name includes a journey to Papua New Guinea, was published in New Zealand,[9] and we might also think about texts like Hone Tuwhare's 'Village on Savaii',[10] Apirana Taylor's short story 'Pa Mai' and later poetry,[11] Cathie Dunsford's *Cowrie* trilogy,[12] and Sullivan's collections.

The connection between Māori and Aotearoa draws on a double genealogy: Māori 'arrival' stories are simultaneously autochthonous (drawn from the ground) and migratory (arrived across the sea). To be clear, at the same time as we are related to *atua* (god(s), spirit power(s), ancestor(s) of ongoing influence) that have always inhabited (and/or fished up) our place, we also remember the *waka* (ocean or river-going vessel(s)) on which our ancestors navigated across the Pacific. In the context of contemporary academic work, in which indigeneity is about having always been in a place and diaspora/migration is about transience and movement, this doubled genealogy might seem like an impossible contradiction, but it is not articulated as a contradiction within Māori texts or cultural practices. A great deal of energy (both contemporary and historical) has gone into exploring the migration of Māori people through the Pacific to Aotearoa. But what happens when the contemporary Māori person travels to the Pacific? Because of the fixedness of Māori to Aotearoa (through Indigenous claims to land), which is in turn fixed to New Zealand (through the occupation of the nation-state of New Zealand, which covers the same geographical area as that understood as Aotearoa), the Māori person venturing to the Pacific is departing Aotearoa New Zealand. In this way the Māori person *departs from* their originary home. But at the same time, because genealogies and cultural/linguistic traditions link Māori to the Pacific (and most locally and especially, Polynesia), the Māori person venturing to the Pacific is retracing migration routes, seeking genealogical and cultural sources and tributaries. In this way the Māori person *returns to* their originary home. In this double-directional mobility between departure and return, Wineera's and Sullivan's poetry both articulates and challenges dominant thinking about the relationship between Māori, the Pacific and indigeneity.

There's something particular about the specific place in which Wineera and Sullivan are located, of course: we know from our training and commitments as Indigenous scholars that land and place are crucially important. Wineera and Sullivan both live in a space we might call 'not-Aotearoa', but they are both also very mindful of the other parallel space they inhabit, the literal ground on which they stand: Hawai'i. For Wineera and Sullivan, this negotiation between Māori, Pacific and Indigenous does not happen in empty space. What is significant about paying specific attention to Hawai'i in this context? Hawai'i is, like Aotearoa, occupied by a First World nation. This means that Sullivan and Wineera have migrated there for reasons other than sheer economic pressures. In the case of Wineera, an active member of the Latter Day Saints church, migration was primarily for religious reasons, whereas Sullivan moved in order to more deliberately pursue a career in academia and writing and Hawai'i offered avenues for this that were not available to him at home. Like Aotearoa, Hawai'i occupies a dual space: Pacific, yes, but also Indigenous in a clearly Fourth World sense.[13]

A Caveat: Identity versus identification

I note that this chapter is included in a volume on identity and with full respect to the editors, I would submit that writing about 'identity' can be difficult: the term has acquired rather bulky luggage in the academy and is used either as a productive or a limiting concept depending on the scholar. The question of the relationship between identity and literature, particularly in Indigenous Literary Studies and Pacific Literary Studies, is also rather difficult. The dominant narratives around the first English-language creative texts produced by Indigenous peoples focus on their expressions of identity: works by Tuwhare, Momaday, Noonuccal, Campbell, Ortiz, Holt, Ihimaera, Grace and so on were understood as being unique because the different *identities* of the writers differed from the 'usual suspects' canon of writers. Further, the texts have often been understood merely as ethnographic documents: as 'expressions of identity' rather than, say, as highly self-conscious and mediated articulations and reading them has been (at times literally) an anthropological act. A huge amount of critical scholarship around identity politics, subject positions, location and connection has used the term 'identity' in order to convey a kind of difference which is simultaneously fixable and flexible. 'Māori identity', then, could shift, as might someone's 'identity as Māori' and yet the idea that 'Māori' is an 'identity' (and experienced by an individual along, perhaps, with gender, sexual, physical and class identities) remains.

I have noted that my own work, which centres around English-language creative texts produced by Māori, Pacific and Indigenous peoples, is often described by other people as being 'about identity' and yet I ponder why this is not a description I use myself. For some reason, describing my work as being about identity feels more like an accusation, a narrowing, a marginalising, than it does an affirmation, an extension, an engagement. It's as if 'identity' is something that's fixed and in my work I just pick it up and prod it a bit, turning it from side to side, peering, evaluating, measuring. It feels like researching 'identity' is something for those of us whose experiences of being Māori do not suit the easy monolith of authenticity – *reo* (language), *tikanga* (culture, customary and correct cultural practice(s)), *tūrangawaewae* (a place to stand), *ahi kā* – and were instead raised speaking English, in urban spaces and so on: doing work 'about identity' is necessary for those who didn't get an identity the first time around. I recall a Sāmoan student walking out of a screening of the film based on Wendt's *Flying Fox in a Freedom Tree* and explaining 'this is my culture – I know this already – I don't need to watch a movie about it'. 'Identity' feels like the stuff of the individual, a navel-gazing luxury rather than the stuff of the collective, political, urgent. Indeed, it feels like something is limiting in the state of identity: something more *fixated* than *fixed*, perhaps.

I have found in conversations about my research and teaching being 'about identity', that it's easier to re-engage the word rather than to ditch it altogether: to describe my work as being about identification rather than about identity. Identification. Articulation. The 'light[ing] of poems'. The 'sing[ing] of fire'. The way I use it, identification is an act, rather than a thing. It reminds us that people are involved in the creation of things, rather than passively being labelled or interpolated by them. Identification is subjective, ongoing, supple, dynamic, negotiable. It is about a 'how' and perhaps a 'why' rather than a 'what'. Identification suggests there are multiple forms, multiple contexts, multiple – well – multiple people. Crucial to my politics as well as to my disciplinary training, 'identification' emphasises the extent to which our worlds are produced by language – surely a central claim of Sullivan's poem about *ahi kā* – and, therefore, the study of language, literature, oratory and poetry is in turn a deep engagement with not only the description but the production of things.

Wineera

In 1978, the first book of poetry in English by a Māori woman was published. The first book of poetry in English by a male Māori writer had been Hone Tuwhare's *No Ordinary Sun* in 1964,[14] the first piece of Māori creative non-fiction was Rewiti Kohere's *The Autobiography of a Māori*,[15] published in 1952, the first fiction by a Māori man was Ihimaera's *Pounamu Pounamu*, in 1972,[16] and the first fiction by a Māori woman was Patricia Grace's *Waiariki*, in 1975.[17] It remained, however, for a Māori woman to publish a collection of poetry in English. When Vernice Wineera's

Mahanga: Pacific Poems was published in 1978, however, it did not as easily slot into the list of 'firsts' as the others had.[18] To be frank, if the poetry had been published but was a little ho-hum in terms of poetic quality, this quietness around its publication might be understandable on some level, but Wineera's collection is packed full of rich, lively and compelling poetry. The themes of the collection are wide-ranging: family, maternity, childhood and children, location and place, teaching and knowledges. The exclusion of the collection from the 'Anglophone Māori canon' is, therefore, on the basis of something else: location, location, location. Wineera's ongoing residence in Hawai'i and her publication in the same place mean she is unlikely to be 'hooked into' the worlds of New Zealand and/or Māori letters by the usual means of literary geography.[19] Ironically, of course, it is possible that this distance from New Zealand and from Aotearoa may well be precisely what enabled her to achieve publication in 1978 when Māori women 'at home' could not.

Inside the front cover of *Mahanga*, bibliographic notes suggest something of the multiple spaces in which Wineera[20] and her work had already circulated: her poetry had previously appeared in *Te Ao Hou* and *Marae* (Māori magazines), *Kula Manu* (BYU-H student/staff creative magazine based in Hawai'i) and *Ensign* (Mormon creative writing journal). *Mahanga* is subtitled *Pacific Poems* and in the preface she is described as 'a sensitive, soul-searching Pacific poet' as well as 'of Māori, English and French ancestors'.[21] In her own introductory poem, she writes:

> The Māori has always been an artist and
> poet and I hope herein to convey in
> English my respect for Māoritanga and
> the Polynesian heritage which enriches my
> twentieth-century life.[22]

In this configuration, the Pacific and Polynesia 'stand in' for Māori (or perhaps vice versa). Even though the slippage between 'Pacific' and 'Polynesian' is rightly contested now, what I am interested in is the inextricability of the specific term 'Māori' from the generic/regional configuration of the Pacific. Wineera's work moves between an Aotearoa consciousness and a Pacific consciousness. Rather than 'journeying out' to consider the rest of the Pacific, Wineera's poetry journeys 'home' from one part of the Pacific (Hawai'i) to another (Aotearoa).

'Pacific Note', which might be described as an 'ode' to the ocean, does not explicitly name any land area and yet Aotearoa is implicitly included in its scope. The ocean occupies a central place in the poet's worldview and this is an important intervention in Māori writing because ocean-centricity (as opposed to land-centricity) is not so common in writing by Māori based in Aotearoa, perhaps because the sheer size of the islands has led to an affinity with geographies and metaphors of land more so than water. The poem starts with the creation/production of an 'us' – a Pacific 'us' – whose common denominator is the ocean:

> It is a curious fact
> that some of us have
> lived all of our lives
> at the ocean's curled edge
> – have breathed with every breath
> we ever took, salted air.[23]

The shared ocean-centrism of the 'us'/'we' is underscored by comparing it with 'others/living out their days/without ever comprehending this fact'. Significantly, the lack of interest that continental people have in the Pacific as a region or indeed the uniqueness of the Pacific world ('and should they/ever confront it, would shrug,/and say something like/"so?"'), is balanced by the poet's own attempt to imagine a reaction to living on a continent:

> I think if I lived
> too far from the ocean
> I would suffer from
> claustrophobia.[24]

This uneven degree of mutual interest between oceanic and continental people could perhaps suggest the emptiness of the Pacific to people outside of that region (an empty space available for atomic testing, available for 'South Seas' fantasies, producing no texts or theories worthy of studying in 'world lit' or 'postcolonial lit' courses) is reversed in the gaze of the Pacific towards the continents.

The ocean itself is a place that both manifests and produces history ('For where would I hear/the surf's steady song/rolling out of the depths/of time?'),[25] an idea that is anachronistically reminiscent of Hauʻofa[26] but also of Walcott's 1979 poem 'The Sea is History'.[27] Rather than being overwhelmingly daunting, the vastness and depth of the ocean becomes a constant in terms of time and space, towards which the poet returns to refocus after petty human interactions:

> And how would I stand
> week-long wrangles
> among my like-kind,
> without the evening
> joy-giving
> tranquillity
> of wind,
> sand,
> rock,
> sun,
> pacific,
> ocean?[28]

The ocean is not solely a body of water, but is a framework for all of the elements: sand, rocks and the sun are included in the 'ocean', just as the islands are included in Hauʻofa's Pacific. Importantly, the original and denotative meaning of the term 'pacific' is mobilised here ('tranquillity'), but rather than echoing Magellan's external observation/assumption of a 'calm' ocean, the ocean itself is the active agent and the 'calm' (the 'pacific'-ness) is something that is sought – and attained – by the Pacific 'I'.[29]

Mahanga includes a number of poems about Aotearoa and these are often self-consciously nostalgic and framed within a context of travel to return 'home'. In 'Toa Rangatira':

> 'I am home,' I said
> to a whip of playful wind
> that trailed my words
> and flung them
> at the wide-eyed tekoteko.
> He gave no sign
> save that carved out
> of defiance.
> Nor would he prance forth
> to lay at my feet
> the fern-leaf symbol.[30]

The speaker of the poem literally speaks – 'I am home' – but the agency lies in the many entities that make up this 'home': the wind and the *tekoteko* (carved human-like figure on the gable of meeting house or figurehead on canoe). While the speaker's actions are simple and passive ('I said', 'my words', 'my feet'), the wind and *tekoteko* are more active and described through physicality: the 'playful wind' 'trailed' and 'flung' the speaker's words; the *tekoteko* is 'wide-eyed' and capable of 'sign', 'pranc[ing]' and 'lay[ing]'. The reciprocal relationship between the speaker and the entities of home – visible, as in the *tekoteko* and invisible, as in the wind – is initiated by the speaker's return and utterance, but requires response.

Lest we read this response as simply having been withheld and lest we, therefore, draw conclusions about the impossibility of full return and continued connection when residing as far away as Hawai'i, we might look more closely at the way in which the 'I' of the poem describes the inaction *as action*. The voice of the speaker has been wrested away and yet she does not understand herself as voiceless: she recognises that despite being disconnected from her words, they have indeed been retained. The wind 'playful[ly]' repositions her words, first quietly 'trail[ing]' but then '[flinging]' them at the *tekoteko*. In this act, then, the wind renders her silent on one level but more carefully and forcefully positions her claim – 'I am home' – on the other. As for the *tekoteko*, the speaker of the poem betrays her own retention of knowledge about the *tekoteko* even as the *tekoteko* himself is not forthcoming. The speaker recognises the action that should be expected – 'pranc[ing] forth to lay at [her] feet the fern-leaf symbol' – and in naming this expectation she creates the possibility for ongoing relationship on the *tekoteko*'s terms. Reading this poem alongside Apirana Taylor's 1979 'Sad Joke on a Marae'[31] is immensely compelling because they both focus on a self-proclaimed dislocated individual engaged in the act of approaching a familial *marae*. In both poems, the claim of ignorance expressed overtly by the poem's speaker is simultaneously undermined by the speaker's knowledgeable articulation of what is not apparently known. Also in both poems, the reciprocal relationship between the *marae* (especially the *tekoteko* and other *whakairo* [carving(s)]) and the individual is unmediated by the presence of other people.

Interestingly, it is in her poems about Hawai'i that Wineera focuses on the ocean itself and her descriptions of the Pacific waterscape are particularly rich. Neatly and anachronistically supporting Hau'ofa's not-yet-written 'Our Sea of Islands', she writes about the ocean as a being: multiple, lovable, active, promising. In 'Watching the Limu Pickers', for example, she describes 'the sea's unruffled skin'.[32] In her longer reflection on Pacific voyaging in her description of the launch of an ocean-going *waka*, 'Hokule'a' contains descriptions of an 'ocean of possibilities', 'an ocean of hospitality' and 'an ocean of welcome'.[33] These descriptions clearly counter the idea that the vastness of the ocean must be threatening and foreboding. Indeed, this relationship with the ocean comes out of intimate and affectionate connection between people and the ocean: 'knowing already the fragility/of the sea's soft skin'. Both of these poems focus on ocean-related activities: subsistence in the case of gathering *limu* (edible seaweed) and navigation in the case of Hokule'a.

Sullivan

Robert Sullivan lived in Hawai'i for a year in 2001–2 and returned to live there with his family in 2004. After his first two collections, *Piki Ake* and *Jazz Waiata*, he worked on the feat of *Star Waka*: a collection made up of 101 poems (100 in the book and one on the cover) and 2001 lines. Published in 1999, the 2001 lines peek over the new millennium and, thereby, the space and time beyond popular focus.

> IN 101 POEMS
> STROKING Y2K
> STANZAS PEOPLED WITH STARS AND WAKA
> AND SEA STROKING PAST TWO THOUSAND LINES[34]

Paying this close attention to the detail of numbering evokes the precision and painstaking attention at the centre of navigation. Each poem retains internal integrity in terms of topic and form and yet they are all tied into a broader structure in very particular and carefully counted ways. This reminds us of navigation, then, but also of *whakapapa* (genealogy(ies)). Next came *Captain Cook in the Underworld* (2002),[35] a different kind of publication: it's the written version of an opera, the lyrics of which Sullivan was commissioned to write. Although each poem marks a shift in perspective and/or time, the dominant narrative is located at the level of the whole book rather than at the level of each poem. In *Captain Cook*, Sullivan brings together two major explorers of the Pacific: Māui and Cook. Rather than Cook and his voyages being understood as singular and precocious, they are tied into a broader context of navigational feats around the Pacific: Sullivan simply subsumes him through incorporation into a Pacific-derived story which is under the creative and metaphoric control of the Pacific. In terms of the connection between Aotearoa and Hawai'i, the relationship is merely implied, through shared 'mythological' and *whakapapa* histories.

Voice Carried My Family was published in 2005 and is another kettle of fish: structured by four sections rather than by an over-arching logic or narrative, the collection roams in very specific ways between Aotearoa and Hawai'i and it foregrounds a range of ways in which that roaming is both prophesied and underpinned by earlier connections and feats of navigation. In three consecutive collections then, Sullivan explores three distinct ways of articulating Māori connections with the Pacific: through the originary and ongoing telling of the *waka* traditions, through the founding stories of Pacific exploration at the regional level with a dual focus on Cook and Māui, and through reflection on the multiple sites and spaces of Māori contact with the Pacific, including in the form of late eighteenth-century European and Polynesian navigators as well as more recent formulations.

Before focusing on *Voice Carried My Family*, we will return for a while to *Star Waka*. This collection has been treated elsewhere and is taught widely but in the context of the present discussion it demands some consideration as a predecessor to *Voice*. *Star Waka* focuses on the idea of *waka*. It centres voyaging, but subtly. Sullivan focuses on voyaging out from Aotearoa and/or from the perspective of Aotearoa. The collection refuses that the history of voyaging to Aotearoa is a one-way process; in 'Waka 89' Māui confirms the meaning of this use of '*waka*': 'without me the waka would be vaka'.[36] After all, '*waka*' were produced only after Māori had landed in Aotearoa and spent some time reworking the Polynesian language.[37]

Sullivan centres a claim that Māori are ocean people: voyagers, navigators, travellers, deeply embedded in specific land because of, not despite, previous migrations. This is significant because contemporary dominant discourses focus on Māori in terms of 'Indigeneity' – and by this I mean Fourth World Indigeneity – and connection to land rather than in terms of migration and connection to water.[38] Sullivan draws close connections between the experience of travelling over the Pacific and *whakapapa*: 'what belongs to water belongs to blood' ('*i*'),[39] 'we all belong to a waka' (xxxii herenga waka),[40] 'There is a Kupe in all of us'[41] (Waka 70) and so on. In the last poem 'Waka 100' he writes about 'each person/ of waka memory …/waka names'.[42] In the second poem of the book, '*i*', he describes the voyages across the Pacific by focusing on the physical act of travelling by *waka*. Rather than agreeing with dominant assertions about the diminished arts of Māori navigation, however, Sullivan argues that the continuation of *waka* traditions is upheld through the ongoing *articulation* of journeys. Just as he later writes about the possibility that *ahi kā* is maintained through linguistic as well as physical occupation of specific space in 'Ocean Birth', in '*i*' Sullivan describes the maintenance of voyaging through literal means:

> In ancient days navigators sent waka between.
> Now, our speakers send us on waka. Their memories,
> memory of people in us, invite, spirit,

compel us aboard, to home government, to centre:
Savai'i, Avaiki, Havaiki, Hawaiiki, from where we peopled
Kiwa's Great Sea [...][43]

This poem moves across time and space: from the physical/past ('navigators sent waka') to the poetic/present ('speakers send us on waka') and back to the physical/past ('from where we peopled Kiwa's Great Sea'). The linguistic/poetic articulation of mobility ('speakers send us on waka') is sandwiched between references to historical mobility. The 'we' of the poem, however, exists across time: while 'our speakers send *us* on waka' in the present day ('now'), '*we* peopled Kiwa's Great Sea'. This reflects an understanding of ancestors living on through successive generations. Further, the desire to move is simultaneously derived from '[speakers'] memories' and 'memory of people in us' 'memories' of historic events (when 'we' peopled the Pacific) coexist with 'memory' of people from those times (ancestors who live 'in us') as it is experienced by 'us' in the present. The act of navigation, in this poem, becomes an historical event as well as a rhetorical and literary gesture. Rather than simply producing a one-way process of moving from literal to metaphoric voyaging, Sullivan establishes and affirms an ongoing oscillation between physical and poetic mobility.

In his remarkable 2005 collection, *Voice Carried My Family*, Sullivan produces a view of the Pacific that oscillates between a view from Hawai'i and a view from Aotearoa. The collection also shifts gears stylistically and temporally over the course of its pages. Rather than seeming confused or disjointed however, this shifting of perspective is immensely generative: Sullivan newly draws links between Aotearoa, Hawai'i, the broader Pacific and indigeneity in order to emphasise connections and disconnections between all of these. The collection is structured in four sections: 'For Gods and Waka', 'For Shadows', 'For the Ocean of Kiwa' and 'For Fires'. Perhaps these four explore four different elements or states: wood (and, therefore, earth), the unseen or hidden, water and fire. Each of these elements in turn produces a different connection between Aotearoa and Hawai'i: shared *atua* and voyaging traditions, shared concepts of the relations between the seen and the unseen, shared connection with the ocean and shared fires (*ahi kā*, poetry, creation). In some ways, the collection negotiates ways of being Māori through various Pacific consciousnesses and recognitions.

While the first two sections continue the work of *Star Waka* and feel New Zealand-based, the third section, 'For the Ocean of Kiwa', has a regional focus and foregrounds the historical figures of Mai and Tupaia, adding Koa and Te Weherua to their memories. The title of this section emphasises not only the Māori name for the Pacific (Te Moananui a Kiwa) but also names an originary Polynesian navigator as he is remembered by Māori speakers (Kiwa) and in doing this Sullivan claims the navigation of the Pacific as an 'always already' activity from the point of view of Māori. The section, which seems to come out of Sullivan's own experience of departing Aotearoa and moving to Hawai'i, is thereby framed as a return at the same time. While we might focus on Sullivan's decision to find an exploratory genealogy in the figures of Mai (Omai)[44] and Tupaia – the famed Tahitian men who voyaged with Cook on his various journeys who are recognised for their significantly early decisions to explore ocean-bound mobility in the late 1700s – we do so within a broader context of Māori mobility and navigation. In 'The Great Hall', the opening poem of the section, Sullivan explicitly seeks an alternative narrative and set of relationships:

> And so I bring a new lens, two, a pair of eyes
> for the mission: Tupaia's and another pair, Mai's,
> two other pairs: Koa and Te Weherua's. Polynesian eyes
> on Cook's several crews.[45]

Describing the new perspective as the 'bring[ing of] a new lens, a pair of eyes' suggests a literal and quite deliberate decision about perspective. The poet is the agent in the poem; he 'bring[s]' the new perspectives rather than simply looking through them or considering them. This is about conscious and purposeful selection of 'a new lens' and 'pair[s] of eyes'; Sullivan's choices are as careful and productive as the quadripartite configuration of the settler nation from which he has just signalled a decision to shift away: explorer ('Cook'), missionary ('Marsden'), soldier ('WWI veteran') and pastoralist/trader ('foundational figures of Canterbury').

In the final section of the poem, Sullivan moves from the generic 'Polynesian' to Māori:

> I looked at the stained glass
> in Canterbury's Great Hall and noticed
> one identifiable Maori at the lowest right
> on whose shoulders stood all the others.[46]

Taking his 'Polynesian eyes' to 'look[ ]' at 'Cook's several crews' as represented in 'the stained glass', the poet sees something new: an 'unidentifiable Maori' who has become visible for the first time, it seems, because of Sullivan's decision to shift his perspective from the settler nation to the Pacific region. Indeed, the only 'unidentifiable' figure in the entire Hall is this one, the one closest to the poet. Once the Māori figure is finally 'noticed' – after all of the other figures have been named – the poet realises that all of the others are entirely dependent on the 'identifiable Maori at the lowest right' after all. This realisation shifts the focus of the whole poem and we step back and realise that all of the weight of the poem rests, concretely and narratively as well as historically and conceptually, on these 'shoulders' in the final line.

Much of the rest of the section goes on to historicise and reflect on the configurations set up in this first poem. The poems range from narration of events that are perhaps unknown to many readers ('Koa was 10 years old amid topmasts and mainstays ... Polynesian')[47] to consideration of the ethics and limits of Sullivan's own decision to write about non-Māori Polynesian historical figures. ('Who am I to extol Tupaia? ... Who am I to say these things?'[48] 'You're in the public domain ... but I can't. I just can't take the middle of your throat /Who would I pay for the privilege?')[49] But Tupaia and Mai are from present-day French Polynesia. What about Hawai'i?

After imagining Mai and Tupaia, as well as the Māori figures Koa and Te Weherua ('the first Maori ever to leave Aotearoa that way'),[50] Sullivan is finally able to talk about Hawai'i. Perhaps he needed to recount and name the stories of the first Polynesians on European ships in order to find precedents for his own journey across the Pacific. After the sequence of poems about these historical figures, then, but still in the section about Kiwa, he writes about his position in a specific space: Hawai'i. 'Pearl Harbour' begins 'I meant this to be a poem about Aotearoa/so forgive me'[51] and focuses on the process by which the US overthrew the Hawaiian monarchy and continues to overthrow the Hawaiian people. The phrase 'I meant this to be ... so forgive me' suggests an initial intention has been averted. At the end of his reflection on various mobile Polynesian figures, perhaps the 'I' of the poem expected to end up with a name, and identification, for the 'unidentifiable Maori': 'a poem about Aotearoa'.

However, it is impossible to write about Aotearoa without recognising the necessarily broader contexts, starting with the context of the place where his feet are located. The slippage between 'a poem about Aotearoa' and a 'poem about Hawai'i' is compelling: in order for one poem to have morphed into the other, a broader claim needs to be made about the substitutability of the two places. The boundary between 'Aotearoa' and 'Hawai'i' is thus permeable on the basis of 'waka memory' – Polynesian *whakapapa* – but also on the basis of shared colonial experience. 'Kuki/Cook' is one example of this shared colonialism. The slippage between Aotearoa and Hawai'i is further gestured towards in Sullivan's corrective when describing the 'Queen':

> ... arrested the Queen. Not Victoria.
> Nor Elizabeth. Lili'uokalani ...[52]

The poet's intervention ('not Victoria./Nor Elizabeth') suggests the imagined reader of the poem will wrongly assume which 'Queen' he is writing about. The English Queens Victoria and Elizabeth stand in for the past and present colonial context in Aotearoa – the likelihood that the reader will misrecognise the Queens (the poet 'mean[s]' Lili'uokalani, after all) supports the extent of the similarity between the two contexts of Aotearoa and Hawai'i at the same time as the colonial contexts (Queens Victoria and Elizabeth vs. 'Congress ... Pearl Harbour ... America') are contemporarily distinct. 'Pearl Harbour' articulates the dual position of Hawai'i and Aotearoa in relation to one another: substitutable and distinct. For Sullivan, although this is 'meant' to 'be a poem about Aotearoa', then, the poem is not only about Aotearoa but is also, inescapably and most overtly, about Hawai'i.

Writing fire in Hawai'i

Writing fire. How do Wineera and Sullivan negotiate the connections and disconnections between these three designations – Māori, Pacific and Indigenous? How do – or might – we read their fabulous poetry in a way that attempts to recognise the possibility (as well as the frustration and implausibility) of an 'AND' between each of these words: how do these writers articulate ways of being Māori *and* Pacific *and* Indigenous? As Māori scholarship moves and solidifies into new places, new conversations, new comparisons, it is crucial that we keep a balanced and ever-increasing view of Māori. In the past few years a great deal of energy has been expended on exploring connections between Māori and other Fourth World Indigenous communities: Indigenous communities subsumed by the First World nation-states of Australia, the US and Canada. This is a good and useful comparative project and I myself have invested heavily in it, through my decision to pursue doctoral studies in the US and to study American-Indian Studies along with English for my PhD. There is a great deal of scholarly excitement about this move and much remains to be done in terms of this comparison. However, we need not be satisfied with Māori scholarship always and only with being 'Indigenous'. We're also from the Pacific. And we need to be clear that choosing to identify with the Pacific doesn't negate or challenge or sideline Indigenous identifications or the possibility of continuing to articulate these. Instead, it enables us to notice *more* and *different* things (migration, diaspora, Polynesianness, sea-centrism and so on) than if we focus solely on those parts of ourselves that are 'Indigenous'.

These two writers are writing fire in Hawai'i. How can our scholarship continually and self-reflexively evaluate its own ability to recognise and foreground the diversity of Māori, Pacific and Indigenous experience? How can we find ways to recognise those complex histories of movement, migration and so on that characterise the Māori diaspora? How can we attempt to recognise, in the telling of each story, all of those stories that are left out in a way that does not undermine any one of the narratives we seek to uncover and articulate in our scholarship but instead provides a rich – if blurred and merely implied – context that further deepens and broadens the scope and stakes of our academic work? 'Indigenous' and 'Pacific' need not be in competition with one another, but they do different work: how can those of us who work in Māori, Pacific and Indigenous Studies bring together the 'ands' where possible, in a way that delights in productive tension rather than in a way that seeks to make things fit together prettily?

Wineera finishes her collection *Mahanga* with a poem that places her own writing in the English literary tradition *and* in the tradition of Māori/Pacific/Indigenous cultural production. She describes 'the ending of this thing' and the narrative ostensibly suggests this 'ending' is of a literature course she's taken.[53] As she packs up the books and notes of a literature class, the speaker of the poem mourns their removal after packing up the things that represent not only the knowledge she has gained, but also the possibility of knowing more:

> three months' time
> is just enough to taste
> a little on the tongue.
> – Just enough to tell me
> I will never be done with wanting more.
> Never done with wanting answers,
> never done with asking.[54]

After packing, her physical environment reflects this loss: 'So now I have a cave of empty shelves'.

> stacked beneath the poets
> in the dark
> at the ending of this thing,
> I've packed my heart.[55]

The ending of the poem most overtly supports her position within the English literary tradition – her heart is now 'packed' in the boxes/piles along with the Western literature she has described so affectionately. On the one hand, then, we might read this as a kind of sacrificial loss: the idea that her 'heart' is now inextricable from those texts she has grown to love. But this is also at the 'ending' of the book *Mahanga*. This poem is about losing one's heart in English language poetry: 'in a pile', 'neatly boxed', 'labelled'. These are all part of the modernist Western project of classifying and classification that Wineera has dealt with throughout her collection. 'Stacked beneath the poets' could be about a consuming passion for these texts *but* also compellingly read as articulating the oppressiveness of this tradition: this is, after all, 'the ending', the final word, the final bundling. Wineera's heart is 'packed' in with all of those Western literary texts and writers and this has left her 'incomplete': she is not lost *in* those texts, but *because* of them. *Mahanga* ends here, after its long discussions of domesticity, family, home, Māori, Hawai'i, Aotearoa. Wineera herself is at the 'ending' of her book, in this location of being 'stacked beneath the poets'. The work of classifying and piling/boxing/labelling is not a culturally or politically neutral process: she has lost herself in it.

Or – is there the possibility of another reading: have we lost her? When we pack up, classify, file and stack the body of writing we call 'Māori writing in English', or indeed the category 'Māori', are we complicit in burying her – and Sullivan and other articulators and articulations of Māori connections with the Pacific and with Hawai'i – underneath the piles of writers and ideas we talk about more prominently? When Wineera claims she is 'never done with asking' is she 'asking' someone else or us? Sullivan asserts and maintains *ahi kā* through his poetry: 'ahi kā/carried by the tribe's forever-story/firing every lullaby' and describes his poetry as 'a fire'. Here, at the 'ending of this thing', I wonder if the 'fire' Wineera and Sullivan produce in Hawai'i can and should warm – and perhaps at times scorch – those of us who are based 'over here'.

CHAPTER THREE

Culture: Compromise or Perish!

Poia Rewi

Multiculturalism is a dynamic influencing cultural change throughout the world, but in New Zealand biculturalism still plays a major role in the development of culture amongst Māori and Pākehā. Since Pākehā settled in New Zealand in the early nineteenth century, Māori and Pākehā have been engaged in continual negotiation. Identity, purpose and coexistence remain problematic, even today. Naturally, attempts at harmonious coexistence have not been achievable without change and compromise. Is cultural transformation therefore inevitable in order to ensure the survival of Māori culture?

The term 'transformation' resonates with change. This change is influenced by many factors: social pressures, legislation, environmental conditions, psychological, ideological or religious shift, 'the media and education'[1] and compromise, just to name a few. I perceive 'compromise' as a settlement of a dispute in which two or more sides agree to accept less than they originally wanted or a condition that a person accepts because the initial goal is unattainable. Compromise has sometimes been driven by the conflict that arose as a 'challenge to survival: to self-respect, to identity and to mana [prestige, power]' of Māori.[2] Does the survival of Māori as a distinct entity through compromise then continue to serve as a prime catalyst for the transformation of Māori culture in the twenty-first century?

In considering these questions, this chapter focuses on *whaikōrero* (the art of Māori oratory) as the platform for cultural maintenance and, in particular, addresses some aspects of *whaikōrero* where change is either underway or imminent as its practitioners attempt to hold on to this dynamic art form while experiencing the pressure to evolve with the culture of the nation. The chapter considers cultural maintenance from both the purist and liberal points of view and approaches the issue of cultural enforcement by asking how and/or who makes the decision as to which cultural practices are relinquished, which are retained, the extent of their retention and when this should take place. I also discuss some internal causes, for example, intracultural pragmatism and their effect on this particular keystone of Māori identity, *whaikōrero*.

Cultural maintenance

Cultural maintenance depends on a strong community life and commitment, as well as the capacity for cultural transmission. It is useful to consider the full spectrum of possible cultural maintenance. For the purist, cultural maintenance might imply rigid attachment to what is perceived as traditional practice and minimum or zero tolerance for cultural variations. Conversely, the liberal individual might be open-minded in accepting, retaining and/or developing changes in Māori culture. The liberal may take the view that all cultures change all of the time, and Māori culture prior to contact with Europeans had already evolved from the cultural practices brought by Polynesian settlers.

The rapid colonisation of Aotearoa New Zealand by Europeans had major impacts on Māori ability to maintain their culture. As the Pākehā population in New Zealand increased over some 100 years, Pākehā became the dominant culture and Māori the minority. As a result, Māori came under pressure to become 'new Britishers: by procreation and by assimilation …'.[3] Intermarriage between Māori and British settlers made cultural transmission between generations more challenging for Māori. But intermarriage, 'once hailed as the way to get the pale brown potato … hastened the learning of the lesson of individualism and the destruction of kin, marae, communal and tribal ties',[4] all of which were viewed as base components of Māori society and within that, Māori culture. These losses had a direct effect on the Māori sense of identity and many first-generation children resulting from bi-racial marriages found issues of identity as challenging then as their second- and third-generation descendants do today. Thus the transmission and maintenance of Māori culture has been an issue for both those growing up within Māori families and communities and for those in bi-racial families.

As well as intermarriage, religion, education, urbanisation and legislation all played a part in undermining cultural transmission and maintenance of cultural practices. Pākehā assimilatory policies and strategies took many forms: cultural accommodation, adaptation, variation, adjustment, development, flexibility, evolution, progress and finally, 'cultural compromise'[5] with its more negative connotation. Whatever the form, culture was at the receiving end.

Of course, since the late nineteenth century there have been a number of attempts within Māoridom to revive the 'dying race' and revitalise Māori culture. Particularly during the last twenty to thirty years, the period of the 'Māori renaissance',

Māori have increasingly pursued their own sovereignty and self determination – a cultural reform internal to Māori society. The establishment of early education in Māori language has been a significant part of this movement. Since the 1980s, too, government responses to this Māori revival have been more proactive, especially with the settlements arising from the Treaty of Waitangi and the establishment and development of institutions and policies addressing specifically Māori needs.

In looking at culture and identity I will use the term '*tikanga*' with reference to Māori culture, a word derived from the root '*tika*', meaning that which is correct, fitting, right, applicable, appropriate, just and fair.[6] *Tikanga* is a set of applied values, most of which are *iwi*-specific, although within *iwi* there will also be variations between different sub-*iwi* (*hapū*) and extended families (*whānau*). Culture generally includes customary practices, language, values and philosophies. It is 'a social process in which individuals participate, in the context of changing historical conditions. As an "historical reservoir", culture is an important factor in shaping identity'.[7] 'Cultural identity is important for people's sense of self and how they relate to others' and contributes to the individual's wellbeing.[8] Identity reassures one's sense of self-worth, confidence, security and belonging. It instills pride. Conversely, to have no culture is to experience a lack of identity. The maintenance or preservation of this *tikanga* is therefore an important factor for Māori as they locate themselves in modern society because it underpins their unique and distinctive identity. In terms of being Māori, I would use the following to describe the effect of cultural impoverishment:

> *Ko te tangata kāore ōna tikanga, he rite ki te rākau kāore ōna pakiaka.*
> *Ka pūhia e te hau, ka hinga noa, ka maroke, ka popo, ka hanehane.*
> People without identity are like the tree with no roots to establish itself firmly. It is constantly at the disposal of the elements.

Having a cultural base and a strong sense of identity provides the Māori individual with *mana*.[9] Therefore, the maintenance of *tikanga* is an important factor for Māori as they seek to integrate themselves into New Zealand society while at the same time maintaining their sovereignty and ethnic identity. Living in a multicultural society frequently calls for compromise and, as for so many other Indigenous people around the world, raises difficult questions over the processes and practices that are required to protect those cultural observances that have been passed down through generations of Indigenous peoples. Does a rigid attachment to *tikanga* arise from the manner in which practitioners value their culture and from their commitment to uphold it as the pillar of their identity? Or is a strict adherence to *tikanga* responsive, a reflection of the efforts mde by Māori to co-exist as Māori in New Zealand's multicultural society? Or is it, perhaps, the result of both? The most immediate question, then, is whether it is more beneficial to exercise flexibility or, conversely, better to remain rigid and uncompromising in order to retain those cultural observances in the purest form possible. For the purposes of this chapter, I will discuss cultural maintenance with specific reference to the Māori cultural practice known as *whaikōrero*: it presents a revealing case study into the types of issues now being confronted, such as gender, division of roles and responsibilities, division of authority between siblings, language of delivery, culture in the workplace and finally, enforcement of Māori protocol.

Whaikōrero is currently one aspect of Māori culture undergoing change. Cleve Barlow describes *whaikōrero* as 'the greetings expressed by elders on *marae* courtyards during assemblies of people'.[10] This form of discourse is mostly seen during the formal rituals of welcome between visitor and host known as *pōhiri*. The *marae* is pivotal in this discussion because of the importance it had prior to colonisation, a time when there were no 'tribal federations, kingdoms or central governments; no supra-tribal tribunals, no courts with executive authority'.[11] *Whaikōrero* may also take on a less formal structure during *whakatau* (ritual(s) of welcome between visitor and host, less formal than *pōhiri*), *mihimihi* (personal introduction, form of greeting) or *mihi whakatau* (rituals of welcome between visitor and host, less formal than *pōhiri*). These are acknowledgements between host and visitor set in a more intimate environment, away from *marae* courtyards and *marae* meeting houses,[12] inside buildings such as halls, lecture rooms, offices and lounges, rearranged as pseudo *marae* on a smaller scale. Regardless of whether they are formal or informal orations, there is a standard procedure. Despite this, there is always potential for unique displays and this is why *whaikōrero* continues to be one of Māoridom's most colourful and dynamic art forms and a key expression of Māori identity.

There are two major understandings of the term *whaikōrero* itself. Katerina Mataira describes *whaikōrero* as an important Māori custom which, prior to European colonisation, was the primary medium of expressing opinion and of presenting topics for discussion so as to enable decision-making by the people on all matters that affected their living arrangements, work, and communal activities in general.[13] If there were any major issues put before the people, each speaker would stand and air their opinion until all concerned had expressed what they wanted to say. They might *whaikōrero*, for example, 'to consider an affront given by another tribe, to determine on war, to make arrangements of peace and to discuss any other affair of general interest, a numerous meeting [sic] was convened and their oratorical powers were freely displayed'.[14] Māori continued to value *whaikōrero* as 'a manifestation of all they still valued'.[15]

The second interpretation of *whaikōrero* is as an exchange or discussion between two separate bodies of people, particularly host and visitor. Ranginui Walker expresses the view that *whaikōrero* originated from the period of inter-*iwi* feuding amongst Māori and that the practice was put in place to assess the intentions of visitors.[16] *Whaikōrero* consequently evolved as a ritual of encounter which then became an integral part of social gatherings amongst Māori. It 'is a true example of "in-group" language, clear only to initiates and this at least in part is the reason it is so highly valued'.[17] *Whaikōrero* is strongly associated with formality: procedures which have been adopted and prescribed and have ultimately become conceptual expectations as a precursor to established behaviour and action. Transgression of these formalities, or the failure to accept a practice such as *whaikōrero*, resonates as a 'slight' because cultural observances such as these form the identity and characteristics that define and distinguish Māori as a unique Indigenous people. Over and above a mere oration, *whaikōrero* involves the physical delivery, the psychological reverence afforded to it and the spirit in which it is expressed.[18]

The photo sequence on the next pages demonstrates the chronological stages of the welcoming process, the *pōhiri*, which is the most formal of Māori welcoming ceremonies in which *whaikōrero* is given a prominent place. The initial challenge, the *wero*, is believed to originate from the earliest period of New Zealand's settlement by Māori when *iwi* were still settling and defining boundaries. In a previous time, when the potential for conflict between host and visitor was always a consideration, one of the major functions of these ritualistic encounters was ensuring the safety of the clan. Now that physical conflict is unlikely, one might easily assert that it is redundant and its purpose, at least in terms of assessing the intentions of the visit, is little more than mere ritual. Why, then, is there persistence of this observation in today's society? Role-playing ceremonies such as these are an attempt by Māori to reaffirm their identity as Māori; they are cultural practices that differentiate Māori from all other peoples in the world. Yoon refers to this as 'geomentality – a particular behavioural pattern in dealing with the environment'.[19] *Whaikōrero* is being maintained as one of Māoridom's most intricate and culturally loaded art forms, especially on the *marae*, as the revered sanctuary where it, among other Māori practices, is given paramount acknowledgement and where it is most fully expressed and appreciated.

Clockwise from top left: *Front view of Painoaiho Marae, Murupara, 2004; Diagonal view of Painoaiho Marae, Murupara, with the* marae ātea, *the courtyard of grass space immediately in front of the* wharenui; *Host people gathered on the* marae, *with a young male member of the host group striding out with his* taiaha *in hand to issue the formal challenge, the* wero, *to the visitors; The visitors have accepted the challenge and proceed on to the* marae ātea; *Kaumātua Koro Tihema, a designated speaker for the host* marae, *delivers his oration,* whaikōrero, *to welcome the visitors; Professor Pou Temara, one of the visiting speakers and a speaker of renown, responding to the* whaikōrero *afforded them by the host speakers.* Poia Rewi

Role complementarity and changing roles

Whaikōrero is a male-dominated area of responsibility on most *marae*. As a result, one issue that has been raised and contested increasingly is gender. Whereas modern Western societies view a gendered division of roles as sexist, such a structure can be seen as a form of complementarity between the sexes: a form of organisation recognised elsewhere in Polynesia. In most *iwi*, women do not *whaikōrero* on *marae*. There are recorded accounts whereby high-born women of the Ngāti Porou, Kahungunu and Te Whānau-a-Apanui *iwi* have delivered *whaikōrero*.[20] Patu Hohepa has also explained that this was acceptable within his *iwi* of Ngā Puhi.[21] Tauroa explains that when women

> who would not normally claim that right [to speak], are accorded that honour by a marae, they will, most often, go to the porch of the whare and speak from there – from the shelter of the ancestor ... women may speak on the marae-atea on special occasions, under exactly the same conditions as men. But they, too, must be accepted by their people as having the necessary mana to speak on behalf of others. This expectation also applies to Ngāti Porou, a tribal area that accepts the right of women to stand and whai kōrero.[22]

There have been two primary assertions with regard to women and *whaikōrero*. The first is that colonisation brought with it Western practices and a leaning towards role division and female submissiveness, whereby the male takes the dominant, speaking role. The second assertion is that it was the old philosophy of Māori to protect women in an environment of potential physical and spiritual threat. Ani Mikaere cautions against the adoption of European views, such as those on gender inequality, in deciding whether or not all women should *whaikōrero*:

> The roles of men and women in traditional Maori society can be understood only in the context of the Maori world view ... Both men and women were essential parts in the collective whole ... The very survival of the whole was absolutely dependent upon everyone who made it up and, therefore, each and every person within the group had his or her own intrinsic value. They were all a part of the collective; it was, therefore, a collective responsibility to see that their respective roles were valued and protected.[23]

And, on the subject of 'physical or spiritual threat', Tauroa comments that the 'tapu [sacred, restricted, under influence of *atua*] of all women requires that they be protected from the possibility of abuse'.[24] This abuse refers to actual physical and spiritual attacks by way of 'cursing' (*kanga* = verbal or *kanakanaia* = inferred). Cursing (*kanakanaia, mākutu, whaiwhaiā*) involves the issue of an incantation, hypnotic inference or projection by willpower, with the intention of affecting the spirit and soul of an individual. This may then affect the psyche of the person who is cursed and result in psychological instability and/or physical weakening, the extreme being the death of that individual. In the woman's case, this will affect her capacity to give birth. This may not necessarily affect only the woman, but may also affect her progeny and so on:[25] 'Women were revered in Māori society for their ability to give life … Therefore, Māori were conscious not to expose women to curses or threats that might be made on the *marae ātea* [courtyard or grass space immediately in front of a meeting house], lest these affect subsequent generations'.[26] The restriction imposed on women in relation to *whaikōrero* (and even the restriction on women being seated on the front seats occupied by designated orators) thus allows the men to absorb the attacks and abuse of opposing speakers.[27]

That the *marae* is synonymous with potential physical conflict, was a point made by the late John Tahuri.[28] Does a woman possess the physicality to enter into physical confrontation, should a challenge be issued to her? As I think of this in relation to pre-European Māori society, I wonder whether aged men well beyond their years of combat would have been worthy adversaries in these instances or was there an age or point of maturation when even they ceased to be the vanguard on the *marae*? Clearly some of today's speakers have been appointed because of their age and wisdom, as opposed to their physical potential to defend their 'ground'. Some women are physically superior to some men and Elsdon Best documented instances where some Māori women defeated their male counterparts in combat.[29] In my own travels, I have seen some physically imposing women who I believe would put up a good fight if called to task by some of the aging orators delivering *whaikōrero* today. In light of the previous comments, it is perhaps doubtful that physical ability or supposed 'physical superiority' would be a strong enough reason for restricting women from speaking in today's climate.

Many Māori women, but not all, accept this restriction. Debate, however, continues: one argument raised is that women are equally and in many cases more eloquent in speaking Māori than men. Another argument put forward in support of women being allowed to *whaikōrero* is the result of some host *marae* experiencing a dearth of male speakers. In such a situation, perhaps permitting women to *whaikōrero* would remedy that shortage to some extent. One might argue that in the absence of men to orate, what would be more or less acceptable: failing to afford oratorical reciprocities or deploying one of the women to discharge this service? In discussing this issue, the argument was raised that when the Mātaatua canoe was adrift, should the female ancestor Wairaka have maintained her position and role as a female and allowed it to be lost to the tide, rather than rescue it as she did?[30] If her uttering of the phrase '*Kia Whakatāne au i ahau* [let me be like a man]', was the licence for her to operate beyond normal activities ascribed to Māori women, why can't this be employed on other occasions? Or would this be viewed as a compromise affecting either the integrity of the host and/or visiting *iwi*?

Perhaps one of the strongest counter arguments to the above is given by John Tahuri, who asks where such compromise might end. Will compromise continue to erode the Māori culture to the extent that the day will come when there will be no culture and no identity left to compromise? One may contest that if there is no compromise whatsoever, we risk foregoing the practice altogether and ultimately effect outright cultural loss. Is not compromise better than full loss?[31]

Compromise and deference

Another keystone of Māori culture is reverence towards elders. With regard to *whaikōrero*, this is expressed in the common practice adhered to, particularly by Te Arawa and Mātaatua *iwi*,[32] that the right to speak rests with the genealogically senior relative. One such restriction for speakers is described in Māori as *kei runga te pāpā, kei raro te tama,* which means the son or junior stands down to the father or elder. Another rule which may be applied is *kei runga te tuakana, kei raro te teina,* the younger sibling defers to the older sibling.

An example of how these considerations come into play may be taken from the blessing ceremony for the new premises in Te Tumu School of Māori, Pacific and Indigenous Studies, University of Otago, in 2006. Two host speakers from Te Tumu had been designated as speakers, I myself being one of them. I thought it appropriate to carefully consider the potential repercussions of my orating. Would any of my elders, as *manuhiri* (visitor(s)), feel that their integrity had been compromised because of my decision to speak before them? The potential was that my participation as an orator from the host side, being a 'junior' to some great speakers, might render them silent. One could argue here that if they persisted in delivering *whaikōrero*, they might be in breach of *iwi* protocols. Being renowned and influential leaders and orators throughout Māoridom, had they spoken, would their action be condoned as supporting the exchange of oratory between senior and junior lines or would this have been seen more as an assertion of their seniority?

In compliance with my own *iwi* restrictions of, first, having a father still alive and orating on *marae* and, second, having three older brothers, I decided not to speak. In retrospect, perhaps I should have tested the situation as a learning exercise. Perhaps this would have forced some particular cultural dynamic to reveal itself and consequently aid in the revival of some other cultural aspect. One Māori expression pertinent to this is *kia ora te tikanga, me takahi te tikanga*: that is, in order for culture to survive, culture must be transgressed. My interpretation of this is that when one particular cultural practice is trampled on, this sometimes prompts a behavioural, cultural response that may not have been practised because it needs to operate under specific conditions.

Over the last twenty-odd years, some senior elders from the Tūhoe and Te Arawa *iwi* areas have suggested providing or allowing fledgling and/or junior orators the opportunity to participate as performers of *whaikōrero*, rather than merely as observers. The motivation for this compromise has been the decline in able speakers as a result of language loss and/or cultural restriction. The concern is that younger generations, in their deference to more senior individuals, have not been getting the opportunity to practise or develop their oratorical skills, with the result that the successful succession of orators has become a challenge. A possible solution touted by some senior Māori elders is to waive the restriction on younger generations so that they be allowed to speak and hence gain confidence in oration while receiving ongoing coaching from the elders present.

Compromise in the length of *whaikōrero*

Compromise in the length of the delivery is an aspect of *whaikōrero* scrutinised by some observers and practitioners with high levels of fluency in the Māori language. For decades, public bodies have questioned and criticised both the need for and the length of some Māori cultural proceedings, such as the *tangihanga* (rites for the dead, funeral) and *pōhiri*. Western society is described as being time-bound, linear and result-focused as opposed to Easterners,[33] and dare I say it, Indigenous peoples, who tend to value an approach that seeks harmony, honours process and values team relationships, almost oblivious to time restraints.

The impact of the Western or Pākehā view is cultural accommodation, as some Māori feel compelled to imitate the host culture and blend in. Imitation of Western culture means accommodating time restraints by doing away with, for example, formal Māori welcoming ceremonies amongst government agencies. The removal of these 'time wasting' Māori protocols has been endorsed by some senior Māori leaders, which may in fact be a step by these Māori towards cultural avoidance. With this pressure, speakers may feel compelled or encouraged by colleagues and peers to cut their orations short. Potentially, the opportunity for the learned speaker to educate is minimised and the prospects for budding orators to observe and learn is also limited as a result of that pressure. And for what reason? All in the cause of expedience.

Environmental conditions can also pressure the speaker into modifying the length of their delivery. For example, on urban *marae*, peak traffic and noise can prove a distraction. The weather, hot or cold, also prompts speakers who host their rituals of encounter outside on the *marae ātea*, to consider the additional strain on the audience and cut orations short. This leads one to wonder whether this is thoughtfulness or compromise? I remember attending a funeral one wet winter's day in the eastern Bay of Plenty. While many sought cover and cut speeches short, the elderly orator from our visiting group 'weathered the elements', so to speak, and rejected offers of raincoats and umbrellas. I can't say whether he cut his original oration short, but it appeared to be a full delivery, leaving everyone at the mercy of the elements.

Now, one could easily be critical of this almost extremist approach by an elder to maintain the integrity of the culture. Was he just an inconsiderate old fool? I vehemently disagree. As a young observer I found the unwavering approach of this elder inspiring. Even if he got sick in the rain, I thought how honourable it would be to 'die' for your culture. It showed me that sometimes cultural maintenance requires extreme measures. It exemplified, at least for me anyway, the commitment by some to maintain the integrity of protocol. I have also witnessed at first hand instances of visiting speakers hearing murmurs around them hinting that they hope the speeches are not too long. In response and to the obvious dismay of the 'hinter(s)', the speakers have deliberately drawn their orations out. At King Koroki's funeral in 1966 Waikato asked Te Arawa speakers to cut their speeches short, resulting in retaliatory interminable speeches clearly intended to do the opposite.[34]

Responses such as these serve to remind us, as Māori, of other cultural practices such as patience and discipline. They focus attention on the importance of the event and the value that the quality of the orations themselves add to the occasion. An oration shortened by either host or visitor can easily be interpreted as a lack of respect for the occasion and/or those being addressed. It is, therefore, of paramount importance that the repercussions of cultural compromise or cultural accommodation be carefully considered to avoid pejorative interpretations of action. That said, it is true that cutting short an excessively long oration probably would not always be viewed negatively in terms of dishonouring the occasion or the participants. It can happen that the speaker may be personally criticised indirectly or in the extreme show of disagreement, the women who make up the body of people that the speaker is supposed to represent may simply begin prematurely singing a song designated for the conclusion of his speech, so putting an end to the lengthy oration.

Whaikōrero and the Māori language

> *A fundamental objective overall for Māori is a sense of self worth as Māori. This cannot be achieved without a sense that to be Māori, to be enriched by one's culture is of high value. In this context the effective recognition of the Māori language is of crucial importance.*[35]

Dr Tamati Reedy reiterates that Māori 'must speak our language. It is our unique expression of our identity. It is our identity in Aotearoa'.[36] Language, said the late Hohua Tutengaehe, is the one aspect that differentiates Māori from all other people in the world. These are but a few sentiments extolling the value of the Māori language to Māori. The importance of language to the Indigenous people, at least in terms of identity, is vital. So, in this heterogeneous country of New Zealand where there are two official languages, Māori and English, should English be accepted during *whaikōrero*? Te Wharehuia Milroy insists that the majority, if not all of the language of *whaikōrero* must be in the Māori language.[37]

I believe the future of *whaikōrero* will see the inclusion of the English language becoming more prominent by the year 2050. Whether this prediction comes true or not, however, will largely depend on the efforts made by Māori and other New Zealand citizens to maintain *tikanga* from a purist view or else reflect a majority decision to opt for the all-encompassing inclusive view of the broad-minded. There are Māori who actively support the use of English during *whaikōrero*. They want the orations to be culturally accommodating and inclusive of everybody in attendance and often encourage the translation of *whaikōrero* from Māori into English and/or important parts of the *whaikōrero* being delivered in English. The purists, on the other hand, view this as demeaning the status of the language. Two old men were actually cried down once for compromising and doing *whaikōrero* in English so that a Minister of Māori and Island Affairs could understand.[38] It angers some that such acts of accommodation are instigated for the benefit of non-Māori dwelling in New Zealand, who often take the time and make the effort to learn languages other than Māori, even though Māori is one of New Zealand's national languages.

On the international stage, it seems that important public figures are often allowed the privilege of speaking in whatever language they choose. Should Māori allow this to happen in New Zealand? Can it be stopped? One decision adopted by the Māori Studies Department at the University of Waikato in the late 1990s was that during the exchange of speeches there would be no language spoken other than Māori until after the formal exchanges had come to an end. In this way, the integrity of the Māori culture, its protocols, the Māori language and the Māori people could be maintained. At present, there is still the preference that 'people would rather provide an interpreter and continue to conduct the proceedings in Māori'.[39] Perhaps this form of accommodation is the best way forward in the interests of cultural maintenance. It neither compromises nor excludes any participant.

The main point is that without the support of the public towards allowing Māori to be prioritised in Māori proceedings, the Māori language itself risks being a language that 'can at best linger on as the language of a closed community, a symbol of a folkloric and oppressed existence'.[40] Differences of opinion do exist about the language of delivery during *whaikōrero* and although narratives speak of cases from the past where the outright opposition to the use of English during formal Māori procedure on the *marae* has resulted in physical bodily attacks on individuals,[41] one cannot really predict the outcome and extent of speaking English during current *whaikōrero*. Nor is it an easy issue to enforce.

Cultural modification and the workplace

As can be gathered from the example above, modifications of formalities have been adopted to accommodate Māori culture outside of its natural environment, the *marae*, and applied elsewhere. The workplace is an area which has impacted on Māori and their cultural practices. Staff at universities, polytechnics and government departments have, to some extent, become increasingly supportive of fostering Māori cultural practices and are working to implement these in institutions. Initiatives include programmes developed with the aim of educating and encouraging people to integrate the Māori language, *tikanga* and the Treaty of Waitangi[42] into their operations. Valuable spaces have been designated pseudo *marae* in order to accommodate the cultural demands of Māori students and Māori staff. Some universities have actual *marae* built on their campuses. These are used for cultural welcoming ceremonies, as congregation areas for Māori and non-Māori clubs and as teaching facilities.

Senior management and Māori academics often work together in order to seek ways to fulfill their role as tertiary providers and to incorporate Māori culture into that academic environment. Māori staff and students do acknowledge the efforts being made in these institutions to address this critical part of Māori identity. This compromise can only be viewed positively as the Western institution is seen to promote the culture of the Indigenous people of the land. It is continually a 'work in progress' and is not always achieved expeditiously and without challenges of its own, but I guess this adds colour to everyday life amidst the Western institution.

It is often the case that this cultural support and promotion requires 'change', more so in the application of cultural etiquette to an environment foreign to that in which it first evolved. In New Zealand, Māori have enrolled in increasing numbers in universities. This means that universities must take notice of cultural requests. The physical structure of university buildings and the human resources employed to facilitate effective learning for Māori are now faced with the concerns expressed by staff employed in a Māori Studies discipline who want nothing less than an environment that is both physically and psychologically safe for Māori staff and students and promotes the best in academic achievement and performance. Māori ask that Māori culture and the Māori language be included and promoted as a means of acknowledging their needs. The workplace may support and provide the opportunity to practise Māori culture, but because the university has its normal mode of practice, there may be a need to 'change' the Māori cultural practice in order to accommodate the physical structure of the university facilities and the Western and academic psyche.

So, are such forms of cultural compromise or cultural accommodation a bad thing? Many Māori advocate that Māori customs should be practised in their true traditional form without compromise. I would tend to agree with this stance on most occasions. And of course one would have to consider which cultural practice was being compromised. Perhaps one may argue that in an era where Māori push for the inclusion of more cultural observances in the workplace which is not, theoretically, a Māori environment, compromise is better than nothing. As the saying goes, '*Engari anō te ngaringari i te korekore?*' – 'Is not a little better than none at all?' There was public discussion recently about doing away with the *pōhiri* ceremony in the workplace because of the demands on time and people. From the point of view of a workplace with minimum resources, having no cultural observances would probably be a more favourable option. On the other hand, in my opinion, the lack of opportunity to offer a Māori cultural experience to non-Indigenous New Zealand people would be detrimental to the education of all New Zealanders, a loss to the wealth of cultural diversity that presently exists around them and a detour from biculturalism.

In an educational institution, I am probably more accepting of compromise because the academy is perceived as a forum whereby knowledge is extended or perhaps challenged, but ultimately I would still prefer to see culture maintained and practised without the inhibitions impressed upon it by a dominant culture, that is, by European practice and law. How else can we educate non-Indigenous people or even uneducated Indigenous people for that matter, about Indigenous traditions and practices when many Indigenous people themselves now live in towns which do not have a high percentage of Indigenous cohorts living in close proximity and, consequently, are not exposed to Indigenous practices at first hand on a regular basis?[43] I believe that compromise of culture is acceptable when it is the 'owner' of the culture who has ultimate control and initiates the change and when it is not a mirror or response to cultural dominance and/or cultural avoidance. Internally amongst Māori, it is the hosts who usually make this decision, an assertion of their identity and their right of occupation, commonly referred to as *mana whenua* (right of occupation, concept that groups with ancestral connection to land may have additional responsibilities).

To police and monitor culture

There is probably no way of discussing maintenance of a culture without commenting on the processes and practices that are required to enforce adherence. If cultural compromise, accommodation or avoidance are not options, then the people whose culture is being adapted need to consider cultural enforcement. So just how much effort or vigilance is actually required? The answer is considerable in both human and intellectual capacity. Even on provincial *marae*, which have been seen by Māori to represent the last bastion for *marae* protocols and hospitality, the ability to fully practise *tikanga* is now under threat from issues such as government laws, health regulations and the national economy. The rising price of fuel poses the question of the economic viability of maintaining cultural practices at current levels. Māori, especially spokespeople, are forced to weigh up the costs of attendance at functions, although I suspect that they may actually deny that cost is a consideration where *tikanga* is concerned.

Enforcement of culture can present itself with potential legal repercussions and interventions. If Māori are of the understanding that the *marae* is an acceptable place for a speaker to 'vent' and 'issue a challenge' before all who are present, there is the possibility that this could prompt physical retaliation at the speaker's expense. For an orator to issue a verbal challenge and then be met with a physical reaction would be unacceptable by law but acceptably Māori, under the old understanding Māori had that '*me marae puehu e marae ai te marae*' – 'for a *marae* to be fully acknowledged as a *marae*, it must have been subjected to confrontation'.

It is easy to set down ideals, but the biggest challenge is whether or not the people to whom the cultural practices belong have the capacity to counteract non-conformity by others, Indigenous or non-Indigenous. What are we, as Māori or as Indigenous peoples, prepared to do to maintain our cultural practices? How much, if any, are we prepared to 'give'? There are purists upholding cultural practices on their own *marae* who are prepared to go to any extreme to enforce adherence to the protocols they, as a unit, have adopted (perhaps over many generations) as being integral practices to their identity as an *iwi* or sub-*iwi* unit. There are Māori at individual or institutional level who, for numerous and varied reasons, are prepared to modify Māori culture. Māori living in areas or countries with low populations of Māori, who are dislocated from localities where Māori practices are a living reality, may not experience the same pressures to comply with cultural practices even if they have observed them many times throughout their own lives. Internal changes are a reality and,

> since it is culturally constructed, cultural identity shifts over time with changing historical circumstances and social contexts. In New Zealand the processual and situational nature of cultural identity is reflected in the highly variable definitions of Maoritanga. The formation of Maori identity has involved continual interaction with and reaction to, Pakeha (of European) identity. Maoritanga sometimes incorporates, sometimes rejects elements of that culture.[44]

Some Māori have viewed cultural shift as neither a predicament nor an issue. The utterance by the late Sir Apirana Ngata in the mid-twentieth century '*ko tō ringa ki ngā rākau a te Pākehā hei ora mō tōu tinana*'[45] encouraged Māori to pursue Pākehā ways, for example in education, and these words are constantly reiterated in speech, in proverb and in song. Although it is debatable whether he also encouraged Māori across that period to give up their own culture, this does indicate that not all Māori in the twentieth century were totally opposed to Pākehā practices. Even the likes of Donna Awatere, viewed by some as an extreme radical, expressed her opinion that Māori must 'offer the Pākehā an opportunity ... to establish an identity as New Zealanders which must be forged not in opposition to us, but for and with us'.[46] The notion of Māori and Pākehā in New Zealand working together must require cultural modification whether this be through compromise or other developments by both parties. Other Māori in the twentieth century sought assimilation because 'they felt they need to belong to the mainstream to be successful'.[47] Even in terms of gender, Māori women have been prominent in formulating identity, sometimes defining and redefining Māori culture through the fostering of Māoritanga (Māori identity, Māori culture, essence of being Māori including all aspects of Māori life) sometimes bridging Māori and Pākehā cultures and sometimes rethinking traditional Māori gender conceptions.[48]

These are just some examples of internal shifts amongst Māori. Ultimately, conforming to the 'mainstream' has meant foregoing some practices viewed as pro-Māori or Māoricentric. Consequently, divisions amongst Māori became evident through the late twentieth century. I recall my years as a university student when Māori afforded classification terms to their peers. These included 'plastic Māori', Māori who have retained cultural practices only 'superficially', for example, those involved merely as cultural performers; 'spuds' or '*rīwai*',[49] likened to a potato, because they are Māori (brown) in the colour of their skin, but psychologically, ideologically and behaviourally Pākehā; 'born again Māori', Māori who, beyond their control, were deprived of any Māori upbringing and knowledge who now have a realisation of their Māori side and are zealously committed to reaffirming their lineage and their identity through culture and language; 'radical Māori', so called because they protested any compromise of culture; and 'Māori *tūturu*' (true Māori), consisting of Māori raised amongst peers with a strong affinity to culture and language as well as being heavily committed to the maintenance of these themselves. All of these categories prompt different reactions to cultural observations, their retention and maintenance, because all of these display varying levels of cultural identity. Social interaction amongst these divisions also varies and two separate Māori subgroups may very well have opposing views about Māori cultural practices and their application.

J. Linnekin and L. Poyer argue that the 'imposition of foreign social models makes cultural identity problematic both in thought and in action'[50] and that for Māori it is already difficult, based on the fact that 'cultural and ancestral differences are at the root of identity …'.[51] A struggle with identity is directly linked to a culture in struggle, therefore cultural maintenance is important for the maintenance of Indigenous identity.

So, does the level of effort and commitment to uphold and enforce cultural observances indicate the degree to which practitioners value their own culture as their pillar of identity? The answer must be 'yes'. The means by which Māori maintain their culture in their own lifetimes and see this extended through the lives of their children and grandchildren will remain a constant vigil for Māori and Indigenous people for all time. There is no single approach to cultural maintenance, but there must be a common starting point for this to occur that the Indigenous grouping must share. They must want to maintain their culture because it is highly unlikely that anyone else will do it for them.

Ehara taku mana i te mana hou
He mana tahito tonu taku mana
I heke mai ki ahau i ōku tīpuna
Hei iwi tuaroa
Hei hā whakaoraora māku ki aku uri
Ki ngā whakapaparanga o te ake ake.

My power, my authority, my Māori majesty
Is not merely of recent times
It takes root from my ancestors long passed before me
To be cherished, appreciated and honoured
An heirloom of noble identity, uniquely Māori
To sustain the generations of Māori into the future.

CHAPTER FOUR

piko ka-sôhki-nitohtaman ka-nisitohtaman nêhiyawêwin
You Must Listen Very Hard to Understand the Cree Language

Naomi McIlwraith

This chapter explores the role of language loss in current debates about Indigenous identity in Canada. Even though it may be argued that there are many ways to express one's unique indigeneity other than through language, people who face the possibility that they will lose their mother tongue repeatedly insist that language is central to their identity. People need language as one of the conventions by which they belong to each other, to carry forward their history, their customs and their hopes to future generations. Among those who feel this most acutely are speakers of, or those who strive to speak, endangered Indigenous languages. Indeed, as K. David Harrison explains, 'Indigenous cultures and languages are among the most threatened globally'.[1] With so much of our reality promulgated through a colonial language, be it in English or Spanish or Russian, both in small nations speaking threatened languages and in the larger Canadian and global society, such uniformity poses serious threats to diversity of perception and expression. Imposed upon by the aggressive forces of political, economic and educational institutions and certainly the insidious influence of the media via the printed word, the Internet, radio, television and movies, Indigenous language speakers in Canada and other parts of the world seek to express their human experience in ways distinct from more homogeneous expressions. This chapter argues that language is central to identity, especially to those Indigenous peoples in Canada who persevere in preserving their ancestral tongues as inimitable mediums for communicating their own truths.

Many have taken up the mantle of language renewal and fortunately Indigenous language speakers are finding solidarity with others who care about rescuing the human knowledge contained within threatened tongues. Academics and activists alike now hear clearly the concerns of Indigenous peoples working to articulate their identity through Aboriginal languages. Indigenous peoples and their supporters recognise the pervasive pressures on language. After briefly considering a few statements from the sociolinguistics literature, I aim to elucidate these stresses by considering language loss as a fracturing process for Indigenous peoples, discussing Indigenous identity as it has been warped by colonial definitions of 'Indian'[2] and pointing to the genocidal foundations of residential schools as playing a destructive role in language erosion. Finally, I share our research efforts here at the Faculty of Native Studies, University of Alberta, in *amiskwacîwâskahikanihk*, as an optimistic example of what can be achieved if language preservationists can muster up the critical energy to raise funds, produce language resources and facilitate peaceful and productive discussions in identifying and managing the conflicts that fuel language debates.

Language, culture and identity

For more than a decade Indigenous language speakers and sociolinguists have disputed the correlation between language and culture or language and identity. Joshua Fishman, arguably one of the most influential of these language scholars, says,

> ... language stands for that whole culture. It represents it in the minds of the speakers and the minds of the outsiders. It just stands for it and sums it up for them – the whole economy, religion, health care system, philosophy, all of that together is represented by the language ... The language symbolizes for us the whole relationship.[3]

Contemplating the decline in Indigenous languages, Fishman describes an 'ethnolinguistic consciousness' amongst speakers who tell him that if they lost their language, 'they would lose a family member, an article of faith, a commitment in life'.[4] Others, like Gegeo and Watson-Gegeo, express similar sentiments: 'Language is essential to identity, authenticity (including people's culturally grounded sense of authenticity), cultural survival and people's learning and thinking processes because it encodes a cultural group's indigenous knowledge and, more important, its indigenous epistemology'.[5] The argument becomes more difficult, however, when language advocates struggle with exactly what a speech community loses if its ancestral tongue succumbs to more invasive forms of communication. Fishman qualifies his statement by declaring that, 'When languages die, people do not stop talking. Cultures do not fold up and silently steal off into the night. They go on and they talk the new language'.[6] Simon Ortiz, an Acoma poet and scholar, agrees but argues further:

'ê-kî-pimicimêyâhk kâ-yîkowahk: *We were canoeing when it was foggy*'.
Canoeing in the fog on manitow sâkahikan *provides an opportunity to move toward mystery and belief, concepts that are difficult to translate from* nêhiyawêwin *to* âkayâsîmowin. Naomi McIlwraith

Acoma people are not identified as Aacquemeh hanoh simply because they are fluent speakers of the Acoma Keres language. They are Aacquemeh hanoh whether or not they speak the language. There are some people, even within the Acoma Pueblo community, who will say otherwise, but such sentiments have more to do, unfortunately, with internalized colonialism, i.e., going along with how Indigenous people are perceived by outsiders and the federal government.[7]

Ortiz is willing to concede that the Acoma Keres language is not a defining characteristic of an Aacquemeh hanoh person. And yet, the deeply felt anguish of others cannot be denied: 'We have been decimated and scattered by war,' said a member of the Tiefo people in Western Burkina Faso in 2004, 'We have lost our identity, and now our language is being destroyed and nobody intends to help us; now we are lost forever'.[8] In presenting statements on the wrongs imposed on them by a dominant and expansionist power, the Tiefo speaker and Ortiz articulate forceful and opposing positions. As persuasive as Ortiz's contention is, however, in particular because his mother tongue is the Native American Acoma Keres language, an undeniable chorus of Indigenous language advocates supports the Tiefo speaker. In Canada, the Task Force on Aboriginal Languages and Cultures presses on with its own mission of protecting what the Tiefo speaker laments he and his people have lost:

> Our task is to ensure that the present generation of First Nation, Inuit and Métis peoples continues their traditions by recovering and strengthening their ability to speak and be understood in their own languages. Our task is also to ensure that the seventh and future generations of our young people will be fluent in their languages and will be able to articulate the traditional knowledge and spiritual beliefs embodied by them.[9]

Specialising in Aboriginal communities, demographer Mary Jane Norris supports the Task Force's assertion that transmission of various First Nations' languages *in the home, from generation to generation*, is critical to their survival. Norris identifies the continuity index as a measure of 'language continuity, or vitality, by comparing the number of those who speak a language at home to the number of those who learned that language as their mother tongue'.[10] The further this ratio drops below 100, the more serious are the causes of a particular language's decline. In fact, continuity may be a more important indicator than population size for a language's ability to survive because, as Norris tells us, 'Although population size is an important consideration in determining the health of a spoken language, if it is not being spoken within the family home it is less likely to be the mother tongue of the next generation'.[11] This intergenerational transmission is crucial to the health of a nation's tongue because children, by speaking their mother tongue, carry forward the knowledge older people in their communities have passed down to them. Norris observes an alarming trend between the 1996 and 2001 census data in Canada: the Aboriginal mother tongue population declined by as much as 3.3 per cent.[12] The traditional knowledge and spiritual beliefs that the Task Force on Aboriginal Languages and Cultures refers to are only a part of what is at stake here. Aboriginal languages articulate an Indigenous person's very selfhood and an Indigenous people's nationhood. Thus, we hear Indigenous peoples passionately defending their territories, their lands, their genders, their knowledges and their languages.

The Indian Act and language loss

Unfortunately, deep and insidious colonial transgressions have resulted in the demise of many Indigenous languages and interference with Indigenous identity in Canada. Hostile lawmakers have, throughout the nineteenth and twentieth centuries and into the twenty-first century, consistently imposed numerous policies and acts to define and restrict 'Indian' identity. Of note, the main goal of the Consolidated Indian Act of 1876 was to assimilate Indians.[13] In other words: eradicate the identities of those they categorised as 'Indians'. Various criteria were and continue to be forced onto Aboriginal peoples as a way to better control and regulate the boundaries of the category 'Indian'. Many of the restrictions of the Indian Act continue to wield the force of law, even today. The more recent Bill C-31 of 1985 (supposed to redress the sexism and racism of the various versions of the Indian Act) contains a second-generation cut-off clause and the messy business of regulating Aboriginal identity in Canada continues to divide Aboriginal peoples. Indeed, Jo-Anne Fiske and Evelyn George describe this misery:

> Collective stigmatization or rejection by one's own culture forces individuals away from cultural foundations that should offer coherent expressions of identity. By its very nature, the Indian Act sets the terms of this stigmatization. Socio-legal distinctions give rise to social disparities: C-31 has become a state of being. INAC commonly refers to persons as 'C-31s.' In their daily talk Aboriginal people ask such as questions as 'Who *is* C-31?' Indeed in our own research this was a continuous expression as researchers and participants alike signalled social distinctions by labelling who was and was not C-31, which communities had residents who were C-31, who had C-31 mothers, etc. Stigmatization and rejection are insidious forms of trauma; they reflect the internalization of colonial biases and create marginalized minorities within minorities ... Identity, contrary to liberal notions of choice and multiple identities, is coercively imposed in negative terms: to *be* C-31 is to be outside of full community membership.[14]

Sadly, the Consolidated Indian Act and its unsavoury reincarnations have bequeathed upon Aboriginal Canadians an alienating and harmful discourse that complicates their ability to assert their Indigenous identity.

Residential schools

Of relevance here is the colonial governments' collusion with churches in establishing residential schools as part of an overt and genocidal assimilation project designed for the 'peaceful elimination of Indians' sense of identity as Aboriginal people'.[15] Cultural genocide is most certainly an apt descriptor for the wrongs meted out to Aboriginal children and their parents when churches and colonial governments conspired in kidnapping children and forcing them to attend residential schools, often prohibiting contact with families for months and even years. While the Récollets, an Order of Franciscans, established a boarding school for Indian youth in Canada in 1620, the most damaging effects came with the official inauguration of the residential school system in the 1870s.[16]

John S. Milloy in *A National Crime: The Canadian Government and the Residential School System 1879 to 1946* and J.R. Miller in *Shingwauk's Vision: A History of Native Residential Schools* provide exhaustive histories of both the assimilative urges preceding and the humanitarian disaster following the residential school system. Both writers describe the horrible conditions, bad food and common abuses Aboriginal students suffered. Worse, death often occurred either from disease, malnutrition or when children attempted to return to their families. Milloy calls tuberculosis the 'white plague' and lists the causes: 'overcrowding in the schools, lax administration, budget shortfalls and poor hygiene and diet'.[17] Milloy says this about the Department of Indian Affairs and the churches' complicity in the goal of 'civilising' Indians:

> That the Department and churches understood consciously that culture or, more particularly, that the task of overturning one ontology in favour of another was the challenge they faced is seen in their identification of language as the critical issue in the circle. It was through language the child gained its ontological inheritance from its parent and community. The word bore the burden of the culture from one generation to the next. It was the vital connection. The civilizers knew it must be cut if any progress were to be made.[18]

Students who spoke their Aboriginal language could expect to be severely punished in the form of a strapping, forced to kneel in a corner for extended periods of time or even to write 500 times that they would no longer speak their Indian language.[19] Miller points to the missionary attack on Native languages as 'part of a broader assault on Aboriginal identity and the individual Native person's sense of worth as an Indian or an Inuit'.[20]

While residential schools are no longer legal in Canada (the last ceased operating in the late twentieth century) the continuing debate on Aboriginal identity and authenticity remains a divisive and destructive inheritance of this racist campaign to eliminate Aboriginals. Consider the confusion of an Indigenous language speaker who returns to her community after speaking a colonial tongue at a residential school for many years and can no longer remember her mother tongue. Some in her community may reject her because they are unable to communicate with her, because they perceive her as inauthentic and because through the assimilative restrictions of her Euro-Canadian education they no longer know who she is. More alarming yet, *she* may not know who she is any more. There is no lack of examples in American legislation that parallels Canadian history in terms of language policy designed to eliminate Indigenous identity. In 1887, Bureau of Indian Affairs Commissioner John D.C. Atkins articulated a callous and excessively narrow position by prohibiting the use of Indian languages at any Indian school in the United States: 'The instruction of the Indians in the vernacular is not only of no use to them, but it is detrimental to the cause of their education and civilization and no school will be permitted on the reservation in which the English language is not exclusively taught'.[21]

Language loss in the twenty-first century

Language death now proceeds at a much faster pace than in the nineteenth century, largely because of the global influences of the Internet, other media and the spread of English as a Second Language classes throughout the world.[22] Provision of these classes all over the English-speaking world is viewed as a necessity, so that newcomers can at least participate in their new environments, though many Indigenous language speakers, linguists and those worried about linguistic diversity will surely disagree. Daniel Nettle and Suzanne Romaine argue that language rights should not be separated from economic and ecological injustices:

> The fact that it is policies directed at the economic roles available to indigenous people – not policies directed straight at language – which kill minority languages is an important one. It confirms our view that language should not be seen in isolation but as one outcome of a general ecological and economic matrix.[23]

This economic and ecological milieu is bound intimately to the desires of Indigenous language speakers to communicate with their offspring in their own languages, to survive in the workplace speaking their own vernacular instead of a colonial language, to remember the name of an important food or medicine produced by their forbears before the species succumbs to short-sighted power-brokers regulating short-sighted economies.

The complexity of this ecological and economic mix intensifies language-recovery efforts on the ground. In some cases, the Indigenous community possesses the resources, including speakers and concerned community members, so that the effort to bring back their Indigenous tongue is a viable enterprise. In other communities, unfortunately, the list of issues is far-reaching and the need for clean water, adequate shelter and safe food takes precedence over language retrieval. Added to these colonially imposed social ills is the frustrating debate over how Indigenous languages should be taught and how to do so on ridiculously limited budgets. In Canada, Aboriginal communities compete with each other for federally provided funds that are woefully miniscule compared to the dollars supporting the maintenance of the two national languages. Such remarks as, 'Oh, you speak that Bush Cree. It's not like our Hobbema Cree' or 'Those people at Frog Lake, they don't speak our Cree at Sweetgrass' and 'That Cree they're teaching at the university, that's not the real Cree!' continue to dog contemporary efforts to set aside regional differences and articulate a practical linguistic strategy that cuts across more recent colonial borders such as the Canadian provinces. In many ways the latter is an appropriate criticism given the university's colonial amnesia regarding the richness and necessity of the spoken word in language learning. Students of *nêhiyawêwin* at the University of Alberta in *amiskwacîwâskahikanihk*, while recognising the usefulness of written assignments, have often criticised the academy for its failure to truly ally with Indigenous peoples in their language-recovery work and lobby governments, industry, the private sector and other funding bodies for appropriate financial commitments toward more than adequate human and textual resources for language instruction. So much energy and time is invested in grant-writing and producing written exercises at the expense of the real work in conversation.

For example, the Faculty of Native Studies at the University of Alberta in *amiskwacîwâskahikanihk* offers a number of Cree classes for speakers and non-speakers. A keen student in these classes can learn a functional vocabulary of nouns, pronouns, demonstrative pronouns, locative suffixes, time passage/conditional markers, reflexive and benefactive verb forms, special suffixes, the intricacies of the transitive animate direct and inverse verb paradigms, how to conjugate verbs in the independent, conjunct and subjunctive modes, change in discourse, relative clause, past, present and future tense markers, even syntax, polysynthesis and reduplication, etc. The academy requires this written work to justify the scholarly

'mîkiwahp waniskânikana manitow sâkahikanihk: *Tipi poles at God's Lake (Lac Ste. Anne, Alberta)'. Covered with hide or heavy cloth, tipi poles such as these provide the structure for the many* mîkiwâhp *that can be seen on* manitow sâkahikan, *located 90 kilometres west of Edmonton, Alberta, where Cree, Métis, and other Indigenous people continue an annual pilgrimage to reconnect with relatives and allies in worshipping* kise-manitow *in Michif,* nêhiyawêwin *and other Indigenous languages.* Naomi McIlwraith content of the courses, just as it does for other languages such as French, Mandarin or Japanese. Many disparities, however, exist between curriculum development and teaching resources for colonial languages and endangered Indigenous languages. Language immersion curricula require enormous financial and human resources and current colonial governments continue to neglect the commitment and investment for such capacity building in Indigenous languages. It is no secret that students can immerse in French or Spanish much more easily than in Cree. Cree teacher Dorothy Thunder, whose mother tongue is *nêhiyawêwin*, has responded to students' insistence on a greater oral component by developing her own pedagogy and professional skills and attending language workshops and conferences, in addition to refining her lectures on a yearly basis.

Thunder brings with her a mother-tongue fluency – *ê-pakaskît* – in Cree and regular participation in Cree cultural events – *nêhiyawîhtwâwina*. Thus far, the Faculty of Native Studies and the University of Alberta have supported her efforts, though this commitment is difficult to maintain given budget cuts and other demands. Thunder has recently adopted Stephen Greymorning's Accelerated Second Language Acquisition methodology, which minimises written work and maximises verbal content. At a recent conference attended by Indigenous language speakers, teachers and learners from all over North America, Greymorning argued that educational institutions are producing great readers and writers of Indigenous languages but very few speakers.[24] Originally developed for the Arapaho language, spoken in various regions of the United States such as Montana and Wyoming, Greymorning's approach is now being implemented in various language programmes throughout North America in an attempt to address this challenge.

Accelerated Second Language Acquisition (ASLA)

A particularly telling demonstration of an ASLA language lesson speaks of the efficacy of thoughtful planning in teaching language. Greymorning permits no English to be spoken in his classroom. He begins with a series of large colour images pasted onto file folders, in pairs. Each image in the pair somehow relates to its mate and each pair of images connects to the pairs of images on either side of it. Greymorning begins with two file folders and four images. Because I know no Arapaho I will use Cree examples and Dorothy as the instructor. Imagine that the first pair of images is a dog and a horse, *atim* and *mistatim* respectively. Using a pointer, Dorothy points to the dog first and says '*atim*'. The students repeat after her several times until she hears them pronouncing the word correctly. Then she points to the horse and says '*mistatim*' and the students follow, repeating the word until they say it properly. Dorothy then points to the dog again and repeats the process, followed by the horse. Once she is sure the students have it sorted it out in their oral understanding and that they hear and know the difference between '*atim*' and '*mistatim*' she goes on to the second pair of images: boy and girl – '*nâpêsis*' and '*iskwêsis*'. Using the same process as for '*atim*' and '*mistatim*', Dorothy points to each image, speaks the word and has the students repeat after her. She does this several times until she is certain the students understand orally the difference between '*nâpêsis*' and '*iskwêsis*'. Now she has four images to work with and she returns to '*atim*' and '*mistatim*' to see if the students still remember these words. Within less than fifteen minutes she is already assessing their comprehension and here is where the real lesson emerged when we observed Greymorning presenting his methodology at the conference in Missoula, Montana in April 2008. He invited an instructor up to demonstrate (not Dorothy) who had used his methodology before and asked her to take the students through this process. When she was satisfied that the students had voiced the nouns enough times to know them, she proceeded with her assessment. She pointed to one of the four images and waited for one of the students to come forward, point to it and speak the word. The students hesitated and Greymorning intervened, saying that testing for speech first is futile; comprehension always comes before speech. By pointing to the image and waiting for the students to say the word, she was testing for speech and pronunciation. Instead, Greymorning stood at the front of the classroom and said in Arapaho, 'Show me the horse'. Now he was evaluating the students' oral comprehension. One of the students stepped forward, pointed to the horse and said the Arapaho word for horse. Greymorning then said in Arapaho, 'Show me the girl' and another student stepped forward, pointed to the girl and said the Arapaho word for girl. In this way, Greymorning was able to determine whether the students had heard each word enough times to store it in their oral memory and in so doing, he was able to test their comprehension levels. If we think about how babies acquire language, this is precisely what parents do: they repeat and repeat and repeat and repeat again until the baby understands. Then the parents repeat again and again until the child begins to speak.

Greymorning has developed and refined this methodology and he now has twenty skill sets, totalling several hundred file folders and images. Anecdotal evidence suggests very strongly that the ASLA method has the potential to produce Indigenous language speakers more effectively than pre-existing pedagogical methods. Dorothy's experience using the ASLA approach in her Cree classes attests to the efficacy of involving the visual (allowing students to see a picture), the audio (permitting them to hear the word repeated numerous times), and the physical.

This 'in-the-trenches,' practical, focused work requires linguistic expertise and a sound teaching pedagogy and demonstrates an effective language approach for institutions.

Mike and Iva Redman provide another example of the use of ASLA in a classroom. Working on the Wind River Reservation in Wyoming, they have developed a highly streamlined process for language instruction that involves increased proficiency for building on previous language acquisition successes arising from the ASLA model. For example, in the Redmans' experience, teaching both the singular and plural forms of verbs is important both for facilitating a more fluid connection between one and more than one object and in preventing code-switching. In Cree, an example of this code-switching would be to rely on the English '-s' to pluralise a Cree noun: one boy is *nâpêw*; two boys in Cree is *nâpêwak* not nâpêws. Emphasising the utter necessity of repetition, these Arapaho language teachers have learned that a foundation is required first before introducing too many verbs. This means that once the students really learn noun combinations they can learn the verbs more quickly.

At the Wind River Reservation, the Redmans and their colleagues streamlined the ASLA methodology so that 300 children a day have some exposure to Arapaho. Kindergarten, Grades 1, 2 and 3 students receive 30 minutes of instruction per day in Arapaho; Grades 4, 5, 6 and 7 students experience Arapaho 45 minutes per day; and Grade 8 students are in Arapaho language classes 60 minutes per day. Arapaho instructors even combine classes, overlapping primary and middle school grades. An amazing thing happens when the Grade 8 students (ages 13–14) begin teaching those in Grade 2 (ages 6–7), illustrating how natural and predictable it is for children of different ages and adults to speak to one another. The Arapaho adult teachers move around the classroom to guide the process and ensure that the eighth-graders are teaching the younger children correctly.[25]

Language revitalisation in the university environment

This monumental effort to recover the Arapaho language speaks both to the cohesion amongst the Arapaho-speaking community on the Wind River Reservation and to the funding, curricular materials, human resources and recognition of the vitality of Aboriginal languages that are crucial to language recovery projects. Fortunately, the Redmans work on a reservation that makes the connection between school and community realistic. In higher learning settings such as at the University of Alberta, linking the classroom to the community is much more difficult, especially when the university Cree seems so barbaric to reserve

Cree speakers or arguments occur regarding how to write in Cree such as whether or not to use Standard Roman Orthography or Syllabics, or we ruminate on just who invented Syllabics anyway and whether or not writing the language down constitutes its theft. Other debates consuming precious time that could be used more effectively in really teaching and learning *nêhiyawêwin* include whether or not non-Aboriginal people should be allowed to work on the Cree language, how much written work compared to oral work should students receive in the classroom, should Alberta scholars use hyphens to mark word and morpheme boundaries and should we mark the long '-ê-' as they do in Saskatchewan and Manitoba.

These discussions are not isolated to Alberta or Western Canada. In Hawai'i, for example, efforts to revive the Hawaiian language have resulted in concern about who the 'authentic' Hawaiian teachers are and how they are produced. Since new speakers of Hawaiian differ considerably in their speech compared to those who speak Hawaiian as their first language, some believe that this 'contaminates the purity and weakens the integrity of the language' when these new speakers become the teachers.[26] In Sheshatshiu, a community in Southern Labrador, Canada, speakers of Innu-aimun (previously called Montagnais by their interlopers) generally learn this language in the home as their mother tongue. However, as in the Hawaiian case, 'the Innu-aimun spoken by elders was highly regarded by nearly the entire population and the Innu-aimun of younger people was viewed more negatively'.[27]

Such conflicts inform our work in the Cree Language Project here at the University of Alberta. Funds from a developmental grant, from the Social Sciences and Humanities Research Council of Canada in 2005, allowed us to host a number of meetings with Cree speakers and those with a vested interest in preserving it and other Indigenous languages in Alberta. In addition to developing more textual resources for Cree language instruction, a major part of our subsequent standard research award (2006) now goes toward exploring these differences. In April and June 2008 we conducted another series of conversations – *pîkiskwâtitôwina* – this time to specifically deliberate on what these divisions mean and how they might be hindering efforts to advance *nêhiyawêwin* and other local Indigenous languages. During the process we heard repeatedly of just how deeply Cree and other Indigenous peoples identify with their languages.

Conclusion

Speakers of Indigenous languages persist in defending their mother tongues as their most precious means of conveying their Indigenous experience. Indeed, Aboriginal languages continue to be spoken in Canada today and this testifies to the resilience of Indigenous peoples in their quest to express themselves freely and forthrightly. Having survived colonial attempts at eradicating their cultures through legislation directed squarely at language and identity, Aboriginal Canadians articulate a powerful position through their distinctiveness as Indigenous language speakers. Indigenous language loss, however, remains a disturbing trend in contemporary Canadian society, as it does globally. 'Loss' seems a particularly inadequate word to describe the decline of languages because of the immensity of what these languages give us in terms of human knowledge. This is especially so for oral languages, since the immediacy of the spoken word cannot be captured in cursive representation. These signs often render the language in European-derived orthographies. The living language is a spoken language filled with history, poetry, music, medicine, wisdom and emotion and the human capacity contained within a language is an infinite repository of what came before and of what lies ahead.

Canadian colonial policy included residential schools, language prohibition, spiritual suppression, identity regulation and a host of other attempts to 'do away' with Indigenous peoples. Current identity laws demonstrate contemporary attempts on the part of modern governments to maintain this assimilation programme and the vehement concern Aboriginal Canadians have for protecting their languages as their means of expressing who they are attests to the centrality of language to their identity. What they stand to lose is so immense that explaining it edges toward the ineffable. A common struggle is to translate a concept from one language to another: some essential quality in the original language escapes the colonial language's ability to express it. Because Cree is a highly inflected language, which is to say that it functions polysynthetically and employs a host of prefixes and suffixes adding layer of meaning upon layer of meaning, word for word translation of anything more complex than a noun is next to impossible. For example, I could quite easily translate *picikwâs* into English: apple. On the other hand, *piko ka-sôhki-nitohtaman ka-nisitohtaman nêhiyawêwin âhpo êtikwê êkâ ka-âkayâsîmoyan mistahi* is considerably more complex. Loosely translated it means, 'You must listen very hard to understand the Cree language and maybe not talk in English so much'.

CHAPTER FIVE

Resisting Language Death – A Personal Exploration

Hana O'Regan

The Kāi Tahu *iwi* (also known as Ngāi Tahu) of the South Island is the fourth largest *iwi* in New Zealand. They have the largest traditional territory of any *iwi*, covering approximately 80 per cent of the South Island. They also have the status of being the *iwi* with the worst language health in the country, with less than 11 per cent of those resident within the *iwi* territory having some level of competency in the Māori language. This chapter will explore the efforts by members of Kāi Tahu to resist the encroaching death of their heritage language over the past fifteen years. It will present a personal account of my own experiences as a second-language learner endeavouring to promote and apply theories of intergenerational transmission of the Māori language within the macro Kāi Tahu context and at the micro *whānau* (family) level. As such, this chapter will aim to present an insider analysis of the struggle for language and cultural identity revitalisation and regeneration of a minority language, with first-hand experiences of the obstacles, challenges and aspirations for language survival.

A language strategy is born

In 1995, a small group of Kāi Tahu language speakers and two invited language revitalisation experts gathered for a three-day planning meeting in an attempt to devise a strategy to revitalise the language within the *iwi*. Over the course of the meeting, the group investigated international examples of language revitalisation and associated theories and were captured by the work of internationally renowned scholar and language expert Professor Joshua Fishman. Fishman's analysis of language decline and strategies to help reverse the shift of language death became the doctrine that provided the basis of the subsequent Kāi Tahu language strategy which emerged from that *hui* (gathering), '*Kotahi Mano Kāika, Kotahi Mano Wawata* – A Thousand Homes, A Thousand Dreams' (KMK). This strategy sought to have at least 1000 homes speaking the Māori language by the year 2025 and so realise over 1000 aspirations of Kāi Tahu people for their language.

The vision was a bold one that was focused on a future generation – bold given the reality Kāi Tahu faced in terms of our language status. With no empirical data to refer to, we set about articulating our collective knowledge on the language within the *iwi* and its then 30,000 or so members, to form a rudimentary environmental scan of the health of our language. We had three native speakers of Kāi Tahu *reo* still alive, none of whom were still speaking *Te Reo* (the language) at that time. *Te Reo* had not been the language of communication within Kāi Tahu *whānui* (wider Kāi Tahu) for fifty years and intergenerational transmission of *Te Reo* within *whānau* had not occurred for eighty years and exceeding 130 years in some areas. Less than one per cent of Kāi Tahu were known to be fluent speakers of *Te Reo*.[1] With these facts in hand and with a vision to guide us, the group set about establishing the foundations to make KMK a reality, driven by an obsessive determination to reverse the tide of language death in our people.

The adolescent years

It has now been over thirteen years since that strategy was launched and eleven years since KMK strategy was formally adopted by the *iwi* council, Te Rūnanga o Ngāi Tahu, in 1997. Since that time, the organisation has facilitated the investment of financial and human resources into the strategy and although the directions have changed over the past decade in terms of the prioritisation of initiatives, the driver has remained constant. Kāi Tahu can now boast a KMK website, a language-planning model and proficiency tests to assist its members in assessing their language levels, language-acquisition resources including language texts and associated audio guides for language in the home and a range of Māori resources to enhance critical awareness around the Māori language. There are now in excess of 3000 individuals and over 1000 homes signed up to the KMK database. Those people have become members of KMK and in doing so have stated their intention to increase the *reo* spoken in their homes and develop their language proficiency.

Anecdotally, we are significantly better off than we were thirteen years ago when we launched our strategy. Back then we could name (personally) around 100 speakers of the Māori language known to the *iwi*. Today we could probably name around 250–300. In 1995 we struggled to identify a handful of Kāi Tahu families known to be raising their children in the Māori language. Now we could safely name fifteen to twenty. Despite these milestones, we still have the worst health statistics for the Māori language of any *iwi* in the country. Although it is healthy

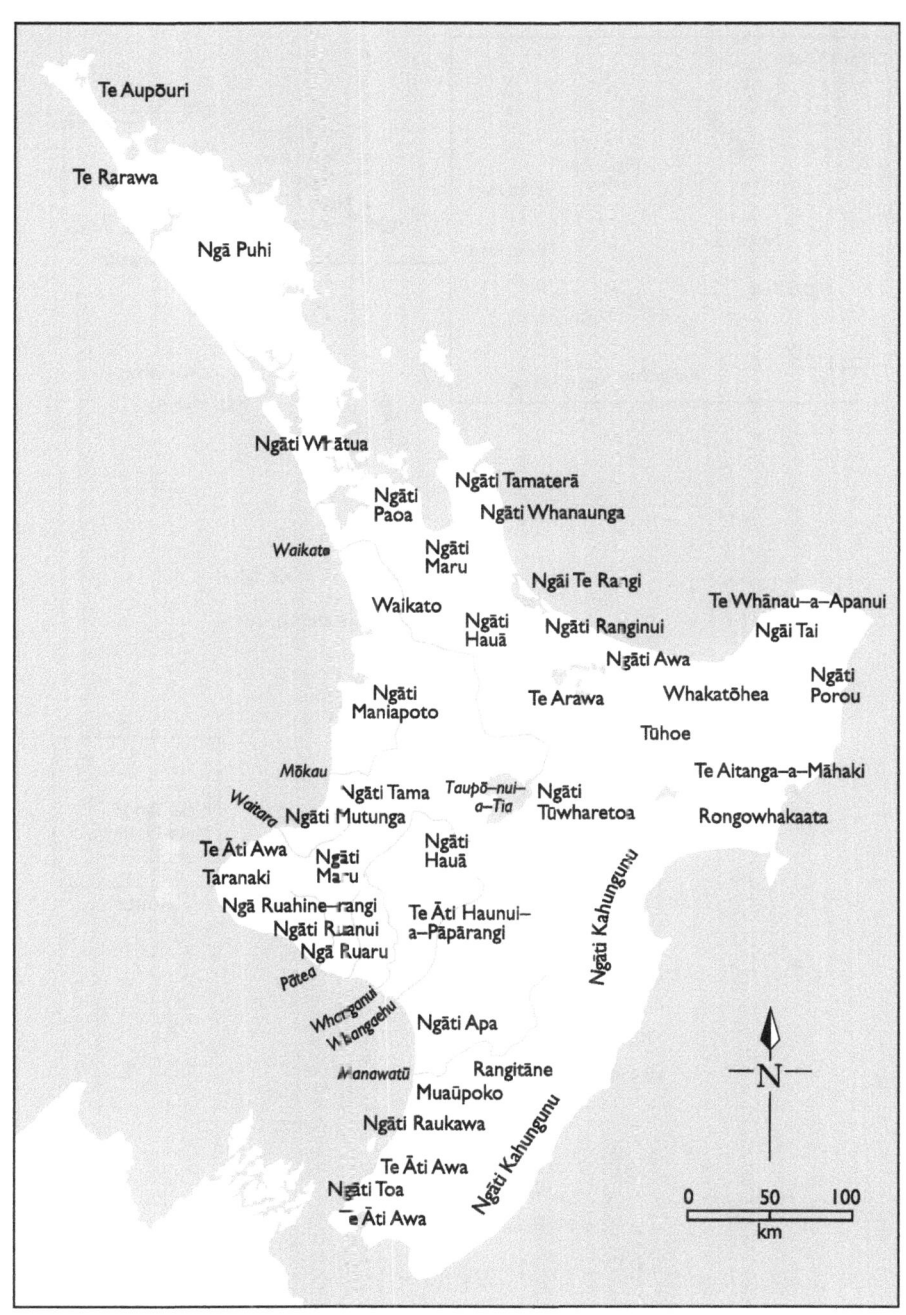

Map of North Island showing iwi boundaries. Allan Kynaston

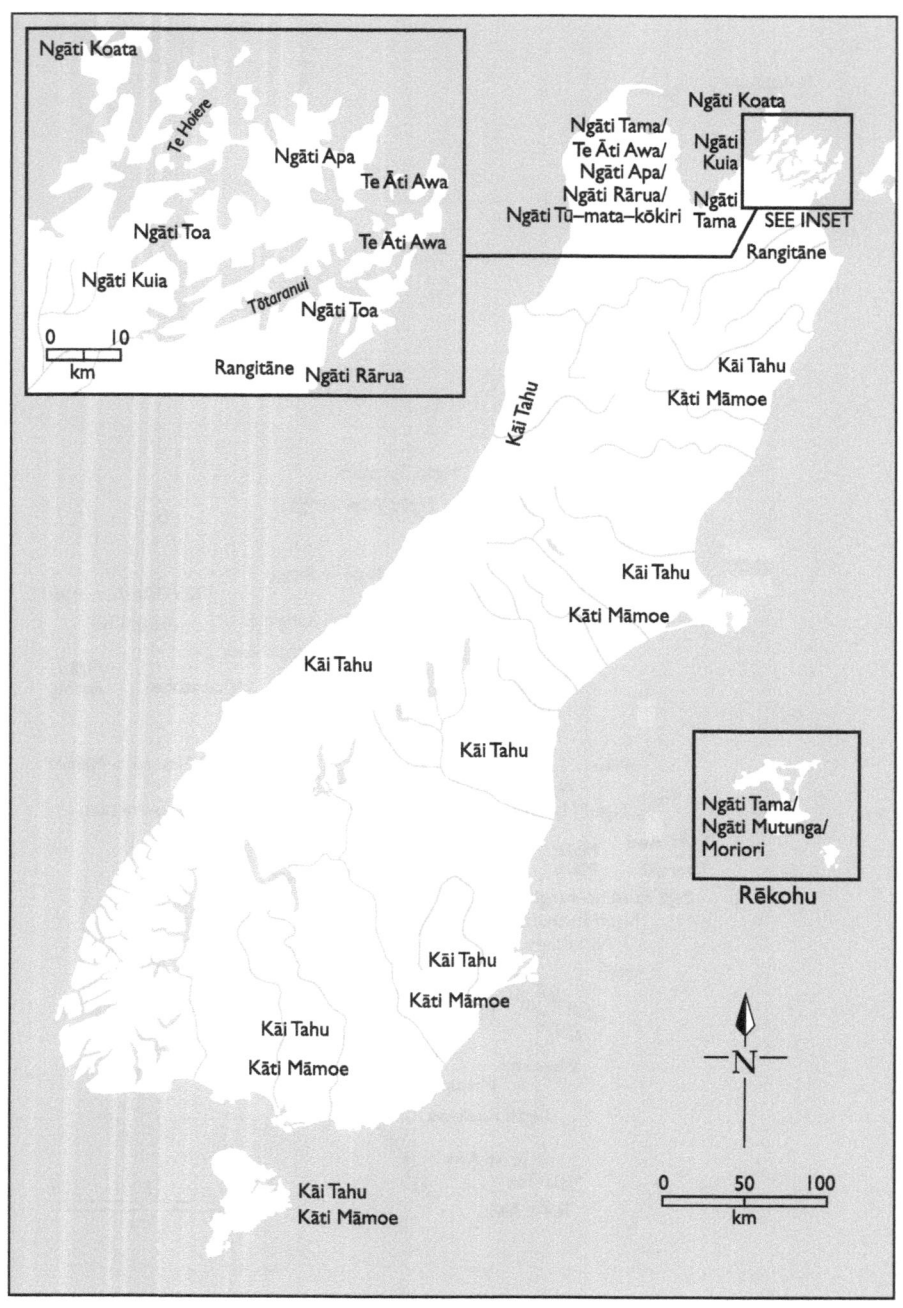

Map of South Island showing iwi boundaries. Allan Kynaston

to at times celebrate the gains, these milestones remain lacking when one places them in the context of global language decline. Complacency can be ill-afforded in the current climate of language death, as internationally we see languages die at an alarming rate: 'The accelerating extinction of languages on a global scale has no precedent in human history ... Languages are far more threatened than birds (11 per cent threatened, endangered or extinct), mammals (18 per cent), fish (5 per cent) or plants (8 per cent)'.[2] Linguists around the world now predict that fewer than half of the approximate 6000 languages spoken today will still be in use in 100 years time. That translates to a language somewhere in the world dying approximately every ten to twelve days.[3] Of course it is positive that we now might have as many as twenty homes raising their children in Māori, but growth from three or four to fifteen in nearly as many years is not fast enough to curb the threatening tide of language death. The rest of the non-Māori speaking Kāi Tahu population, now numbering approximately 40,000, are continuing to grow and the speakers are becoming even more of a minority than before.

The struggle is very real and it affects people in a very personal way as it is inextricably tied up with perceptions and articulations of one's cultural identity. In order to gain an appreciation of the dramatic nature of that battle to resist language erosion and regain language proficiency, it is appropriate to look beyond the somewhat impersonal layer of *iwi* statistics, to focus on the more personal realities faced at the *whānau* level where efforts to raise children to speak Māori can be seen and the associated challenges analysed.

The language family tree

My own family and experiences can provide a focus for such an analysis. My great-grandparents were both Māori. They were born in the 1880s and died in the 1940s. Both sets of their parents (my great-great-grandparents) were native speakers of Māori but they did not raise their children in the language. Over 120 years ago, the major language shift away from Māori to English occurred in my family. My great-grandparents, Taare Bradshaw (the first) and Rena Harawata, had my grandmother, Rena Ruiha. They commonly used phrases and commands in Māori along with the odd curse, but English was the dominant language at home and by that time the dominant language in Māori communities in Te Waipounamu (the South Island of New Zealand, literally 'the place of greenstone'). In the 1930s and 1940s, most of our elders were still quite capable of performing the necessary cultural rituals in the Māori language, but English remained the vernacular.

My grandmother picked up some of the sayings and commands, terms and pronunciation, but her exposure to the language was even less than that of her parents and so the decline continued. She married my Pākehā grandfather and they had my father. He can recall spending time with his maternal grandmother and hearing her use her limited *reo*, mainly commands. His mother would call him by his Māori name. He knew he was Māori. He knew he was Kāi Tahu, but he was raised to have no functional ability in the language. Many Māori find it hard to comprehend the extent of language decline within Kāi Tahu and even harder to imagine that Māori being born over 100 years ago were not being born into Māori-language homes. This was, however, the reality for many Kāi Tahu families living in Te Waipounamu and for some, the time gap extends beyond 150 years. The challenge that this reality then poses for those *whānau* is significant when the issue of language revitalisation is considered.

When the heritage language has not been a part of the family's inherited legacies for so many generations, a person cannot simply delve back into the recent catalogue of memories and experiences to retrieve it. The linguistic memories of surviving generations in or about that language do not actually exist. The jokes, sayings, idioms and terms of endearment all have to be learnt from scratch. Although there may still be manuscripts, written records that hold many keys, the kind of language used is usually limited. It tends to be dominated by a high degree of formality: poetry, histories, songs and traditions and descriptions of events and people. Although there is often much prose, it is rare to find whole dialogues of 'ordinary speech' between individuals on which intergenerational language can be modelled.

Despite the richness of knowledge that can be obtained from these treasured manuscripts, for those who aspire to speak the language and re-establish it as the vernacular within the home, these manuscripts' greatest contribution will be in the associated cultural and personal historical knowledge that can be obtained from within, along with models of syntax and lexicon particular to that language or dialect. There is still no way of knowing, however, how things were said: the intonation, where the emphasis and word stress might be found or the ways they laughed and why. For the descendant of a language silent for generations, nothing comes easily and naturally. Everything must be sought, everything must be learnt and these are often combined with a great deal of speculation, conjecture and assumption on the part of the language reviver.

In the 1960s (eighty years after that first major language shift occurred in our family), my father embarked on learning Māori as a second language and therefore started to turn the tide. All his five children were born by 1973 and none were to be raised in a bilingual context. The sayings and odd command, grace at meal times, a few Māori songs and Māori names had remained culturally persistent and survived the preceding three generations, but beyond that there was nothing. Whilst learning Māori himself, my father increasingly exposed his young children to new words, sayings and phrases. Three children went on to formally study Māori at secondary school and two of those children sat national examinations in Māori.

Of all the children, I was the youngest and therefore fortunate enough to be growing up when my father's language acquisition was on the rise. I was exposed to more Māori-language environments on a more regular basis. The only child to attend a Māori boarding school, I began my first Māori-language class being quite sure I knew Māori, even if I was more of a receptive bilingual as opposed to a productive one. At the age of twelve, my ability to comprehend what being 'fluent' in another language meant was, to say the least, severely inadequate. Being raised in a largely monolingual context in a predominantly monolingual and geographically isolated country meant that my proficiency in another language had never been challenged. I was, therefore, of the belief that knowing a number of phrases, the odd prayer, a number of words and some songs, meant somehow that I was able to speak Māori. My home environment also failed to challenge me in this regard as I was able to comprehend most of what I was being regularly exposed to. It was not until I arrived at a Māori boarding school and was introduced to girls who were functionally proficient in Māori that I was confronted with the harsh reality of my language ability.

After four years of formal training in the Māori language at secondary school, I left for Thailand and proceeded to learn more Thai in four months in that immersion environment than I had Māori in four years. Returning to tertiary study in New Zealand, I continued my formal training in the Māori language for a further three years. By the end of my undergraduate study, I had achieved a level of proficiency that allowed me to compose traditional-style chants in Māori, write essays in Māori, compete in formal debates, read and edit Māori newspapers from the 1800s and do so with a medium to high level of accuracy. My meta-linguistic skills were functionally passable, if not plausible. By nineteen years of age, I was tutoring others in Māori language at university and, by twenty-one, had assumed the position of lecturer in undergraduate studies in Māori language and Māori creative writing at university.

One might be forgiven for imagining, therefore, that I had attained near native fluency in the Māori language by this stage and although that might have been the case in certain domains, my language ability was not as broad or extensive as I allowed myself to believe. The issue was that I had not really thought about Māori language outside of the familiar formal context. I had, on occasion, engaged myself in Māori language immersion courses where I tutored during the day and played cards and ran concerts at night. They were often a struggle but because the small group of us who were teachers were, on the whole, more proficient than the student participants, we developed a false sense of security in our language and were largely unaware of what we did not know.

Remember also that the previous twelve years of formal language learning was centered on the text-book language of the day, which had been largely standardised – stripped of dialectal references and void of that which might confuse. It had largely been simplified for the burgeoning group of second-language learners who were attempting to reclaim their language. We had not yet heard of a *kīwaha* (idiom). *Kīrehu* (idiom with obscured meaning) were another eight years away. We knew of *whakataukī* (proverb(s)) and used them in speeches and debates, but had not considered their application in non-formal language contexts. I had only ever assessed and been assessed in terms of my own language proficiency in a few very limited domains – but within them I had scored sufficiently high.

In her book, *Bilingualism in Development*, Ellen Bialystok refers to the complexities of assessing proficiency of second-language speakers:

> ... research that has ostensibly examined the viability of the critical period hypothesis for second-language acquisition has usually examined one or two aspects of language proficiency but made claims about the question at large ... A more differentiated approach to explaining proficiency would allow us to say what it would mean to function like a native speaker across several domains and then to evaluate the success with which language learners approximate those performances.[4]

It is seemingly easy to place yourself in her diagram and measure your proficiency in a given domain, based on how capable you are at controlling and analysing language in different contexts:

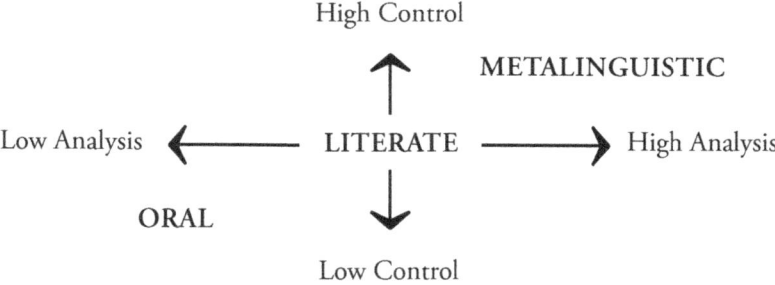

Figure 1. *Three domains of language use indicating values on analysis and control*[5]

When one starts exploring those language contexts further however, it becomes more difficult and, as Bialystok suggests, it is inaccurate as an indicator of proficiency by itself. As an example, Bialystok goes on to place tasks associated with certain roles and functions into the above diagram. Using this model, a disk jockey assumes a position in the top left-hand quadrangle, as that role requires a high level of control but generally little analysis of language. The task of simultaneous translation is placed in the top corner of the top right quadrangle because it requires a high level of control and a high level of analysis. Lecturing assumes the midway point of the same quadrangle since slightly less control and analysis is required. This model places adult conversation diagonally opposite, in the midway point of the bottom left quadrangle, requiring comparatively little analysis and control. Children's conversations inhabit the lowest position of that same quadrangle, with the lowest level of analysis and control required.[6]

If we were to add in written uses of language to this picture, things like writing poetry and writing for study would be in the top right-hand area. If I were to assess myself against these domains, I might say that the way I use my *reo* places me in this top right-hand area. I lecture in and about the Māori language, I write poetry and compose songs, I am able to do simultaneous translations on a basic level. On the more informal side of the spectrum, I am able and have at times run radio shows and interviewed and been interviewed in panel discussions like one might expect to find in the top left-hand box. What I find most challenging, however, is the kind of proficiency required to perform the tasks in the lower left-hand corner – ordinary children's conversations. In all my years as a learner and teacher of the Māori language, I never had to talk with children in the language for any sustained period and had not considered the range of language required to engage intergenerationally in informal contexts.

My father had started to turn the tide within our family from generations of Māori language deprivation to a path of acquisition in our heritage language. I had continued to move further down this path and immersed myself in language goals and activities. It was natural, therefore, when embarking on the next stage of my life as a mother, that Māori language would play a significant role. That choice has proven to be the single greatest challenge in my language acquisition career. I made a pledge to myself and to each of my two beautiful newborn babies as I cradled them in my arms. I promised that I would raise them in Māori and that their Māori language would not be something they had to fight for and struggle to learn. I did not want my children to have to deal with the kinds of identity conflicts and struggles that I myself have had to confront. I was determined that for them it would be a normal part of who they were, it would be natural and it would be theirs.

A commitment to Māori language and the transmission of it to the next generation had become inextricably tied in my mind and heart, to being a good mother and being Kāi Tahu – neither of which I believed to be up for negotiation. From the birth of my first child in July 2003, I adopted the OPOL (One Parent One Language) strategy by default, learning subsequently that such a strategy was actually recognised and practised.[7] We naturally fell into this methodology of intergenerational engagement as the children's father was not a speaker of Māori and, although Māori himself, had been adopted at birth and had not grown up in a Māori cultural or language environment. As a result, being a household that spoke only Māori was not an option we had at our immediate disposal. Although their father did make early efforts to keep up with our daughters in their first years, he was unable to substantially sustain it beyond their first years and, therefore, remained an English-speaking parent.

Beyond the classification of OPOL, it has been difficult to place our family into one of the many classifications of bilingualism identified in much of the literature on bilingualism, second-language development and language revitalisation. Like other Kāi Tahu families in our situation, the patterns, scenarios and characteristics often do not seem to match or cross over. This can become problematic for the language learner or transmitter embarking on the investigation of strategies to support a particular language situation. Although there is a wealth of information available on raising bilingual children and supporting the bilingual and multilingual family, along with literature concerned with preserving and developing endangered languages, it has proven more difficult to find sources that reflect examples similar to the Kāi Tahu situation: that is, raising bilinguals in a context where no or very few inter-generational models existed for the preceding three to five generations.

Within the majority of cases, Kāi Tahu simply did not 'fit the picture'. As an example, when discussing the various 'faces of bilingualism', Bialystok refers to Romaine's six patterns of home language bilingualism. Type 1: one person, one language; Type 2: non-dominant home language/one language one environment; Type 3: non-dominant home language without community support; Type 4: double non-dominant home language without community support; Type 5: non-native parents; Type 6: mixed languages.[8] If I were to assess my own family against these bilingual family 'types', I would place us in categories 1, 3 (to a degree of 80 per cent) and 5. Within the literature, the assumption is made that both parents are able to speak each other's language but choose to use certain languages with their children or that both adults are able to function in two languages.

My own immediate family's characteristics are as follows: one parent (mother) mL (minority language) speaker but mother is second language speaker of minority language; one parent (father) ML (majority language) speaker; two children (aged four and five), children's first words/sentences: Māori (mL), language of communication/relationship language between children in and outside of the home: Māori only before they turned three-and-a-half and four-and-a-half at which point English became increasingly used in creative play together, Māori remains dominant relationship language between siblings; language of communication/relationship language between parents: English.

In terms of our family's capacity to create a competently functional bilingual household, many would look at the factors above and believe that all the necessary requirements were there and in fact the evidence of success is there too, insofar as the children's language of communication with each other and their mother is still dominantly Māori – the minority language in our community and wider society. What is harder to assess is the sustainability of that language and how long this will remain the case. Over the past year, I have noticed an increasing tendency for my daughter (now recently turned five) to mix her language, not when speaking to different people of different languages, but instead to use an English word when she does not know its Māori equivalent. Although Māori is still her language of choice in the home environment, she is already finding it cannot keep up with her knowledge of English vocabulary. As a second-language speaker of Māori myself and as her main provider and modeller of that language to my children, I am increasingly struggling to fill the gaps.

Resisting language shift to the majority language from the minority language is a daily battle. To highlight the seemingly simple nature of this 'resistance struggle', I will draw on an example of natural interaction between my daughter and I that occurred not long ago. A discussion was taking place in the car on the way home at the end of the day and my daughter was getting impatient at the delay. She suggested that I hurry up and questioned why I was waiting so long – the Māori word for 'traffic jam' simply evaded me. I was able to give her an immediate response – '*Kāore e taea e au te neke e kō, kua kikī rawa te rori i te waka*' – 'I'm unable to go girl, the street is too full with cars'. The concept seemed simple enough and certainly common enough, but I had no memory of ever coming across a situation where I had had to use the term in Māori.

It would be two days before I found a moment to sit down with an English–Māori dictionary to locate an appropriate word, but that was to present its own set of challenges. I was able to find the word '*tiamu*', a transliteration for the spread 'jam' and the definition for 'jammed' as in jamming one's fingers was '*tāmi*'. The difficulty here was the concept of traffic jam and the notion of being 'jammed in' was not one of the options given under the explanation of 'jam'. It would be another week before I stumbled, by chance, across an example of 'traffic jam' under the base word 'traffic'. There I found the translation '*taero waka*', with '*taero*' meaning to obstruct or to get in the way of something. I was familiar with the term from one of our *iwi* proverbs, '*Kā taero o Tū te Koropaka*' – 'The obstacles of Tū the Koropaka', and could immediately associate it with the notion of being blocked up and unable to move because of the vehicles in front of you. Despite this knowledge of the formal use of the term, it had taken me over ten days to find out that I was able to use it in an informal discussion with my three-and-a-half year old. If you then consider how many new words one might find oneself needing to research in any given day when engaging with two inquisitive preschoolers, the daily reality becomes rather daunting.

At any one of those junctures, it would be easy to revert to my first language, English, in order to explain the concept or to give the name of the desired object. To persist in Māori is for me the harder option and one starts to question whether the quality of the engagement is being compromised because of my insistence that the second language be my one language of communication with the children. Another challenge is the need to 'fix' words that I have taught them when they are later found to be incorrect or not the most appropriate for the required purpose. In this instance, one becomes concerned about the integrity and perception of integrity from the child's perspective of the language being transmitted when the proverbial 'goal posts' are prone to shifting or sometimes collapsing altogether. These dilemmas and tests tease and taunt the mind of this second-language speaker on a daily, even hourly, basis. The stress levels inevitably rise because this is a mission, a commitment I do not want to fail. I am in a quandary. The language I love and yearn to speak well, to live in, to play in, to be in, is a language I have not been raised in, a language I am severely limited in when communicating with my own children and yet that has been my main purpose in acquiring the language in the first place.

Consider then, that I am one of a small group of Kāi Tahu living in our territory who could feature anywhere on this chart. Most of my peers, like me, have learnt the Māori language as a second language. Of that group around fifteen to twenty of us are attempting to raise our children speaking Māori as their first language. We have a handful of Kāi Tahu reaching their late teens to early twenties who have been educated through *Kōhanga reo* (early childhood immersion language nest(s)) and *Kura Kaupapa* (immersion language primary school(s)). These people are competently bilingual. In nearly all cases, however, it has been the formal education environment that has been the Māori-language environment for these children, with Māori being the language of communication in their homes for only a few. In most of the aforementioned cases, the parents are neither native nor near-native in terms of proficiency. These individuals, therefore, are likely to still experience similar challenges to mine if they choose to raise their children in the Māori language, as they would not have had that language modelled to them in their own lives.

There is another group of youth who are currently in or have just recently left Māori immersion primary schools and who will, upon leaving secondary school, have achieved a much higher level of proficiency than the current generation of parents of young children. These numbers are, however, still very small, with less than 5 per cent of Kāi Tahu assessing themselves as proficient speakers of Māori. With so few households committed to developing home bilinguals, we are still in grave danger of the *reo* that our Kāi Tahu speakers use being confined to the limited domains of formal education and cultural rituals.

So what does this mean for the realisation of our *iwi* language vision? There is a very real challenge that we must face as an *iwi*. If we do not make a concerted effort to reintroduce *reo* back into the homes, acknowledging the sheer input and effort that is going to be required to support intergenerational transmission of the Māori language, then we are in fact sentencing our language to death. If this is the case, I am not sure that we will be able to resurrect it in the future as we do not have what I believe to be the essential characteristics required to achieve such a feat. We must also acknowledge the barriers we will face in achieving this goal, whilst being careful not to be overwhelmed by them. We do not live in a defined geographical area. More often than not, we do not even live in the same neighbourhoods. The traditional communities that could support language retention and survival are isolated and few in number, often with limited economical opportunities for families to secure a living. We have been successfully integrated and assimilated into the dominant society and dominant language. We do not have sovereign control over significant areas where we can determine language domains and establish laws to protect and develop our language. We are, therefore, at the mercy of mainstream politics and institutions.

Another barrier is our own cultural diversity and lack of *iwi* cohesion. We do not belong to a single religion, which can often be another way that people draw together to commit to a cause. We do not have a national identity as part of the Kāi Tahu nation. With our Land Claim, an unbroken petition against the government that endured for over 150 years before settlement in 1996, now fading from memory, many Kāi Tahu believe that we have even lost the shared cause that served to unite the dislocated communities and families for so long. Post-settlement, Kāi Tahu have shifted into a phase of distribution of dividend earned from the collective assets and for many this has become the basis upon which their affiliation to the *iwi* is articulated. For a significant proportion of the *iwi*, being Kāi Tahu has little or nothing to do with speaking *reo*, let alone an obligation or a commitment to it or to being Kāi Tahu in a cultural sense. At the *iwi* level, these factors seem significant, but at the local family level, they are overwhelmingly so.

Fewer than 5 per cent of Kāi Tahu speakers in our territory identify themselves as proficient speakers of *reo*. Nearly all of those speakers are second-language learners and have had limited exposure to natural, native-language models of generational language; we have extremely limited resources that can model generational language to us on a regular basis, with only a handful of native speakers surviving, most of whom reside in the North Island; we are highly integrated into mainstream society with regard to housing and lifestyles; we live in isolated communities or are fragmented within urban communities; no high-density areas of Kāi Tahu speakers remain; there is limited community support and few domains that expose home-bilinguals to natural, native language at appropriate age levels.

These negatives seem daunting when one considers the need to add the usual list of challenges of raising bilingual children, some of which are described by Baker in his book *A Parents' and Teachers' Guide to Bilingualism*: language mixing, language refusal and reluctance to talk, language and community isolation, language rejection, and the effects of school and peer pressure on language use.[9] Baker goes to a great deal of effort to talk of the benefits of raising bilingual children and discusses the challenges involved in raising a child in a minority or non-dominant language, whilst still suggesting the goal is achievable:

> … bilingualism inside the child can be effectively sustained through the language of the home being different from the language of the community. However this will be a challenge and a constant journey that moves across bright mountain-tops and dark valleys … Determined parents should not be deterred by their language being an island in the home.[10]

This of course assumes that the parents have enough language at their disposal to keep the island above water at the best of times.

Most of the literature readily available tends to deal with the issues of implementing a strategy of intergenerational transmission. It assumes that parents can already speak the language concerned or at least are near-native in proficiency of the said language. The question most pertinent to Kāi Tahu, therefore, is what model of home-bilingualism should we be encouraging our families to adopt and how can we support them with it so as to resist encroaching language death? Whilst we desperately need more *whānau* committed to raising their children in Māori homes in order to achieve a critical mass of competent bilinguals, we also need to make sure that we are not limiting Kāi Tahu children because of the quality of language of the parents and, therefore, the quality of interaction the children engage in.

The question needs to be asked, how do you achieve a macro strategy of intergenerational transmission of Māori without a generation of native speakers? And when it comes to assessing the quality of *reo* of those who do speak, where do you draw the line? Baker's response to the question 'My second language is not perfect. Should I speak it to my child?', might endorse the sentiments of many Kāi Tahu who believe they should not make the effort. It really depends on how perfect or imperfect your language is. One thing is for sure: if you are a bad model of language for your child, you should not speak that language to the child. If a child begins to learn incorrect linguistic structures or inexact expression from you speaking a second language, you may be undermining rather than helping the child's language development. Instead, consider speaking the first language to your child, knowing that many skills and competencies learned in the first language (e.g. ideas, meanings, concepts) transfer easily to the second language.[11]

However, Baker does go on to suggest that if you are a new parent and can keep up with your child's language needs whilst actively engaging in further language acquisition yourself, then you are still able to be a valuable model to your child. Perhaps his most concerning judgment for Kāi Tahu is this one:

> The reality is that it is very difficult for most mothers (and fathers) to speak a second language to their child. It feels restrictive and frustrating. The wealth of wise colloquial sayings, family stories, local jokes and colorful tales, are all stored and can only be authentically conveyed in the first or mother tongue. The transmission of the parents' heritage is best recounted in the mother tongue. That storage of experience in the mother tongue from birth to parenthood seems of low worth if a second language is used with that child.[12]

There is, however, a significant difference between the Kāi Tahu situation and the examples Baker describes. For us, the second-language speakers are the only transmitters of the heritage language. Even if the strategy we are forced to employ is that of artificial or non-native language transmission, the choice is it's either us or not at all. Such sentiment may lead those Kāi Tahu currently sitting on the proverbial fence to decide against making the investment into a strategy to create a Māori-language home – it is simply too hard and an unachievable goal. I can empathise with this position, as indicated earlier in this chapter, because I struggle to do just that every day and if I am struggling, then I can only assume it is equally challenging for those of similar proficiency and experience.

For me personally, however, there is no choice because the choices exist only in a vacuum of excuses. I know I will never in my lifetime achieve the same depth of understanding of the Māori language as a native speaker. The closest I can hope to achieve is as 'near-native' as possible. I also know that my children's language will be limited by my own language proficiency and that I will have to continuously look at ways to balance their language diet with other experiences, resources and influences. I am fully aware of the associated frustrations that my peers and I will face in our combined efforts to turn this fight of resistance into a fight for survival and language prosperity. But I am also fully aware of what may be lost if resistance fails.

I have now been actively learning *reo* for over two decades. The kind of language I have learnt has helped me to become a language teacher, a writer and a poet. It has aided me with my duties to perform my cultural rituals upon my *marae* and in formal Māori contexts. The biggest gap, however, has been in learning the language I require to be a mother to support intergenerational transmission in my own home and, therefore, to give my *reo* a real chance of survival. I know I am one of the lucky few within my *iwi* who have been given opportunities to learn the Māori language and acquire a level of proficiency. I know I am one of an even smaller group who have made the commitment to create a bilingual home. I am more convinced now than ever that if Kāi Tahu wants to once again normalise *Te Reo* and have a people that truly own and give life to their language, then it is not sufficient to merely look at investing in the development of proficiency. There must be recognition that what we need is targeted proficiency and the most crucial domain where targeting is required is in the home.

Of course I understand that it is important for the culture and our identity to build the capacity of our *marae* so that our people can engage in rituals, customs and practices with confidence and pride. But if we do not adopt a position of urgency to support the efforts of those currently striving to give effect to intergenerational transmission in the homes, then we may find that the challenge will prove too great for some and the *traffic jams* become too overwhelming and isolating. If we get to that point, then the opportunity to develop a critical mass – a wave, albeit small – of first-generation Kāi Tahu speakers of Māori in our lifetime will be lost. We then run the risk of losing the language altogether as a marker of our culture and identity. If that happens, then we will arguably be seriously compromised in our ability to assert our collective cultural Kāi Tahu-ness, as so much of our historical cultural knowledge and practice will have become increasingly beyond our collective grasp:

> As languages fall out of use into forgetfulness, entire genres of oral tradition – stories, songs and epics – rapidly approach extinction … We stand to lose volumes: entire worldviews, religious beliefs, creation myths, observations about life, technologies for how to domesticate animals and cultivate plants, histories of migration and settlement and collective wisdom.[13]

What is needed to resist such a state is a concentrated effort to create opportunities for young parents and parents-to-be to learn the language required to raise their children as first-speakers of Māori. We need to create more domains where those young families can interact, network, discuss strategies and find support amongst each other. We need to invest in targeted resources to support intergenerational transmission. And we need to be aware that time is not on our side.

Language revitalisation circles constantly echo the words of Fishman around the need to take a generational approach when investing in language regeneration and revitalisation. To paraphrase, language can be lost in one generation, yet it takes three generations for language revitalisation to occur. If I turn my thoughts to my *whānau* and our own experience, the first part is right. It took only that first generation to lose the language. It then took a further three generations to realise what had been lost before two more generations would be consumed in trying to turn the tide. For my *whānau*, at least another two generations of effort and commitment will be required before we can say, 'our *whānau* are native speakers of our *reo*'.

My hope is that I am still alive to hear my grandchildren or great-grandchildren argue and tease and cry and laugh in our language. I dream of the day when I might read an article written by one of my own grandchildren where he or she is discussing the intricacies of Kāi Tahu *reo* and is doing so in the language itself. The hope is that at that stage *traffic jams* are a thing of the past and instead the focus is on celebrating a living, dynamic, rich and strong Kāi Tahu language.

CHAPTER SIX

Towards a Model for Indigenous Research

Jim Williams

'e pakihi hakinga a kai
A plain, if properly searched, will reveal its foods
or
Seek in the right places or starve

In 1844, Bishop Selwyn described Canterbury[1] as a 'featureless plain with few trees and a little scrub, quite incapable of sustaining human life'.[2] However Māori sources, in particular H.K. Taiaroa, record the area as containing some 1800 *mahika kai* (site where work is undertaken on food resources such as hunting, harvesting, etc.), involving 114 different foods.[3] Selwyn simply did not know what to look for, nor did he recognise the import of what he saw. In Aldo Leopold's words: 'His reaction depended not only on the quality of what he saw, but on the quality of the mental eye with which he saw it.'[4] This is a good analogue for a research methodology: the researcher needs to know what to look for, where to look and how to recognise what is found.

Most research into the traditional[5] ways of Indigenous[6] peoples has been conducted by outsiders, generally Europeans, and has therefore been informed by another worldview. However, information is often encoded in culturally specific ways and may be ranked as highly important by those who fully understand its significance, yet an outsider may undervalue or even ignore it. These Indigenous understandings will differ from group to group and a research methodology must, therefore, take culturally specific meanings into account.

The relatively new discipline of Māori Studies borrows from the research methodologies of a number of other disciplines, including Anthropology, Archaeology, History, Linguistics and Art History and integrates these according to the Māori worldview. There is now a considerable corpus of work in this area, mainly focusing on social, linguistic and ethical questions and contemporary issues. Very little theoretical material is available that applies to the 'traditional' pre-European contact period, however. Mason Durie, Bill Dacker, Hirini Moko Mead and Ranginui Walker all use traditional information in various publications but none of them propose a methodology. To date, only Royal (whose bibliography is particularly useful), Stokes, Tucker and Tau have set out research models incorporating traditional information in an abstract framework.[7]

This chapter outlines some of the issues associated with the analysis and interpretation of traditional information available in the form of place names, *waiata* (song(s)), *whakataukī*, *whakapapa*, manuscripts and contemporary interviews, as well as published sources. The focus is on Māori language material because one of the particular strengths of sources such as *waiata*, *whakapapa* and *whakataukī* is that they have usually been repeated verbatim. Like manuscripts, they are effectively frozen in time, unlike contemporary oral evidence, where the stories are retold in each generation. The contemporary oral record of past events must be compared with everything else, since much Māori tradition is political in nature and this political perspective can change over time.

As will become apparent by looking at specific published examples, different forms of traditional evidence can seem to contradict rather than complement each other. Highlighting some of the pitfalls involved with these sources not only serves as a caveat for new researchers to the field but also demonstrates the need to adopt a methodology that incorporates both the etic (outsider's view) and the emic (insider's approach). At the risk of proposing an awkward neologism, I propose an 'etmic' approach for the study of New Zealand Māori traditional topics. This entails a familiarity with the strengths and shortcomings of both perspectives, arriving at a point where the researcher can see both the wood and the trees.

Somewhat ironically, as the old *whakataukī* goes, '*Kaua hei titiro ki Ngā Whatu*' – 'Don't look at Ngā Whatu'. Whenever our *tūpuna* (ancestor(s)) crossed Raukawa Moana[8] the expedition was said to be doomed if the correct protocols were not observed. Usually this involved wearing 'chaplets'[9] or 'hoodwinks'[10] of leaves, which were strewn upon the waters following *karakia* (prayer(s)) recited in the vicinity of Ngā Whatu (O Te Wheke a Muturangi), The Brothers Islands. First-time travellers were required to avert their gaze or remain 'hoodwinked', until the *karakia* were finished[11] lest disaster struck, demonstrating the importance to our *tūpuna* of always doing things correctly, that is, always having a prescription, such as is advocated in this chapter.

Etic perspectives

The etic view lacks that special 'insider' understanding gained from prolonged exposure to a culture and can, therefore, lead to misinterpretations or even omissions of evidence. Once made, an error is likely to be perpetuated if others follow the original without any independent checking. As Ngāi Tahu *kaumātua* (elder(s) of either sex, old man) Sid Cormack explains, 'There are many mistakes made in recording history. Some happen because the speaker is misunderstood, some because of the coupling of names of different individuals or of separate incidents into one story. Some errors are intentional'.[12]

A particularly complex example of a mistake being perpetuated is described in detail by Harry Evison regarding the usage of the name 'Kaiapohia' for 'Kaiapoi' *pā* (fortified village).[13] The somewhat derogatory word 'Kaiapohia' was coined by Ngāti Toa at the commencement of the inter-island wars during the early nineteenth century and 'many writers, academic as well as non-academic, have been using *Kaiapohia* as if it were an authentic Ngāi Tahu name for the historic pa'.[14] Etic perspectives, of course, depend primarily upon the written record. Examples follow from various disciplines that have valuable etic perspectives on Māori events.

Archaeology

In an article published in the *Journal of Polynesian Studies* in 1995, Ian Barber observed that 'By the mid-20th century, archaeological interpretations and data had come to subsume and even sideline, Maori oral history in the scholarly construction of early Maori culture sequences'[15] and concluded with the comment that New Zealand Māori archaeology 'has a self-identification as a prehistoric discipline in largely ignoring tradition as evidence'.[16] In the main part of his discussion, he makes the point that more recent studies in traditional history, linguistics, biological anthropology, biological and earth sciences and other disciplines have made it unlikely that 'archaeological syntheses ... will ever return to the position of authority achieved over much of the earlier 20th century'.[17]

In what amounts to an early (1978) attempt at incorporating the emic perspective of traditional knowledge into an etic discussion, archaeologist Foss Leach made some quite speculative inferences from a number of published *whakapapa*.[18] Without access to appropriate insider genealogical knowledge, the use of whakapapa can be a trap for the unwary. Another archaeologist, Atholl Anderson, brought together information from diverse sources in an attempt at an interdisciplinary study in 1983, although in organisation and argument it is still weighted heavily towards archaeology.[19] His written sources were almost all published ones; nineteenth-

Map of South Island showing some key rivers and settlements. Geomatics NZ Ltd

century manuscripts were not used. His use of genealogical material was limited, although he drew on *whakapapa* to clarify relationships referred to in the narrative and pointed out that the resulting genealogy was not a *whakapapa*.[20] Other traditional sources of information, such as *waiata* and *whakataukī*, were not drawn on and his analysis of place names was less than cursory. And, in keeping with where the discipline was at the time, he commented that 'No attempt is made here to re-examine the southern Maori traditions as they have been recorded', suggesting that 'the complex points of detail in which they vary could eventually turn out to be of considerable significance'.[21] Anderson's subsequent work on southern Maori has borne this out and has benefited from his inclusion and examination of insider knowledge.[22]

A good example of traditional knowledge both complementing and supplementing archaeological interpretations involves what I like to call 'The enigma of the *tuatua*'. *Tuatua* are bivalve shellfish which often feature in middens but tend to be in dense layers, separated by layers of other food refuse, such as the shells of other shellfish. Archaeologists for years questioned why *tuatua* occur in large numbers, but only sporadically. Reference to modern Māori almost certainly resolves the question of why *tuatua* were eaten at certain times, then not for a number of years: they don't taste good! In fact, *tuatua* are exceptionally nutritious but were eaten only in times when more preferred foods were in short supply, an interpretation that was not available to archaeologists without inside knowledge.

Early histories/ethnologies

While the earliest recorded histories were written from the extremely advantageous standpoint of having access to *tūpuna* who had traditional knowledge, many errors occurred when they were recorded and as stated above, many, once made, were perpetuated. As mentioned, Evison completely debunks the 'Kaiapohia' name which had become the de-facto standard used by most writers over the years, beginning with Canon James West Stack.[23] In 1859, Stack was asked by Bishop Harper to become Superintendent at the Christchurch Diocesan Māori Mission. Born in the Thames district in 1835 and raised in various North Island mission stations, Stack was a near-native speaker of *Te Reo* and ideally placed to collect authentic traditions.[24] His knowledge of North Island dialects proved to be a double-edged sword, however, and whilst he collected much valuable material (and Kāi Tahu will always be in his debt) he was responsible for a number of unfortunate misunderstandings which have been kept alive. His eschewal of Māori material such as *waiata* and *whakapapa* is more than just poor scholarship, it is monocultural myopia.

One of the more significant of these misunderstandings is the Waitaha confusion which Adkin extrapolated from Stack, leading to suggestions of two waves of ancestors with that name.[25] Waitaha, the Southern *iwi*, in fact descend from Rakaihautu who arrived here on 'Uruao' canoe forty-four generations prior to Te Maiharoa.[26] Waitaha, the eponymous ancestor, was ninth in descent from Rakaihautu. Stack's oft-repeated error is that 'they were descended from the individual named Waitaha who was on "Te Arawa"'.[27] O'Regan explains, 'It is important to note that this Waitaha is not the same Waitaha who descends from Hei, a brother of Tama-te-kapua in the Arawa traditions'.[28] Stack had spent enough of his early life amongst the Arawa peoples to have some familiarity with their traditions. However, he lacked the depth of insight to recognise that ancestral names were not unique and accordingly, as with the Waitaha example, he conflated quite unrelated traditions on the strength of a name that was common to two or more stories. Perhaps only the understanding of an insider or an accurate recording of the tale without editorial commentary could have prevented this.

Another of Stack's deficiencies was the superficiality of his research and his assumption regarding the homogeneity in South Island traditions. Just as Māori oral tradition is not homogeneous across all *iwi*, neither does South Island tradition have one single, definitive version. Stack admitted quite frankly to lacking an understanding of how Māori society was structured: 'It may prevent misapprehension if I here state that in tracing the history of Ngai Tahu, I have purposely avoided alluding to the exploits of particular hapus [sic] – a favourite practice of the Maori analyst, but fraught with confusion to the European reader'.[29] Ironically, it is this very matter of orientation or *hapū* (sub-group(s) of *iwi*) perspective, that adds meaning, rather than confusion, to the researcher who can understand these multiple, contributing threads of tribal history.

Another problem associated with the works of missionaries is the fact that they had their own agenda to advance: the conversion of Māori to Christianity. Missionaries saw it as desirable to overcome anything that was an obstacle to this process and Stack seems to have felt a need to so deal with the recent memory of Te Maiharanui, *Ūpoko Ariki* (Paramount Chief) of Kāi Tahu, who was treacherously killed during the wars with Ngāti Toa and their allies in the second decade of the nineteenth century. An example of this impediment to objectivity can be clearly seen in White,[30] who acknowledges Stack as his source and in Jacobson: '[Te Maiharanui] will always be remembered by the story of [his] cruel and evil deeds'.[31]

In contrast with these missionary accounts are those recorded by what Katherine Urry describes as 'educated gentlemen who had an interest in natural history ... their accounts often contain quite detailed ethnographic information on Maori culture ... much of the usefulness of their work stems from a tendency to describe, rather than interpret what they witnessed'.[32] Edward Shortland, a doctor, is a very good example of this type of person. His book, *Southern Districts of New Zealand*[33] abounds with examples of objective reporting, as well as many comparisons with North Island Māori, which show Shortland to be a most reliable reporter on Māori practices and fully cognisant of *iwi* differences.

Some published accounts comment upon and question the lack of homogeneity within the various *iwi* accounts, but few have sought an explanation. One who did was J. Herries Beattie (1881–1972), an indefatigable collector and publisher of Māori material. From the 1890s to the 1950s, he sought out and interviewed the most knowledgeable South Island Māori elders. His interpretations seem to be minimal and were often refined in the light of further information and greater understanding.[34] Significantly for his time, although he used the term 'Moriori' to describe the early *iwi* who settled Te Wāi Pounamu (variation of 'Te Waipounamu'), he did so without any of the connotations that have caused it to become synonymous with cross-cultural bias and politico-racial hegemony. Indeed Beattie recorded in 1941 that one informant told him, 'Don't call us "Moriori". The real Moriori came down from the North Island and went to the Chathams. We are not Moriori but Waitaha and Kati Mamoe'.[35]

Beattie usually classified his informants as Kāi Tahu, Kāti Mamoe or Waitaha and accepts multiple versions of traditions as in the naming of Aoraki (the highest mountain in New Zealand). His overall approach is summed up by the following: 'North Island historians have erred in accepting statements from representatives of the last migration instead of undertaking the really difficult task of hunting up lore from the descendants of the older stock'.[36] He goes on to comment, 'the alleged extinction of the Kati Mamoe is surely one of the falsest yarns ever foisted on the people of this country'.[37] This statement is corroborated by the 1844 census figures in Shortland where he records twenty-one Kāti Mamoe, from two different *hapū*, living at Waiateruati, well north of the area where the greatest numbers were said to be.[38] One of these *hapū*, Kāti Rakai, was in fact a Waitaha *hapū*, that of the prophet Te Maiharoa. Tikao tells us that Kokiro, the mother of Te Maiharoa, was of the Kāti Rakaihautu *hapū*.[39]

Academic works

Many academic works on *kaupapa Māori* (Māori topics, strategies and practices [of research] carried out according to appropriate Māori cultural protocols) have been based primarily on material initially collected by early Pākehā and the later works of non-Māori scholars. In particular, there are dangers when Māori language material is not included and especially when the Māori worldview is ignored. For example, a full understanding of *Te Reo Māori* (the Māori language) provides an insight into the full significance of Māori place names, such as 'Waiateruati', Opihi, and Tikoukou. Waiateruati is located close to the mouth of the Opihi river, the name of which refers to the prolific growth of *tī* (cabbage tree(s)), from which *kāuru* is prepared, in the catchment of the three rivers which make up the Opihi river system; Tīkoukou refers to the multitude of cabbage tree stumps just inland and to the north of Waiateruati, such multiple names emphasising the main product of the district. Indeed, Maungatī and Te Ahi Kāuru are also within a short walk, and even Temuka (properly, Te Umukaha) nearby may have supported other place-name evidence as one explanation is that it, too, refers to the ovens used to extract *kāuru* from the *tī*. A number of other South Canterbury place-names also refer to aspects of the *kāuru* harvest.

By the middle decades of the twentieth century, many academic writers on Māori topics lacked the language and cultural insights that could provide deeper understandings. However today, with the expansion of Māori language and culture in schools and tertiary institutions, these limitations are no longer valid excuses for using models developed in other disciplines. In this more enlightened time, thanks especially to the Māori renaissance since the 1970s, an increased number of scholars in Māori Studies, History and Anthropology, such as Bruce Biggs, Ranginui Walker, Judith Binney, Michael King, Anne Salmond and Jeffrey Sissons, have contributed to a pan-disciplinary approach to scholarship. Accordingly, it is timely to offer suggestions for a model that might help to bridge the disciplinary gap.

Emic perspectives

The purpose of this section is to examine features of the emic view and contrast it with the etic. The emic perspective is often claimed to be somewhat subjective, since it offers an insider's view on the subject. Subjectivity, though, is not necessarily a disadvantage. Freire writes: 'For me the concrete reality is the connection between subjectivity and objectivity; never objectivity isolated from subjectivity … that is, how the people in this area perceive themselves'.[40] Accordingly, the following describes how the 'insider' view can add to the interpretations of evidence from etic sources.

Some of the clearest examples of bias arising from subjectivity can be seen in the extant, alternative accounts of inter-*iwi* warfare. The following example illustrates how subjective perspectives may determine the history related. It concerns the early nineteenth-century battle at Kapara-te-hau between Ngāti Toa (and their allies) and Ngāi Tahu. The battle is known variously as: Waka Taupopoki, by Ngāti Toa; Tutaetahi by Ngāi Tahu; and Oraumoa or Orauaiti by Pākehā historians. Buick writes that Ngāi Tahu have called it 'Rau moa iti' but there does not seem to be a Southern source for this name.[41] There is substantial difference between the two *iwi* versions, particularly with respect to Te Rauparaha's (a Ngāti Toa chief) own role. Burns, who endeavours to synthesise previous accounts, comments on the work of other historians and says that none of them tells the same story.[42] Stack advises how Te Rauparaha was almost caught and escaped only by diving into the sea and hiding amongst the kelp.[43] The Northern version, however, is quite different. According to Buick, Te Rauparaha swam out to a canoe that had not yet landed and ordered several of the occupants out to make room for himself and increase the speed of the vessel.[44] Burns, giving the witness account of his son, Tamihana Te Rauparaha, relates that Te Rauparaha endeavoured to launch a canoe but was unsuccessful and swam to one that was already on the water.[45] Perhaps the son could be expected to withhold a matter of discredit to his father, such as ordering his kinsmen overboard, if Buick's (above) is the Ngāti Toa view. Thus, there will not necessarily be a single emic view, since: '*Ehara i te takata kotahi anō i oho ai i neherā*' – 'There was more than one person alive in olden times'.[46]

Before proceeding, I want to add some observations concerning the use of Indigenous languages. It is essential that minutiae described in the language of Indigenous people is not masked by cultural misunderstandings. Traditional concepts are sometimes viewed by folk today in a watered-down way. This can be due to a lack of equivalent English vocabulary or as a result of early translations of customary concepts made to suit a missionary agenda. It is likely that all Indigenous cultures have unique concepts that underpin their worldviews. Many Indigenous concepts reflect an emic outlook that exposes perspectives missing from the view of the coloniser. For example, there is the Māori concept of '*mana whenua*', which encompasses the idea that groups with ancestral connection to land may have additional responsibilities, beyond those of other members of their *iwi*.

Care must also be exercised when accepting common translations. In their zeal to convert the heathen, early missionaries provided some rather corrupt translations of Indigenous concepts. '*Atua*', for instance, was usually translated as 'gods' without necessarily conveying the Māori belief that special ancestors could continue to influence events involving their descendants, long after their own death. The word '*tapu*' was translated as 'sacred' when the term applied to subjects that were under restriction, including those due to physical or spiritual pollution. Some examples of various types of culturally recorded information follow with comments on their strengths and weaknesses.

Kōrero tuku iho: Manuscripts

Oral narratives are reinterpreted each time they are told, according to the perceptions of the time. To give an example, according to the nineteenth-century *kaumātua*, Te Wanikau Tapiha,[47] when Tu Te Urutira was returning the captured Hineroko to her own *iwi*, Kāti Mamoe, her father asked her 'who are the *iwi* of your man?' Hineroko replied 'Kāti Kurii' (the people of the Kaikōura region). Carrington acknowledges access to the Te Wanikau material, but advises, 'These records were translated for the author by Mrs Hariata Beaton'.[48] Now, Mrs Beaton was in fact the grandniece of Te Wanikau Tapiha and her version of events could be expected to be the same. Carrington goes on to say, 'Mrs Beaton assisted in editing the information ... [she] amplified and explained every detail of the story'.[49] Comparing this passage with Carrington's retelling of the story,[50] the reply is 'Ko Ngai Tahu Pōtiki' (the people of Ngāi Tahu Pōtiki). It is likely that this reflected the cohesive effect that the land claim, under H.K. Taiaroa, had upon the disparate sections of Ngāi Tahu in the late nineteenth century, that is, between the time of recording the Te Wanikau version and the time of Mrs Beaton's contribution to Carrington. Indeed, there are a number of occasions where Carrington uses Ngāi Tahu for the group Te Wanikau calls 'Ngāti (or Kāti) Kurī'.

In the example above, contemporary values have intruded on the telling of the story with significant consequences and furthermore, Mrs Beaton (or more likely, Carrington himself) seems to have censored the story. For example Carrington notes, 'The reference to hot coals is to a purely domestic incident the full details of which have not been recorded'.[51] However, Te Wanikau tells us 'you threatened that you would cook my penis in the hot coals'.[52] The general details of this incident are still relatively well known within Ngāi Tahu today. Māori since last century have been well aware of the different view Europeans have towards matters of a sexual nature and, accordingly, are inclined to tailor traditional stories to suit their idea of a rather more delicate ear. Biggs comments, 'Maori legends are not remarkable for the amount of humour they contain and their main relish is decidedly Rabelaisian, while euphemism is not a characteristic of the language'.[53]

Another difficulty in using manuscripts concerns the confusion over names, as seen in a comparison of the two versions of the Kāti Kurī story given above. Te Wanikau uses the interrogative '*Unutai?*',[54] an old Ngāi Tahu idiom meaning 'What is it?',[55] or alternatively, 'Who are you?'[56] Tikao also tells us that the expression was obsolete by his time. This is almost certainly the '*inutai*' in the Williams dictionary, but unfortunately, Williams's source is not given.[57] Presumably Mrs Beaton was not familiar with the idiom and the fact that it was written with a capital letter may have led her to believe that it was a proper name since Carrington rendered it as the name of a woman.[58] Proper names can be a problem generally. Sometimes it is not clear whether the name is personal or relates to a place, battle, canoe or even weapon. In many cases the same name might be used for any or all of these categories. That which is quite familiar today as, say, a personal name, may in fact have been bestowed to commemorate an event or thing from the past.

Old manuscripts in Māori also present problems in terms of legibility, spelling and words that may be combined or split in unusual places. The use of capitals is often erratic (as in the possible error involving *Unutai* above) and punctuation may be incorrect or even non-existent. Nevertheless, a researcher who perseveres, and who is vigilant in ensuring that all interpretations are checked out, will find rewards. Carrington provides more clarity in some areas and Te Wanikau has additional detail in others. It is valuable, indeed, to have the opportunity to cross-check.

Another obvious difference involving manuscripts is one of focus. We need to consider whose perspective is being described. Again with regard to the Kāti Kurī story, Te Wanikau (or, more probably, his scribe, Tame Green) declares in the manuscript's title: 'The History of Ngai Tahu (Ngati Kurii [sic] clan)' that the story is told from a Ngāti Kurī point of view. Carrington purports to be telling the 'History of Ngai Tahu' without qualification, yet effectively he is telling the same story and from a similar, if updated, perspective. The history is still primarily a Ngāti Kurī one and many other primary *hapū* of Ngāi Tahu are all but ignored.

Whakapapa

> *Polynesians possess oral traditions that reveal sophisticated understandings of the world and their place in it. These typically take the form of an elaborate cosmogony beginning with the origin of the universe and the primal parents, then continuing to trace the descent of living and nonliving, material and immaterial phenomena, including humans.*[59]

Whakapapa is the name given to the genealogical tables that give the relationships between all things, providing the actual and notional basis of all cultural taxonomies. It is the backbone of Māori epistemology and extends to the ancestral period in the manner of more familiar genealogies. In pre-contact times, Māori memorised and understood considerable amounts of *whakapapa*. It was an intimate form of knowledge, manipulated mentally, recited orally as appropriate to the audience and with no particular convention for its presentation.

Whakapapa are, therefore, highly significant from an emic point of view but would-be researchers need to be wary of taking them at face value. Charles Royal, for instance, says he was taught that in the case of his famous Ngāti Raukawa ancestor: 'Poututerangi, son of Whakatere who, in turn, is son of Raukawa'.[60] However, Te Rangihaeata and Matene Te Whiwhi wrote the lineage as Raukawa to Poututerangi to Whakatere. Royal believes 'that Te Rangihaeata and Matene Te Whiwhi recorded the wrong whakapapa *deliberately*',[61] perhaps because of the potential for abuse if it should fall into the wrong hands and in the secure knowledge that their own people would not be led astray, as the information was 'basic general knowledge'. The etic researcher, using only the written record, cannot be expected to discern this.

Royal goes on to suggest that genealogical information contained in Māori Land Court records likewise needs to be used with caution:

> Sometimes claimants laid deliberately fabricated information before the court in order to support their claims. As all Māori Land Court judges until the 1970s were Pākehā and, therefore, had limited knowledge of tribal histories and traditions it was possible to get away with presenting false information, therefore, the minute books should be used with some caution.[62]

This would seem to be something of an over-generalisation as some Māori Land Court judges, like W.E. Gudgeon, were particularly knowledgeable about Māori traditions, though admittedly from their own particular viewpoint.

Ruka Broughton also alludes to deliberate alterations being made to *whakapapa* in order to support an Aotea origin for Ngā Rauru. He is reluctant to make an outright accusation but says,

> I suspect that the areas where the inconsistencies occur, which are mentioned above, certainly indicate that the particular lineage has been tampered with ... It does appear that the genealogies of Ngaa Rauru were changed about in order to connect the Aotea canoe or rather the crew, to the chiefly line of Rauru.[63]

Deliberate falsification of *whakapapa* is not the only trap. We also need to have regard to the difficulty of understanding exactly what it was that the original recorder was endeavouring to say. In the nineteenth century, when *whakapapa* first came to be written down, there was no accepted convention; rather like Alice in Wonderland, our ancestors knew exactly what they meant even if subsequent readers have been left bemused.

The following extracts from Ngāi Tahu *whakapapa* illustrate some of the difficulties regarding interpretation.

Whakapapa 1
Rakaiwhakaata = Manawatakitu = Manawaiha = Manawamaaruru

Armed with knowledge of only European family trees, one might wonder at the number of marriages and ask who are male and who are female. Somebody with a general knowledge of *whakapapa* might speculate that Rakaiwhakaata possibly married the three Manawas and that they could be three sisters because it is such a recurring pattern. However, other explanations are possible and to the uninitiated, the table is quite unclear.

Similarly, in *Whakapapa* 2, gender is not indicated, though the generations are clear. And, there is no indication which member of the pair in the next generation is the son or daughter of the parents shown. Possible conventions could be: that the male (or the female) is always shown first; or alternatively, that the offspring of the parents above is shown first regardless of gender. We have no indication as to which convention has been followed or even whether the pattern has been consistent. In this case, the convention followed is of showing the offspring first regardless of gender but this is not universal.

Whakapapa 2
Hikaororoa = Urupa
Tumaikuku = Uemate
Rongokote = Tahupitopito
Manawatakitu = Rakaiwhakaata

Whakapapa 3
Marukore
Tuuhaitara
Tamaraeroa
Huirapa
Pahiirua
Tahumataa
Tamaraeroa
Te Aohikuraki

Whakapapa 4
Marukore = Tuuhaitara
Tamaraeroa
Huirapa
Hinehou
Hinekuuhaa
Hinepuutauhinau
Pahiirua
Whakapuna
Tahau
Whakaata
Te Hauwhakakino
Tahumataa

Whakapapa 2 can be compared to *Whakapapa* 3 and 4, which are from two different manuscripts but describe part of the same genealogy. The initial reaction from an etic viewpoint would be: they cannot both be correct! Yet they merely reflect different conventions for writing down the *whakapapa*.

The brothers Tamaraeroa, Huirapa and Tahumataa are normally regarded as having been born in that order, but sometimes, Tahumataa is said to be the *tuakana* (eldest sibling or cousin of same sex), as it was he who avenged the murders of Tamaraeroa and Huirapa, so his line carries the *mana* that we might expect to belong to the *mātāmua* (first-born). The story is referred to in Ngata and Te Hurinui where the misunderstanding regarding primogeniture is perpetuated: '*E haere ana a Tahu-matua* [sic] *me tana ope ki te ngaki i te mate o ōna tēina o Tamaraeroa rāua ko Huirapa*'.[64]

Broughton also comments upon the lack of consistency in the treatment of (especially) siblings in written versions of Ngā Rauru *whakapapa*.[65] He argues that only one recorded version is quite clear:

> Rangikaitu says that Poumatua was the son of Puruora, but Tautahi claims that Puruora was an older brother of Poumatua. This is not to say that Tautahi is correct, but rather that he is the only tohunga [priest, spirit medium, expert] who actually sets the names out in detail and in some sort of order to show the sibling connections. Perhaps this may be due to the fact that his scribe prodded the old man with questions and really delved into the actual details of the genealogy.[66]

This suggests an alert and involved recorder, rather than one who is passive. There is, of course, a danger in this: the recorder may be tempted to embellish the account.

Ngata is quoted in McEwen as stating that some *whakapapa*, especially some of the very old ones, were '*tatai hikohiko*'; that is to say, they jumped around like electricity.[67] Biggs draws attention to the fact that in Cook Islands' genealogies there are usually fourteen generations between Toi and Ruatapu.[68] However, McEwen points out: 'the maximum which I have encountered in New Zealand is 6 (generations), yet every one of those 14 Cook Island names is found in one or other New Zealand tribe's version of the whakapapa'.[69] This suggests that a certain amount of inconsistency may be expected, especially with regard to the conventions used and in deciding who to include.

Not all *whakapapa* lines are of equal mana. This is particularly so in the event of conquest and eventual subsumation of one group by another. 'Ngāti victor' lines will dominate those of 'Ngāti vanquished', *except where there is some other source of mana*. We see this in the *whakapapa* (1, 2, 3 and 4), where Manawatakitu and Marukore are from Kāti Mamoe, the vanquished. However, they constitute an important focus in the *whakapapa* as Tuhaitara, daughter of Manawatakitu and wife of Marukore, is the eponymous ancestor of Ngāi Tuhaitara, a primary *hapū* of Ngāi Tahu in Canterbury. Significantly, it is through her that the *mana whenua* was transferred from Kāti Mamoe to Ngāi Tahu and, accordingly, this line of *whakapapa* is just as significant as the line from Tahu Potiki, which it joins through the marriage of Manawatakitu to Rakaiwhakaata. In later generations we find the names Manawa (for men) and Takitu (for women) being often repeated, another example of the key role of these two ancestors to Ngāi Tahu and an illustration of how sources of *mana* are regularly re-emphasised. The same pattern recurs, for example, when the name of the Ngāi Tara *tūpuna wahine* (female ancestor(s)), Irakehu, reappears for the eponymous ancestor of Ngāti Irakehu (Banks Peninsula). The particular strength of *whakapapa* is that they permit the ordering of events. In the absence of a Western-style calendar, Māori ordered events by generation, somewhat like those older histories that began, 'In the reign of ...'. In the oral tradition, *whakapapa* provided the backbone to the stories.

Place-names

> *Cow-country place-names are lewd, humorous, ironic or sentimental, but seldom trite. Usually they are subtle enough to draw enquiry from new arrivals, whereby hangs that web of tales which, full spun, constitutes the local folklore.*
> (Aldo Leopold)[70]

Māori place names make many contributions to tradition, sometimes confirming stories and, at others times, providing independent clues to past events. A feature of Māori place naming is that the *mauri* (personality, life principle) of *tūpuna* (ancestor(s)) is often said to have become one with the land. According to the Māori view, this may be stated as '*whakapōhatutia*' (turned to stone) and so the place is said to in fact be that *tūpuna*. The supreme example of this is Aoraki, the story telling how Aoraki's canoe became the South Island and Aoraki and his brothers become four peaks in the Southern Alps. Other important *tūpuna* have had their names used as place names: Tūhaitara appears as a name for at least five peaks and three fishing grounds off the South Island. All are mnemonic devices, providing clues to traditional stories. Another common theme of Māori place names is to focus on some essential aspect of an area. South Canterbury is replete with names associated with the production of *kāuru*, an important carbohydrate south of the horticultural region. Collectively, they indicate the traditional importance of the region.

'Etmic' approaches

The incorporation of emic material with the etic, forming what I coin the 'etmic' approach, requires an understanding of the worldview from where the material originated. In particular, such a model should include inquiry into Māori-language material and, usually, the perspective of the modern-day descendants of the research subjects, else misunderstandings are likely. The following are examples of etmic studies that have met with varying degrees of success.

Margaret Orbell, in her comments on the *waiata*, 'He Tangi Mo Te Iwi-Ika',[71] attempted to use emic material but, by-and-large, trod the same etic path as others. Although she exhibits some local knowledge in identifying Tahu-Kumea and Tahu-Whakairo as being from 'a South Island version of the myth of Tāne', she states: 'The poet … begins by lamenting the death of her husband, Te Iwi-Ika'.[72] She does not seem to realise that 'Te Iwi Ika' is a Southern name for all Māoridom, a fact which leads to a whole further perspective on the *waiata*.[73] Indeed much old knowledge is still retained among the local people despite Orbell's insinuation that only the paper record remains.[74] Had she approached the descendants of the people from whom the *waiata* was collected (by Judge Chapman around 1894) this error of interpretation probably would not have occurred. By contrast, Bill Dacker, in preparing *Te Mamae me te Aroha*, consulted extensively with Southern Ngāi Tahu and did not accept published information without question.[75] Rather than illustrate his book with photographs or drawings from public archives, Dacker peppered his book with family photographs of the main players. The result is a book that is very consistent with the insider view and shows understandings uncommon in most works.

Conclusion

> *Ko te kōkōmuka te rākau i tunua ai te moa.*
> *There is a proper use for everything and only by means of correct usage can the optimum result be obtained.*

While this chapter is very New Zealand-Māori specific, the principles could apply to a study of the traditions of any Indigenous peoples. For, from my perspective, it is only through consideration of all forms of evidence available that a fully comprehensive picture emerges. What the emic may lack in terms of objectivity is complemented by the etic approach. Where the etic must rely on interpretation, the insider perspective can fill in some of the gaps to aid in that interpretation. Broughton makes an important point:

> According to the elders, conflicting opinions and dissension do not necessarily blur the truth. In oratory the length of the speech does not determine the quality of its contents and often in lengthy speeches only a few important details may be extracted. Here lies the exercise. A great deal of information, some conflicting and confusing, was given by the old people, then there are the manuscripts and also the published materials, but the greatest task was to sift the facts from what may be regarded as opinion.[76]

Clearly, this sifting is greatly facilitated by the understanding that comes with some foreknowledge of the topic area, whether that knowledge derives from the insider's perspective or the outsiders', but to have both is a considerable advantage. Further, Broughton's first sentence is in direct contrast to Anderson, who recognises that the variations 'could eventually turn out to be of considerable significance' but does not explore them. Stack deliberately put aside genealogical material. Orbell failed to seek a contemporary, emic viewpoint. It is argued that, in all cases, a more comprehensive result could have been obtained from an 'etmic' approach, where the advantages of etic research are combined with the insights and deep knowledge of insiders about their place and their ancestors.

CHAPTER SEVEN

Rediscovering the Hidden Heritage from Ancient Mangaia

Michael P.J. Reilly

Mangaia is one of the largest islands of the Cook Islands group in the South Pacific. Until the late nineteenth century it was an autonomous polity, governed by powerful chiefs who received advice from the resident agent of the London Missionary Society (LMS), which first evangelised the island in 1824. From 1888, Mangaia became part of the British Protectorate over the Cook Islands, an arrangement ostensibly made to protect the Islands from French invasion but in reality intended to facilitate the growing trade between these islands and Britain's New Zealand colony. In 1901, New Zealand annexed the Cook Islands, which remained part of the country until achieving autonomy in 1965.

The LMS in Mangaia was supervised by Pacific Islands missionaries until the first English mission family arrived in 1845, to be followed in 1852 by William Wyatt Gill. He was to supervise the local church for about twenty years, working with local pastors, notably his coadjutor, Mamae of the Ngāti Vara *kōpū* (clan), who acted as one of Gill's instructors in *te tara Mangaia* (the Mangaian language) when they served together in the village of Tamarua. Their working relationship led them in subsequent years to embark on a project to record Mamae's own knowledge of Mangaian society prior to its transformation by the adoption of Christianity.

This chapter explores a particular story that Mamae wrote for Gill and which Gill then translated for publication in 1876. Looked at side by side, the two texts reveal a lot about the perspectives the men brought to their shared work. Part of a larger body of ethnographic writing, the dominance of Gill's version reflects the hegemony of Europe throughout the world during the later nineteenth century. His English translation speaks to the aspirations of mission societies as well as those of European colonies, such as New Zealand, of founding their own versions of empire in the islands of the Pacific.

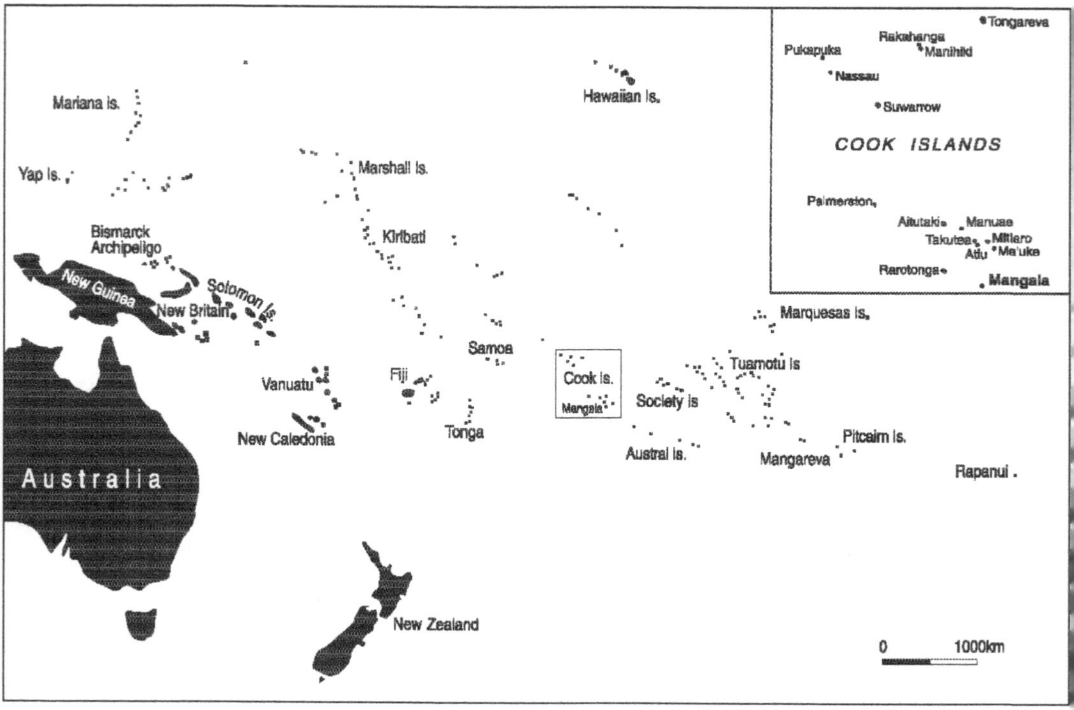

Map of the Cook Islands and wider Pacific. Les O'Neill

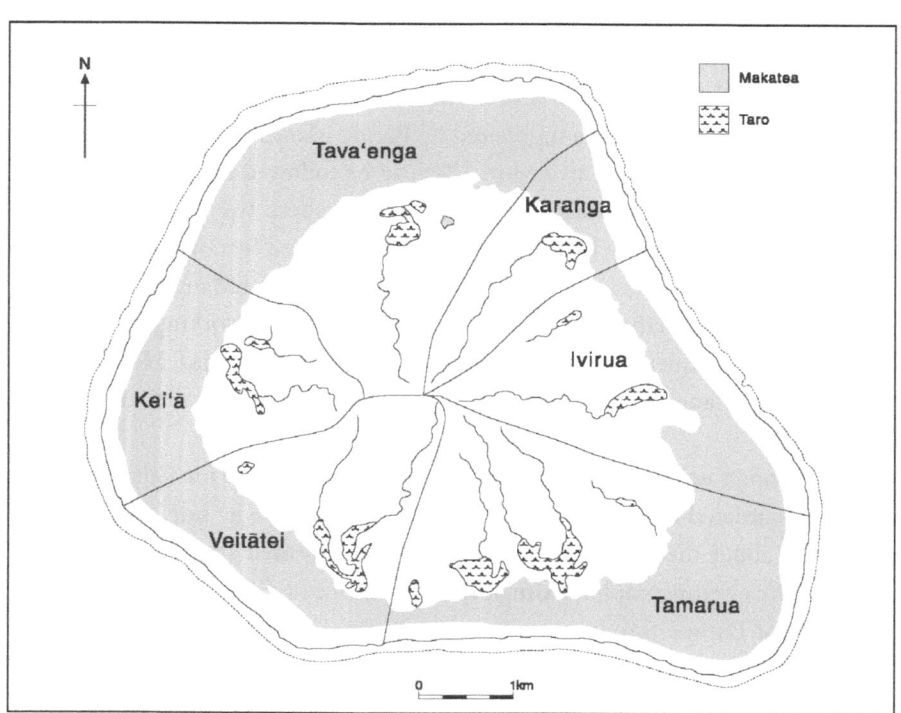

Map of Mangaia. Les O'Neill

Rediscovering and reconstructing Mamae's narrative expresses the aspiration of contemporary scholars, such as those in Māori Studies in New Zealand, to seek out what Sidney Moko Mead calls 'Te Wahi Ngaro (The Lost Portion of the Heritage)' in order to reintegrate the sum total of *mātauranga Māori* (Indigenous knowledge inherited from ancestors) for future generations.[1] At one level, discovering Mamae's vernacular text in the archives evokes the resistance of Indigenous languages which continue to be heard in spite of the dominance of colonising languages such as English. At another level, however, there is a more complex interplay in operation between the two texts, reflective of the two writers' collaborations as LMS church ministers. The stories can be read contrapuntally, to use Edward Said's term, as one text foregrounds England's evangelical readers and the other highlights local social and cultural understandings. Mamae's own life and writings suggest that Mangaians of his generation embraced a composite cultural identity, where the values and achievements of the ancestors co-existed with full and enthusiastic participation in the local LMS church. The following section is my summary of Gill's version: some passages directly quote his own words.[2]

> The story occurred during the time of Ngāuta. The brothers were kinsmen of the high-ranking Taia. The elder brother, Kōtū, lived with his aged parents in the district of Veitātei, located in the south-west of the island. His younger brother, Kōā, lived on the other side of Mangaia, in the district of Karanga, amongst his mother's family. The brothers were very close and visited each other all the time. One evening Kōtū and Kōā both decided to go and visit the other. Their pathway crossed the highest hill in the centre of Mangaia, called Rangimōti'a. By the time each of them climbed to this central point it was quite dark and had started to rain. In those days travellers at night made sure to wrap their head and faces up in *tapa* cloth. When the brothers met on Rangimōti'a beside a large *toa* (ironwood) tree, they failed to recognise each other. The track was narrow, allowing only one person to pass that place. The two figures stood facing each other, waiting for the other to step aside. 'It was', Gill explains, 'a point of honour not to step out of the narrow pathway to oblige another: to do so would be an admission of inferiority'. They engaged in some pushing and shoving, but still neither moved aside. The two now began to wrestle, each attempting to grab the opponent's long hair (their head coverings having fallen off) in order to break their neck. In the struggle, they fell off the track and rolled down the hillside, their fall broken by the soft covering of fern and grass. Kōtū landed on top of Kōā and attempted to break his neck. Kōā, weakened from the fall, could not resist

and called out the name, either of their father or according to some, that of his elder brother. '"Alas; Kōtū, I perish!"' Realising who it was, Kōtū released his grip and the brothers 'wept with shame and grief'. The place where they stood in the isolated and swampy valley of Mataʻare is now marked by an *'ara* (pandanus) tree. Kōtū insisted that they should go to Veitātei and inform their father, Eve, of what had happened.

The reference to the ancestors, Ngāuta and Taia, helps locate this text. Ngāuta was the leader of the Tongaʻiti *ivi* (people), descending from senior lines within its most senior *kōpū*, also called the Tongaʻiti. He held the *mangaia* (the highest chiefly title) an unprecedented seven times, probably in the middle decades of the seventeenth century.[3] Gill understood that Ngāuta granted Taia, probably a chiefly supporter, the *mangaia* title following their second victory against leaders from other kin groups.[4] Thus Gill assumed that Kōtū and Kōā were 'persons of mark' in the early part of Ngāuta's reign as *mangaia*.[5] During the period of such a reign, the island was in a state of peace: the carrying of weapons was banned.[6] This requirement explains why neither of the brothers is armed. In these circumstances, wrestling was used to determine a victor.

The internal evidence within the text demonstrates that it is a composite work, based upon several Mangaian language versions recounted to Gill. Not surprisingly, his text includes items of information that would have been of more value to a non-Mangaian reading audience. One concerns the explanation of customary usages, such as the wearing of a *tapa* cloth at night, perhaps as protection against Mangaia's numerous mosquitoes. More importantly, he provided his foreign readers with word-pictures of the physical environment through which the brothers passed. For example, he described the particular *toa* tree which stood beside the mountain path, remarking that it was 'a large ironwood tree, the gnarled roots of which yet remain', that at the time of the story 'then waved its light and graceful limbs'.[7] Of the fall down the hillside, Gill noted that the two men suffered little, partly because of the 'gradual slope', but more especially because the sides of the hill 'are entirely free from projecting roots of trees and stones and are clothed with soft fern and coarse grass'.[8] When Kōtū almost succeeded in killing Kōā, Gill reported that he intended to hide the body in 'a morass, now planted with taro', suggesting that in the mission period, such remote valleys in the hilly interior were brought into production.[9] The site of this struggle was marked in Gill's day by a pandanus tree, probably planted deliberately to remember this historic incident.

These descriptions point to Gill's familiarity with Mangaia's landscape, which he explored very thoroughly during his twenty years' service there. On all these journeys, on foot or by horse, he was frequently accompanied by Mangaians who acted as guides, directing his attention to items of historical interest. For modern readers, these descriptions provide valuable information, not only about the changes effected during the nineteenth century, but about the look of the place in former days since many features of that older world, such as the ancestral walking tracks across the mountain, remained in active use.

Gill's own interpretation of this story reveals his professional concerns as a missionary then home on leave in England. He thought the story 'an emblem' for the kinds of 'unhappy contests' and 'sectarian prejudices' occurring amongst various Christian churches.[10] I should stress that he referred to relations between Protestant churches, since, like other English people, he thought Roman Catholics no better than heathen idol worshippers.[11] Gill interpreted the cry to the father or elder brother as a call upon God or a 'common brotherhood' which would stop the conflict and draw the opposing churches together in a shared bond.[12] The visit to Eve was read as the testimony of formerly divided churches who related 'the strange story' of their terrestrial errors and misunderstandings to their heavenly Father.[13]

If Gill's interpretation has more to do with contemporary English church politics, still he evidently felt comfortable enough using what he called elsewhere, a 'pretty story' from Mangaia, in order to make an important point to his English readers.[14] Such good people, he seems to suggest, might learn something from the mouths of Christianity's most recent converts. Here Gill resumed his missionary role, with the difference that he used a Mangaian story to mildly reprove English Protestants. For Gill, his scholarly research of Mangaia's traditions formed an integral part of his evangelical mission: to enlighten those who dwelt in darkness whether they lived in London or Tamarua.[15]

Mamae's version of the story is found amongst Gill's papers,[16] confirming that it formed part of the men's project to record the old stories and songs which Mamae had inherited from his grandfather, Koroa, a *mangaia* titleholder.[17]

> 'E tuatua nō 'e tokorua puke tangata, nō roto i te kōpū o Te Kama, 'e tuakana tēta'i, 'e teina tēta'i. Tērā tō rāua puke ingoa, 'o Kōtū te tuakana, 'o Kōā te teina, e no'o te tuakana i Karanga, e no'o te teina i Veitātei. I tēta'i rā, kua 'aere te tuakana i te a'ia'i e 'ātoro i tōna teina i te Tapere i Veitātei, kua pērā 'oki te teina e 'aere a ia i te 'ātoro rāi i tōna tuakana i te Tapere i Karanga. Kāre 'ua tēta'i i kite ē tē 'aere mai rā tēta'i, kāre katoa 'oki tēta'i i kite. I nā te maunga mai tēta'i, i nā te maunga mai 'oki tēta'i. E tae mai rā rāua tēta'i ē tēta'i, 'ārāvei ake rā i runga tēta'i maunga, 'o Rangimōti'a te ingoa, tei rotopū ia maunga i te 'enua. Inārā kia vaitata rāua i te 'ārāvei, kua tū mai rā tēta'i, tū atu rā 'oki tēta'i, kāre

tētaʻi e pā i te ara, kāre ʻoki tētaʻi e pā. Tē manako rā tētaʻi e ʻakaruke te ara nōna, e pae a ia i te ʻiti, kua pērā ʻoki tētaʻi. E mai te aʻiaʻi e turuaʻaipō rāua i te ʻakapērā ʻanga. Kua tupu tō rāua riri tētaʻi ē tētaʻi. Kua tautātā rāua, e riri nui tō tētaʻi, e riri nui ʻoki tō tētaʻi, taka atu rā rāua i raro i tētaʻi ngāʻi ʻakaʻaka. ʻE vao, ʻo Mataʻare te ingoa. Kua vaitata i te ao i reira. Inārā ʻia ʻakarongo te tuakana ē, kua ʻakaea te teina i te vaʻa. Kua kite a ia ē, kua pau te riri nui. Kua rave riri nui mai rā a ia i te ūpoko e ʻaʻati i tōna ʻua. Kua auē ʻiōra te teina, mā te kāpiki i te ingoa o tōna tuakana, nākō ake rā, Auē Kōtū ē, ʻā mate au ē! Kia rongo a Kōtū ē, ʻo te reo ia o tōna teina, tuku ake rā i tōna ūpoko, auē katoa ʻiōra rāua, ē kia oti tō rāua auē ʻanga, arataki atu rā te tuakana, ʻoki atu rā rāua i Karanga i ō te tuakana rā.

Mamae, like Gill, concluded his story with a song excerpt referring to the brothers. According to Gill, this 'scrap' of song was sung around 1818 by Reonatia, a couple of years before he became the last person ritually sacrificed to inaugurate a *mangaia*'s reign. Gill thought its 'crabbed style' was a sign of its 'antiquity'; he estimated it to be 'about 300 years old'.[18] Mamae's song is dotted with Gill's annotations (reproduced in the notes), suggesting that he discussed word meanings with Mamae when preparing his own translation.[19]

Tērā te potonga peʻe i ʻatua nō rāua[20]
Nāʻaku rāi e kake
I ō te puku roā i Tavaikura,[21]
Ko ʻakarērē Kōā ē![22]

ʻIa ua ē i, ʻia ua ē, tō reirē
I kakea Kōtū ē i kākē![23]

Tū e tū ʻakariri ʻo Eve ē,
Tū e tū ʻakariri ʻo Eve ē[24]
ʻUa ʻakaāuriri! Ki tē kānotau ē[25]
Tei nunga te mārama ē!

Both versions of the story of the two brothers refer to two significant clusterings of Indigenous cultural themes. The first of these thematic clusters is topographical in nature and refers to the descriptions of the land through which the two brothers passed on their journeys. The second concerns the nature of the relationship between these two brothers and associated social values.

Topographical theme

The story locates both brothers in Karanga and Veitātei, two of Mangaia's six *puna* (districts). These are the classical wedge-shaped land divisions found in many Polynesian islands which all fanned out from a central point on Rangimōti'a, their boundaries running along the valley ridges to the sea. As the *puna* are associated with events that occurred during the earliest period of Mangaia's history, we can assume that these land divisions were ancient ones. *Puna* also referred specifically to the inland valleys filled with irrigated *taro* plantations. In pre-Christian times, most people lived here in clusters of houses and associated *marae* (sacred sites) on the ridges and higher ground before their post-conversion migration to three coastal villages (Oneroa, Tamarua, Ivirua). Each *puna* contained a number of *tapere* (sub-districts), resembling slices of land, which incorporated the various food resources including cross-sections of the *taro*-producing valleys. *Taro* (*Colocasia esculenta*), known locally as *māmio*, forms the staple food on Mangaia as elsewhere in the Pacific. These *tapere* were occupied by one or more kin groups under a ruling chief. The two brothers are described as visiting each other in their respective *tapere* within these *puna*. They would have been moving between households within these food-producing valleys.

Besides being the point of origin of the island's *puna*, Rangimōti'a had many other special associations for Mangaians in the pre-Christian era. It is still known as '*te pito o te 'enua*' 'the centre of the island'.[26] Mamae elsewhere recounted how the founding *tupuna* (ancestor) of Mangaian society, Rangi, travelled about the land and climbed the highest peak in the centre of the island, naming it Rangimōti'a after himself, and in effect, taking possession of the land from its guardian spirits.[27] This was the place where one of Rangi's own *tupuna*, Te Manava-roa, lay buried.[28] This *atua* had produced Vari-mā-te-takere, mother of Avatea, her first born. Avatea married a woman of the land, Papa-ra'ira'i, and they produced Rongo, who, marrying his own daughter, Tavake, produced Rangi.[29] For Mangaians this might be considered their most sacred descent line from which all humanity emerged.

> Te Manava-roa
> Vari-mā-te-takere
> Avatea = Papa-ra'ira'i
> Rongo = Tavake
> Rangi

Rangimōti'a is always called a *maunga* (mountain) in Mangaia. It retained a special status for the people, becoming a sacred site for certain important rituals associated with the inauguration of the *mangaia* title holder.[30] To cross the mountain was, therefore, to pass through a highly venerated place named after the founder of Mangaian society. Until the 1840s when a coastal road was built under the supervision of the missionary George Gill, all travel across the island had to pass through this *maunga* region.[31]

The central line of hills or *maunga* divides Mangaia into two parts, commonly referred to as the northern and southern sides of the island. Karanga was one of the three northern *puna* while Veitātei was one of the three southern ones. Te Manavaroa's body forms the central hills, while his arms and legs are the ridges extending out to divide off the districts from each other.[32] Mangaia is often described as 'the fish of Rongo' or '*Te ika a Rongo*', in commemoration of Rongo, their most important *atua*. In this conceptualisation, both Karanga and Veitātei are described as being the '*pori*', the 'body' or 'belly' of the fish. The northern half of the island is thought of as the left side (*kaui*) and the southern half is considered to be the right-hand side (*katau*). In formal terms, Karanga is called '*te pori o Rongo i kaui*' (Rongo's body on the left), while Veitātei is '*te pori o Rongo i katau*' (Rongo's body on the right).[33]

This story, therefore, establishes an opposition between the two brothers, further complicated by a switch of locations in the two versions. According to Gill, the contrast is between a younger, junior brother on the northern, left side and his elder brother located on the southern, right side of the island. For Mamae, the situation is reversed, with the *tuakana* living on the northern side in Karanga and his *teina* on the southern side in Veitātei. Gill's variant may have resulted from his using other versions derived from people who lived in *puna* on both sides of the island. Other traditions allude to significant political differences between those kin groups dwelling on the northern side of the island and those on the southern side.[34] Mamae's story may represent a southern perspective since all his mission service, in Oneroa and Tamarua, took place on the south side while the ancestral lands of his own *kōpū*, Ngāti Vara, lay in two Veitātei *tapere*.[35]

Sociological theme

Mamae placed the two men within their proper social context when he explained that the brothers belonged to the Te Kama *kōpū*. This was a clan traditionally associated with the northern *puna*, Karanga.[36] Not surprisingly, Mamae located the *tuakana* in this *puna* since the older, senior child would be expected to grow up amongst the leaders of his community. In the two generations before Ngāuta's reign, Te Kama had sought to seize control of Mangaia by attempting to take the *mangaia* title from its previous holders, the Ngāriki *ivi*, who descended from Rangi and his brothers, Te 'Akatauira and Mokoiro. Despite a number of battles, Te Kama was unable to gain a decisive victory. In the time of Ngāuta's predecessor as *mangaia*, Te Kama is considered to have been decisively destroyed as a military force.[37] However, other traditions indicate that Te Kama remained in control of Karanga and its food resources during the reign of Ngāuta and his immediate successors.[38] Thus Kōtū lived in an area dominated by his own kin group and its leaders.

Mamae's placing of Kōā in Veitātei is not altogether surprising as the final battles fought by Te Kama in an attempt to obtain the *mangaia* title occurred in localities within this southern *puna*.[39] No doubt after their first defeats which took place in Karanga, numbers of Te Kama had escaped southwards, perhaps to family connections there, in order to rebuild their strength. Mamae's story about the brothers indicates that some Te Kama remained in that *puna* once Te Kama was finally defeated, perhaps living with relations from other kin groups. Kōā's southern residence may, therefore, represent a survival strategy. Other *kōpū* under pressure resorted to similar devices, with survivors living under the protection of relations in other kin groups.[40]

A key theme of this story is the special relationship that exists between older and younger siblings or cousins of the same sex, called *tuakana* and *teina* respectively. The emotional impact of this story about the mutual misrecognition and fight between this dyad is premised on readers understanding the normal relationship between the partners in this important kinship pair. Gill, as an outsider, writing for an English audience, explained that the brothers were 'tenderly attached to each other' and visited each other constantly.[41] In his conclusion he referred to 'this singular midnight encounter between two brothers who had ever entertained the warmest affection for each other'.[42] While Gill did not elaborate on the wider cultural significance of this bond, Mamae made it clear that the whole drama of the unfolding events depended on the strong affection felt between *tuakana* and *teina*.

Other Mangaian traditions highlight how *teina* were expected to support and look out for the interests of their *tuakana*.[43] The *teina* is presented in such stories as following the directions of their elder; for example, executing their instructions. The stories assume a profound trust between them. The *tuakana* partner is expected to reciprocate by supporting the *teina* partner, respecting their position and not exploiting or demeaning them. While the *tuakana* is genealogically superior in terms of rank, these stories imply that the close affective bonds between a *tuakana* and *teina* prevent any abuse of that relationship occurring. Hence when the story refers to the impasse between the two men on the mountain, when neither would yield to the other, the reader is expected to understand that this contradicts the whole nature of that fraternal bond.

Gill highlighted how status considerations prompted the attempts to find a violent resolution to that impasse when he stressed that neither individual could give way to the other without admitting inferiority. In other words, the act of stepping aside implied a deferral to the *mana* of the other individual. Neither of them would willingly do this, since both men were, as Gill stressed, of high social rank. Of course, if Kōā had known that the other man was in fact his *tuakana*, Kōtū, he would have willingly done that as a gesture recognising the greater *mana* inhering in his *tuakana* as the first-born son of their parents.

Both texts highlight the emotional reaction of the brothers when they finally recognise each other. Mamae, in his characteristically more laconic style, described how they wept together ('*auē katoa 'iōra rāua*'). Stephen Savage defined *auē* as 'to cry, weep, lament, bawl: to utter a shrill loud sound especially as of one in pain or who has received a sudden shock or fright'.[44] Mamae implied that this shrill lamentation continued for a long while; there is no Anglo-Saxon economy with the emotions. This response is not surprising since both brothers, especially the *tuakana*, would have recognised just how close he had come to committing murder. If Kōā had not cried out for his *tuakana*, itself an indication of their mutual affection, then Kōtū might have inadvertently slain someone bound to him by the closest of family ties. As Te Rangi Hiroa observed: 'The killing of relatives during peace … was particularly abhorred'.[45] The consequences for their *kōpū* if Kōtū had killed his brother would have been serious. In such circumstances, Te Rangi Hiroa remarked, a 'blood curse' fell upon the family, leading to their eventual demise.[46] This may explain why Gill reported the brothers going to tell their father about what had happened. Presumably, as the head of their family, he may have been called on to ritually clear away the possibility of such tragedy befalling the brothers or the wider *kōpū*.

In reflecting on the differences and similarities between the versions composed by these two friends, it is tempting to imagine their own relationship as a *tuakana* and *teina* pair when Mamae taught Gill to *tara Mangaia* (speak Mangaian) or when Gill supervised Mamae's pastoral work. While referring to two particular men from a defeated *kōpū* that would soon disappear, Mamae's version provides cultural markers, which help us reconstruct the dynamics of the *tuakana* and *teina* relationship. Gill, the stranger, was drawn to the emotional power of the story, but deliberately turned away from its Mangaian context and instead used it to admonish English Protestants to abandon their unseemly inter-church squabbles. Mamae resists this universalising of the story and locates it within a Mangaian cultural framework. When Gill describes this local world, it is to draw attention to details of the countryside. Did he sense the danger for a missionary in engaging too closely with the cultural values of that other world? The Mangaian characters in his story are made to carry messages intended for another place, their island society depicted as amongst the new converts in a greater Protestant world order. Even so, there remain moments when Gill reveals his own personal engagement with Mangaia in his landscape vignettes and in the way he embraced this story in order to correct wayward English believers. In those moments his own identity as an evangelist seems less pure and closer to the hybrid identity of Mamae and other Mangaian church members. While the richness and vitality of this story fades a little in the process of Gill's translation, it is restored through Mamae's own words, thereby returning another piece of Mangaia's hidden heritage to the present as part of the knowledge base for a new generation.

RESISTANCE

CHAPTER EIGHT

Indigenous Political Representation and Comparative Research

Janine Hayward

Comparative research is an empowering component of 'research as resistance' for scholars in Indigenous studies. This chapter investigates a simple observation evident when comparing Canada and New Zealand's Indigenous representation: Māori have been represented through the guaranteed Māori seats in the national legislature since the late 1860s, while First Nations are negotiating self-government with the federal government on a case-by-case basis. The comparativist asks, why are these contemporary experiences so different? The answer is revealed through comparison of colonial histories, particularly the degree to which the Indigenous peoples were engaged in or excluded from the emerging nation-state and the degree to which they enjoyed the rights and privileges of British subjects. But this comparison also reveals an important similarity that may be overlooked in a single case study: in both cases self-government and national representation appear to have been treated as mutually exclusive. Māori and First Nations have engaged in one, it seems, at the expense of the other.

Having established and explained this observation, this chapter explores whether or not self-government and guaranteed representation are mutually exclusive for First Nations in Canada and Māori in New Zealand. There are many forms that self-government and guaranteed representation can take. For simplicity's sake, this discussion defines these in terms of the models used in New Zealand and Canada: in other words it asks whether, in principle, it is problematic for First Nations to have guaranteed representation as Māori do and for Māori to exercise some 'law-making' capacity through self-government as do some First Nations. This debate is further advanced in Canada, where guaranteed representation has been advocated in a variety of ways. Therefore, this discussion focuses on bringing the New Zealand debate 'up to speed' in terms of considering the implications of Māori achieving some 'law-making capacity' through self-government in the future.

There are two important things this discussion does not do, which must be acknowledged. First, it does not ask or answer the prior question whether First Nations can make a case for guaranteed representation and Māori can make a case for self-government. Second, it is not the purpose here to make a case for self-government and guaranteed representation *per se*. Both these questions ought to be asked and answered by Indigenous communities themselves. Rather, the point here is simply to 'clear the way' for these important discussions and to determine whether First Nations and Māori can engage in both forms of representation concurrently, *should they choose to do so.*

Guaranteed representation and self-government: Comparing New Zealand and Canada

Māori voters at Rotorua, about 1908. Auckland City Libraries, A14995

Canada and New Zealand's colonial histories are of interest to many comparativists who have documented and examined their many similarities and differences.[1] This discussion begins with the observation that Canada and New Zealand have, at very different times, accommodated representation for their Indigenous peoples in very different ways.² The 1867 Māori Representation Act made provision for four guaranteed Māori seats in New Zealand's House of Representatives. The electorates for these seats overlaid those of the general seats and Māori voted for candidates from a separate Māori roll. The legislature's motivation in creating the seats is contested. Irons Magallanes neatly describes the creation of the seats as a 'political bargain' made possible by 'a convergence of political factors'.³ As was also the case in Canada,⁴ communal property was a major obstacle to Māori exercising a right to vote. The Māori seats and the Māori roll were originally temporary measures designed to bridge the gap until Māori communal land title had been individualised, allowing Māori to meet the property requirement for voting and move to the general roll. But the seats were extended indefinitely, which suited the needs of settlers and Māori: for settlers, the four seats effectively constrained the influence the (then) large Māori population could have on the legislature in its early years, while Māori felt their interests were better protected by seats accountable to Māori electorates.⁵ The seats survived the passage of time and in the 1990s were reformed to bring the size of the Māori electorates in line with those of the general seats. Currently there are seven guaranteed Māori seats in the New Zealand legislature. The seats are still a contentious aspect of New Zealand politics. As recently as the 2005 general election campaign, many of the political parties advocated reviewing the need for the seats in future. Given that the seats are not a protected provision of New Zealand's constitutional arrangements, their future cannot be taken for granted.

Turning to the Canadian experience, self-government has long been an objective for First Nations people. The history and contemporary reality of the struggle to assert rights to self-government, which First Nations argue were never relinquished, is complex, fraught and inspiring. Accepting that this issue is expertly considered elsewhere,⁶ the purpose here is to explain the Canadian Government's formal position on First Nation self-government. Prior to 1995, several self-government arrangements were developed in Canada: the James Bay and Northern Quebec Agreement (1975), the Sechelt Indian Band Self-Government Act (1986) and the Yukon First Nations Final Agreement (1993).⁷ In 1995, the federal government formally recognised the inherent right of self-government as an existing Aboriginal right. The policy limits the jurisdiction of Aboriginal self-government to matters internal to the group, integral to distinct Aboriginal culture and essential to self-government operations. This includes governing structures and membership, marriage, adoptions, education, health, housing, social services, Aboriginal law enforcement and policing, property rights, land and resource management, agriculture, hunting, licensing and local transportation. The policy recognises that different groups of Aboriginal peoples (problematically defined as First Nation, Métis and Inuit, see Chapter 1) have different circumstances (some have treaties and others do not, some have a land base and others do not) that will require different packages of self-government rights to reflect their needs.

Māori, First Nations and the rights and privileges of British subjects

Guaranteed Māori representation and First Nation self-government reflect the relationships these Indigenous peoples established with settlers during first contact and particularly with colonial governments during early nation-building. To put it bluntly, Māori were represented within the government because they exercised the rights and privileges of British subjects, while it is probable that First Nations exercise their own limited forms of self-government because they were not granted British rights and privileges (particularly the franchise) until the 1960s.

In 1840, Māori were granted the rights and privileges of British subjects in Article Three of the Treaty of Waitangi, signed with the British Crown. Article Three is the least controversial and most overlooked of the Treaty articles. Attention has focused instead on Article One, by which the Crown established government in New Zealand and Article Two, which guaranteed to Māori their chiefly authority over lands, resources and other prized possessions. The English version of Article Three states: 'In consideration thereof Her Majesty the Queen of England extends to the Natives of New Zealand Her royal protection and imparts to them the Rights and Privileges of British Subjects'. Despite being an unusual treaty provision, this is generally not seen as a remarkable aspect of New Zealand's colonial history. As New Zealand historian Claudia Orange notes:

> Elsewhere in the British Empire, native races were supposed to enjoy the status of British subjects, although they were not always treated accordingly. What was remarkable in New Zealand was that this was explicitly stated and the expression of humanitarian idealism thus publicised. However, the implications of accepting the 'rights and privileges' of a British subject (that Maori would be subject to British law and committed to certain responsibilities) were not emphasised.[8]

Perhaps the most significant implication of Article Three was the inclusion of Māori in the franchise and the creation of the four Māori seats in Parliament from 1867. But the 'certain responsibilities' Māori also acquired have been the price that

Māori paid for those rights. Māori attempts to assert their chiefly authority under Article Two of the Treaty were generally greeted with hostility by the settler society. As Cox's study of Māori political unity reveals, the state resisted independent Māori expression of self-determination in the late 1800s, such as the Māori Parliament and the King movement, and made provision instead from time to time for Māori participation within the state in a variety of ways.[9] Through the late 1800s, as Māori rapidly lost the land from which to express their chiefly authority, their British rights and privileges became an assimilating force that framed Māori expressions of culture and identity outside the state as radical and divisive.

It is difficult to quantify the full impact of Article Three on Māori since 1840, but some of the obvious outcomes are more readily apparent when the New Zealand case is compared to the experiences of First Nations in colonial Canada. The 1763 Royal Proclamation (which set the boundaries for the new colony of Quebec) refers to British protection for Indian Nations, but also sets them apart from 'all our loving subjects'. The treaties subsequently signed with First Nations were written in the language of land 'surrender' and did not convey the rights of British Subjects to First Nations as the Treaty of Waitangi did for Māori. These treaties often, however, set aside reserved lands which First Nations retained with considerably more success than the reserves set aside for Māori which were largely lost by 1910.[10]

In 1867, the same year that the Māori Representation Act was passed in New Zealand, the British North America Act provided Canada's federal government exclusive authority to legislate in relation to reserved lands. The subsequent 1876 Indian Act ended any confusion about the place of Aboriginal people in the new colony; 'status' Indians were not enfranchised, so had different rights. From this time, laws and policies encouraged First Nations to relinquish their 'Indian' status and embrace the rights and privileges of Canadians (which First Nations resisted).

It is this combination of factors – Māori inclusion in the state and lack of geographic isolation and First Nations' physical and political exclusion from the developing society – that makes the respective forms of representation in contemporary society unsurprising. What is harder to explain is why Māori attempts at self-government and calls for guaranteed representation for First Nations have been unsuccessful. As Māori scholar Mason Durie notes, Māori have exercised some limited forms of self-governance at the *iwi* and community levels, many of which originated in the 1980s when the government sought to 'devolve' many state functions to organisations outside the state in order to be more efficient.[11] But the New Zealand government has not engaged in negotiations with Māori to recognise and accommodate more comprehensive forms of self-government. In particular, there is no public debate about the possibility that Māori might exercise some law-making capacity, as First Nations are negotiating in Canada.

The debate about guaranteed representation for First Nations (in fact for Indigenous people generally) has enjoyed some currency in Canada. In 1991, the Royal Commission on Electoral Reform and Party Financing recommended the creation of Aboriginal constituencies for federal elections to the House of Commons. In 1992, the constitutional negotiations known as the Charlottetown Accord was defeated in a national referendum. It included proposals to enhance Aboriginal representation in the House of Commons and other Canadian institutions. In 1996, the Royal Commission on Aboriginal Peoples raised concerns that the previous proposals for enhanced representation were not compatible with self-government. The Commission recommended a 'nation-to-nation' proposal that Aboriginal peoples have a third House in Ottawa, complementing the Senate and House of Commons. Finally, in 2004, the Law Commission of Canada recommended the introduction of MMP in Canada. It also tentatively supported the notion of Aboriginal Electoral Districts as recommended by the Royal Commission on Aboriginal Peoples in 1991.

Both the New Zealand and Canadian cases reveal evidence of a 'trade-off' in representation rights, forcing two divergent results. In engaging with the state, Māori possibly unwittingly undermined their case for self-determination, as state responses to their initiatives show. First Nations, on the other hand, strengthened their case for self-government by emphasising and even protecting their exclusion from the state, at the expense of their representation and engagement in provincial and federal legislatures.[12] But today, circumstances are significantly different in both countries and these historic assumptions and attitudes need to be reconsidered. Māori continue to achieve Treaty of Waitangi settlements on a case-by-case basis with the New Zealand government. Post-settlement *iwi* have, arguably, the status, resources and institutional arrangements to allow them a greater capacity than ever before to exercise increased control over aspects of their own affairs. First Nations have been enfranchised since the 1960s without relinquishing their treaty rights and those groups concluding self-government negotiations with government can potentially enjoy both self-government and engage in provincial and federal politics. And yet, in both cases, the colonial legacy appears to continue to constrain public debate about representation.

Self-government and guaranteed representation: Mutually exclusive?

Why is it that New Zealand and Canada seem to act as if self-government and guaranteed representation are mutually exclusive for Indigenous peoples? Two distinct but related issues have been raised. First is the problem Aboriginal scholars and commentators have raised regarding identity as it relates to representation. That is, identifying with a sub-group in society precludes or complicates concurrent membership within a larger constituency. This is particularly so when the smaller group identity feels threatened. Gerald Taiaiake Alfred, for example, takes the position that it is impossible to be both a citizen of an Aboriginal Nation (with inherent rights to self-government) and a citizen of the Canadian nation (represented in the provincial and federal legislatures).[13] Similar arguments have been made with regard to First Nation peoples voting in provincial and federal elections: 'I don't vote in elections in France. I don't vote in elections in Ethiopia. Why would I vote in Canada? They are all foreign nations'.[14] Similarly, there is evidence that Māori engagement in the larger constituency has precluded their capacity to also act independent of the state. Durie notes that national self-governance has not become a reality in New Zealand because the Crown sees Parliament as the only source of authority for all New Zealanders and there is substantial fear amongst non-Māori that self-government is an expression of separatism.[15]

The second concern about exercising both forms of government concurrently regards the 'fairness' of self-governing peoples also having representation in shared institutions. Canadian theorist Will Kymlicka suggests that it is problematic for Aboriginal MPs elected in specially created Aboriginal districts to decide federal legislation from which Aboriginals exercising self-government might be exempt. He cites examples of 'reduced representation' for groups that exercise self-government and also have some form of representation at the national level.[16] Kymlicka 'over-simplifies' the case thus: self-government for Indigenous peoples seems to require reduced representation on federal bodies which legislate in areas of purely federal jurisdiction from which they are exempted. He concludes that the logical consequence of self-government is reduced representation, not increased representation. 'The right to self-government is a right against the authority of the federal government, not a right to share in the exercise of that authority'.[17] This, he argues, is the reason that Aboriginals who claim self-government often oppose seats in the House of Commons because this might give government 'the sense that they can rightfully govern Indian communities'.[18]

So, what are possible responses to these two concerns? First, Williams addresses First Nations' suspicion of shared citizenship in Canada when she asks, 'is it truly the case that the goal of self-government is incompatible with the goal of enhanced representation in shared institutions in Canada?'[19] Directly addressing concerns such as those expressed by Alfred, she explains:

> Citizenship as shared identity seems to presuppose an ordering principle that subordinates group or cultural identity to the identity of shared citizenship in cases in which the two conflict. If accepting Canadian Citizenship entails putting aside Aboriginal identity in such cases, many Aboriginal thinkers want nothing to do with it. Since political representation in shared institutions implies shared citizenship, they would prefer to forego it in favour of self-government.[20]

To avoid the position Alfred and others take, Williams advocates for a different conception of citizenship that does not threaten First Nation identity. She advocates for 'citizenship as shared fate'. She explains: 'What connects us is a community of shared fate is that our actions have an impact on other identifiable human beings and other human beings' actions have an impact on us'.[21] In this way, First Nations can be citizens of their own nations and at the same time citizens of Canada, with whom the fate of First Nations is so closely tied. In more pragmatic terms, Alan Cairns warns that if the identity argument (as espoused by Alfred and others) enjoyed universal Aboriginal support, their small communities would be isolated and Canadian governments would have no incentive to be concerned about their fate.[22] Finally, Aboriginal scholar John Borrows has pleaded for Aboriginal engagement in full civic life. He says 'ideas of citizenship have to be rooted in notions of mutuality and interconnectedness'.[23]

Second, with regards to the 'fairness' of self-governing nations also having representation in shared institutions, opinions are also at odds with Kymlicka's concerns. Ovide Mercredi (Grand Chief of the Assembly of First Nations) has said '[t]here is no inconsistency in Canada recognizing our collective rights of self-government and us still getting involved and maintaining our involvement in the political life of the state, which means getting involved in federal elections'.[24] Williams addresses Kymlicka directly and responds that: 'the limited jurisdiction of self-governing First Nation communities, the large off-reserve population, plus the obvious importance of federal and provincial laws and policies for all Canadians, Aboriginal or otherwise, suggest that isolation from the federal, provincial and territorial political process would be unfortunate for First Nations'.[25]

Williams's rebuttal to Kymlicka deserves closer consideration as she exposes many problems with the position he himself admits is over-simplified. First, what are the 'laws' Kymlicka has in mind when he wishes to reduce Aboriginal representation in the shared institutions? The federal policy clearly states that self-governing nations are not nation-states and their jurisdiction is limited to matters internal to the group (as discussed above). And as Williams notes, it is difficult if not impossible to imagine a regime in which Aboriginal people living off-reserve could be wholly covered by Aboriginal jurisdiction exercised through self-government on reserve'.[26] Therefore, does it seem 'fair' that *all* Aboriginal people should have reduced representation in shared institutions on certain issues because those matters are subject to laws created by just *some* Aboriginal self-governments?

Moreover, in adopting Williams' vision of citizenship as shared fate, Kymlicka also simplifies the role of the representative. His proposition assumes that representatives have the right to influence only those laws that affect them. This is clearly not so of representatives in general seats; why must Aboriginal representatives in Aboriginal seats be judged against standards not applied to general representatives? Are they not still members of the shared society, with a 'shared fate' with other citizens? Williams's response to Kymlicka demonstrates that possibly the best way to determine whether self-government and guaranteed representation in shared institution can co-exist is to consider how the scenario might play out in a real case.

Is Māori self-government possible with Māori seats?

As discussed above, there has been some public debate in Canada about the possibility of representation for Aboriginal people; a stumbling block to implementation has been the perceived conflict with the goals of Aboriginal self-government. The equivalent debate has not enjoyed such a public profile in New Zealand. Durie points out, however, that Māori currently practise limited forms of self-government at the local level, particularly in the provision of health, education and social services.[27] Self-government in this context is essentially Māori having the funding and institutional support (created by central government law or policy) to deal directly with Māori communities in ways considered appropriate for Māori. It is not self-government in the sense of Māori having the capacity to make laws for their own constituency. So what might the consequences be if Māori in New Zealand exercised self-government similar to that being negotiated by First Nations in Canada?

The Tsawwassen First Nation, in British Columbia, have agreed to the terms of a modern treaty that is typical of the sort of self-government being negotiated through the modern treaty process in British Columbia. The process and terms of treaty-making in the province and elsewhere in Canada are deeply contested. However, for the purposes of this discussion, the question is not whether the new governing authority of Tsawwassen and other First Nations is the best possible outcome, but rather whether their self-governing capacity should diminish their right to representation in shared institutions.

The treaty establishes the Tsawwassen First Nation as a legal entity with the capacity, rights, powers and privileges of a natural person. *Iwi* in New Zealand are similarly required to assume a legal personality in concluding settlements with the New Zealand Crown. Ngāi Tahu, for example, was one of the first *iwi* to reach a Treaty settlement with the Crown. In order to receive settlement assets from the Crown, the *iwi* adopted a legal identity via legislation in 1996. In addition, the Tsawwassen treaty also creates Tsawwassen government and stipulates how members will be elected and what their responsibilities are to their people. Again, this is not so dissimilar from the obligations accepted by Ngāi Tahu in the 1996 Act which prescribe, amongst other things, the status of Te Runanga o Ngāi Tahu (the *iwi* council), the membership of Ngāi Tahu constituency and their entitlements and the provisions for electing representatives. The Act stipulates that the Runanga Appointment Committee will be elected in a democratic manner, by postal ballot, by its members.

The modern treaties being negotiated in British Columbia include many provisions similar to the treaty settlements Māori are making with the New Zealand Crown in terms of the return of land, financial redress, cultural recognition and protection and changes in resource-management regimes. But the law-making capacity and the ability to delegate that capacity sets the modern Canadian treaties apart from New Zealand's treaty settlements. Tsawwassen government, for example, has the authority to make laws *on Tsawwassen lands* in relation to (amongst other things): adoption of Tsawwassen children in British Columbia; child protection services and child-care services; education in the culture of Tsawwassen First Nation; post-secondary education provided by a Tsawwassen institution; practice as aboriginal healers; health services, including public health; and social services including income assistance, services related to family and community life and housing. The Tsawwassen government can also make laws on Tsawwassen lands relating to nuisance, trespass and threats to public order, peace or safety which the Provincial Court of British Columbia has jurisdiction to hear under Tsawwassen law. A Tsawwassen institution may provide Community Correctional Services for persons charged with or found guilty of an offence under Tsawwassen law.

In the New Zealand context, the first objection to imagining Māori exercising this level of self-government is likely to be that *iwi* such as Ngāi Tahu, despite owning lands and properties, do not enjoy an *exclusive* territory as do First Nations with reservations. This is problematic to the extent that the law-making relates to laws exercised within a designated territory, as opposed to laws that pertain to certain people no matter where they are located. Suppose, for a moment, that in the absence of an exclusive territory, a self-identifying constituency can fall within a jurisdiction that is, on some matters, different to the jurisdiction governing the general populace. To put it another way, imagine that those individuals who have registered as Ngāi Tahu for the purposes of the treaty settlement, also consent to coming within the jurisdiction of a Ngāi Tahu government in relation to some very limited matters internal to the group. An obvious example from the Tsawwassen treaty is adoption: imagine if Ngāi Tahu 'government' as democratically elected by the Ngāi Tahu constituency, could pass a law regarding the adoption of Ngāi Tahu children which was different from the law governing the rest of New Zealand. Two questions arise from the Canadian experience of this debate: would this challenge Ngāi Tahu members' identity as 'New Zealanders'; and second, would it require that Ngāi Tahu have reduced representation on matters of adoption law in the legislature?

It seems highly unlikely, given the long history of 'shared fate' Ngāi Tahu has with the greater citizenry in New Zealand, that exercising self-government would derogate from their engagement in the state. In fact, it might be that public recognition of Ngāi Tahu through the exercise of self-government would increase the legitimacy of the legislature and its representatives in the eyes of the *iwi*. In this sense, self-government and national representation may be complementary and mutually reinforcing.

The second question, Kymlicka's problem with the legitimacy of self-government and representation, requires us to continue the proposed scenario. Imagine that the legislature, which includes representatives from the Māori seats, sought to review its adoption laws. Kymlicka's contention is that Ngāi Tahu should have reduced representation in regards to adoption laws that will not apply to them. As Williams foreshadowed, this is problematic for several reasons. First, the relationship between the Māori representatives in the legislature and Māori exercising self-government is not as simple as Kymlicka's proposition assumes. His concern supposes that Ngāi Tahu are also directly represented in government, which may not be the case. In fact, the Māori representatives in the legislature have multiple *iwi* affiliations. Ngāi Tahu might not be able to point to any one MP who 'represents' them in the legislature. It would be difficult, in New Zealand, as Kymlicka would see it, to decide which representatives are to be denied influence over adoption laws that will not apply to them. As Williams also noted in reference to First Nations, not all

Māori (in this case) will be affected by self-government and not all self-governing Māori may choose to pass their own adoption laws, given the opportunity to do so. But Kymlicka's proposition is also troubling in that it assumes that representatives vote only on matters that affect their group and that it is sensible then to extend this principle to also apply to self-governing Aboriginal people, to avoid some sort of double standard arising. This is clearly not the case. All representatives are always voting on laws that will not directly affect them; why should self-governing Māori (for example) be the only group expected to reduce their influence in the legislature to appease his concern? Admittedly, the example of adoption law, as an exercise of self-government, is very limited. But it is difficult to see how this example, at least, either challenges Ngāi Tahu identity or leads to an undemocratic and undesirable outcome.

Conclusion

Comparative research is highly valuable to Indigenous studies. Its strength is its capacity to reveal the implicit assumptions researchers make about their own case studies. The perils of comparison are also important to recognise; familiarity with one case study invariably leads to bias and imperfect interpretations of the less familiar cases. But these shortcomings, once acknowledged, should not detract from the tremendous potential comparison offers, particularly to scholars in Indigenous studies. The relationships between Indigenous peoples and their respective governments, such as those in New Zealand and Canada, share a fundamental similarity that makes the differences between them all the more striking and revealing.

Comparison is a valuable research method for scholars in Indigenous studies. In isolation, New Zealand's preoccupation with guaranteed representation for Māori has unnecessarily limited the scope of debate to exclude the possibility of self-government for post-settlement Māori. Canada's focus on self-government, on the other hand, overshadows issues of representation in Parliament at the expense of real debate about the importance of Indigenous influences within government. Viewing these two cases comparatively helps us to understand that these contemporary political debates are the result of historical colonial government policies that placed Māori inside, and First Nations outside, the state. It may also help each to be inspired by the other's successes and forewarned by the other's misfortunes.

CHAPTER NINE

Urban Indigenous Governance Practices

Shalene Jobin Vandervelde

In Canada, urban Indigenous[1] populations are increasing and they face social, economic and political disadvantages while battling to create unique spaces for Aboriginal community and governance within wider Canadian society. Edmonton, Alberta, currently has the second highest municipal Aboriginal population in Canada, at 52,105 residents, growing over 10 per cent in the last five years alone.[2] With such a large Aboriginal population, Indigenous governance is fast becoming a central issue in the region.

The Institute of Governance (IOG) explains governance as 'a process whereby societies or organisations make their important decisions, determine whom they involve in the process and how they render account'.[3] David Newhouse reveals that there has been little research examining the structures and processes around urban Aboriginal communities, particularly around the institutions of urban Aboriginal life.[4] In a survey of Aboriginal organisations conducted in Edmonton, Toronto and Winnipeg, the majority (79 per cent) of respondents reported following an Aboriginal philosophy in their organisation, although the features 'tended to be vague, fragmentary and imprecise'.[5] The authors of that study concluded that 'this aspect of urban Aboriginal organizations remains unclear'.[6] In light of this scholarship gap, the following research was undertaken to better understand the unique attributes of urban Aboriginal organisations. In 2005, under the guidance of an advisory committee, and guided by participatory-action research (PAR) methodology, insights of the board, staff, and members of Bent Arrow Traditional Healing Society were gathered through focus groups and two questionnaires, which were given to all fifteen programme participants operating within the organisation. These were supplemented with key interviews. This chapter synthesises this research, exploring the guiding philosophy behind the organisational governance of the Bent Arrow Traditional Healing Society and how this non-profit agency is part of the dynamic development of Aboriginal community governance in Edmonton.

Edmonton

The history of Edmonton is rich and deeply rooted in Indigenous culture. The region is better known to some as *amiskwaciwâskahikan*,[7] which means 'Beaver Mountain House'[8] in *nehiyawewin* (the Cree language). Archaeologists have speculated that Indigenous peoples have inhabited the Edmonton area for up to 12,000 years, in seasonal camps and permanent villages.[9] In addition, Indigenous peoples have long known *amiskwâciwaskahikan* as a place for hunting, trading, sundance ceremonies, feasts and other cultural events. The area of the city now called Rossdale Flats was once referred to as *pêhonan*, which in Cree means 'the waiting place' or 'the gathering place'. This area was considered sacred land and functioned as a meeting place for many nations including the Beaver, Nakoda, Cree, Blackfoot and by the 1700s, the Métis.[10]

Edmonton is still a gathering place for many Aboriginal peoples. The Aboriginal population in Edmonton self-identifies as 52 per cent Métis, 44 per cent North American Indian, with the remainder being Inuit or multi-ethnic.[11] The First Nations population includes Cree (63 per cent), Stoney-Dakota (10 per cent), Ojibwa (9.7 per cent), Chippewya (3.5 per cent), Slavey (1.7 per cent) and other First Nations (12.1 per cent).[12] First Nation languages commonly heard in Edmonton include Cree, Stoney, Chipewyan, Saulteaux, Dene, Beaver, Blackfoot and Sarcee,[13] with Cree being the most common.[14] There are over sixty-two Aboriginal organisations in Edmonton serving this population, including community associations, representative groups, social and health services, women's groups and various educational, cultural, business, employment and housing organisations.[15] Urban Indigenous peoples are becoming increasingly vocal about the need for these organisations to provide culturally relevant services, and for a mechanism by which these groups can collaborate in meaningful ways.

Urban communal governance

In analysing perspectives from dialogue circles using a qualitative approach, Robert Groves discovered that Aboriginal people in Edmonton find the highest practicality and desirability with urban communal governance,[16] 'the major features of which are the involvement of all urban Aboriginal residents, without regard to status, treaty, specific nationality or other criteria, in the formation of a common authority for governance over whatever institutions or jurisdictions may be capable of being negotiated, delegated or successfully asserted as a matter of right.'[17] The Royal Commission on Aboriginal Peoples has a virtually identical idea of community governance, which they term a 'Community of Interest' model, and believes this mode of Aboriginal government could potentially serve a broad range of government functions and services, such as education.[18] In the Community of Interest model, a key feature is voluntary membership. The other defining characteristic is that ownership and access to a land base is not a mandatory factor.[19]

Edmonton is at the forefront of the innovative urban Aboriginal governance initiatives occurring across Canada. Over the last few years, Aboriginal organisations, community groups, representative organisations and governments have been developing a process and structure by which to collaborate and develop solutions on topics and issues of interest to Aboriginals living in the Edmonton area. This collaborative mechanism, which fits both Groves' urban communal governance approach as well as the Royal Commission on Aboriginal Peoples' Community of Interest model, is called Wicihitowin: Circle of Shared Responsibility and Stewardship. Fluid and responsive to the needs of the community, it formed in order to unite organisations such as the Bent Arrow Traditional Healing Society into a network of like-minded peoples focused on city-wide strategies to meet the needs of urban Aboriginal peoples.

Urban Indigenous space

One of the distinguishing factors for Aboriginal peoples living in the city is that they do not have access to their own land base.[20] Having a recognised and designated connection to a specific place is important, as it allows Aboriginal peoples the space to practise traditions and ceremonies A crucial step, then, in creating Indigenous community space involves increasing access to spaces to practise ceremonies and cultural traditions in an urban environment. Aboriginal peoples have recently begun to assert that all land in Canada is traditional to Indigenous peoples.[21] Even if you live in Edmonton, a metropolitan city of 1,024,825,[22] you are still walking and living in traditional Indigenous territory. Through lobbying and partnership development, significant progress has been made in allowing Aboriginal people in Edmonton access to land for ceremonies and other cultural events and practices. The Indigenous Cultural and Ceremonial Land Area Project (ICCLA) is an Aboriginal-led partnership between the Indigenous Elders Cultural Resource Circle Society (IECRCS) and the City of Edmonton. The ICCLA project provides land within the City of Edmonton for traditional ceremonies, activities and resources.[23] Aboriginal Elders[24] also use this space to offer mentoring and teaching opportunities to Aboriginal and non-Aboriginal people and organisations.

The Bent Arrow Traditional Healing Society has likewise seen the need to access land for the use of ceremonies and cultural teachings. Bent Arrow bought a piece of land west of the City of Edmonton, which they use for cultural camps, various programmes and regular ceremonies. Bent Arrow also provides access to the land to their staff and to community members of both Aboriginal and non-Aboriginal backgrounds. The development of Aboriginal organisations such as Bent Arrow is vital to Indigenous peoples without their own land base, as they provide an atmosphere where Aboriginal identity can be encouraged and expressed in a supportive environment.

Bent Arrow Traditional Healing Society

The concept of governance is relevant to both community-based models such as the newly developed Wicihitowin: Circle of Shared Responsibility and Stewardship, described previously, as well as the organisational governance of individual groups such as Bent Arrow.[25] In both cases, urban Aboriginal governance is grounded in traditional[26] practice, which is crucial for ensuring cultural continuity in a metropolitan place.

The Bent Arrow Traditional Healing Society is a non-profit, urban-based Indigenous organisation 'committed to building on the strengths of Aboriginal children, youth and their families to enable them to develop spiritually, emotionally, physically and mentally so they can walk proudly in both the Aboriginal and non-Aboriginal communities'.[27] The Society began in 1993, when co-founders Brad and Shauna Seneca[28] recognised a need in Edmonton for culturally relevant social services. Initially they received funding from a federal programme called Pathways to provide a programme to youth between the ages of fifteen and twenty-four who wanted to return to school, enter training or find work. This programme was successful and with the encouragement of the community and Aboriginal Elders, Bent Arrow was then established. The organisation takes its name from an Indigenous story. Brad Seneca explains,

> When we were trying to find a name for a youth program that was working with youth from many broken homes and families I remembered the story my grandfather told me of the hunter and the warrior. These youth who had ventured off their path or journey in life were not lost or broken, but like the warrior if he did not take time in preparation of his arrows he would miss his target and his family would suffer because of his hurriedness. I saw these

youth not as broken but like the arrow that was slightly bent. The warrior could fix the problem of his arrow by making a new one. We could help the youth with their problems so they could learn to walk a straighter path and hit their target also. They were not broken just a little bent. This is the reason for the name Bent Arrow Traditional Healing Society.[29]

Since its establishment, Bent Arrow has grown to over ninety employees. It currently serves more than 3,000 children, youth, adults and families annually and offers support and services in the areas of education, health, housing and employment. It administers over fifteen different programmes that focus on the physical, emotional, intellectual and spiritual needs of the community. These programmes range from services such as the Rites of Passage school (combining academic work, spirituality, culture and life skills), to Circle of Hope (providing holistic support for survivors of the residential school system and their families). One of the unique aspects of Bent Arrow is how all involved with the Society commit to living healthy lifestyles. For example, since there are people in the community with addictions, everyone involved in the organisation has decided to commit to a sober lifestyle to be authentic in their roles as helpers: 'Brad and Shauna walk their talk. I've now been here since 2000 and I've seen consistency through this time. Bent Arrow abides by values and traditions. It's a family here. Bent Arrow is very good at nurturing'.[30] Throughout the interviews, a common theme was how Bent Arrow is a community: Richard Woodman explained that when he is at Bent Arrow, his connections with people make him feel like he is back on the reserve, 'The thing that is different about Bent Arrow is that there is a community here ... a family. We are all here to do our part'.[31]

Underlying Bent Arrow and many other Aboriginal organisations is the belief that community-based Aboriginal organisations provide culturally appropriate services[32] and create space for cultural continuity and community building in urban spaces.[33] The programmes that Bent Arrow operates have been created and developed specifically for Indigenous people. They nurture the spiritual, emotional, physical and mental aspects of people's lives, their family and their community, based on the teachings of the Medicine Wheel. People who are involved with Bent Arrow become part of the Bent Arrow family and community: 'Miracles happen here every day. Every day, I am honoured by someone who shares with me what they've accomplished ... what they've achieved. That's the gift of this place'.[34]

Community-based research

Indigenous community-based research can be constructed as a decolonising tool to empower local communities.[35] This type of methodology helps the community itself make its own definitions. The community also takes a leadership role in all phases of the research process. Linda Tuhiwai Smith explains that such community-action research 'not only enable[s] communities but also enable[s] indigenous researchers to work as researchers within their own communities'.[36] Participatory-action research (PAR) was the overarching methodology in this study, where Bent Arrow was actively involved throughout the project as a partner. PAR has been defined as '… inquiry by ordinary people acting as researchers to explore questions in their daily lives, to recognize their own resources and to produce knowledge and take action to overcome inequities, often in solidarity with external supporters'.[37] With PAR, the process can be as important as the results. The analysis phase is something different from other methodologies, in that it incorporates 'learning to perceive social, political and economic contradictions and to take action against the oppressive elements of reality'.[38] A central premise of this research was to support the Bent Arrow community in knowing that their knowledge is valuable and to use academia as a vehicle to assist in external recognition of this wisdom.

As the organisation has grown rapidly from two employees to over ninety, Bent Arrow also saw the need to describe the philosophy and governance model of their organisation in written form. As well, the founders were interested in knowing whether their guiding philosophy continued to be reflected in all of their programmes. The information in this chapter is thus focused on the guiding principles and values that inform Bent Arrow's governance processes and is not intended as an in-depth analysis of the programmes. Rather, the scope of this research project is about understanding and communicating the high-level vision and philosophy that permeates the work of the society.

The Medicine Wheel

To understand the values and beliefs that guide Bent Arrow one must appreciate the teachings of the Medicine Wheel. Although each Indigenous nation has its own language and cultural practices, some ceremonies, symbols and beliefs are held in common by many different Indigenous nations. One teaching common to many Aboriginals in Canada is that of the Medicine Wheel or four-directions teachings. A Cree Elder explains how our language is interconnected to the wisdom of the Medicine Wheel:

> We are called *iyiniwak*. That is the foundation of who we are, our identity. We are supposed to heal ourselves and others and *iyiniwaskamkaw*, that is, our relationship to our land, our connection here. *nehiyau* [a First Nation person] is the four directions, *newoyak*. There are four parts and those are our four directions and that is in our language. Additionally, '*newoyak ehoci pikisweyan*' [is] I speak from the four directions, so you are always honouring your four directions. That is the philosophy of it. The four directions are [that] we have to be caring, sharing, we have to be honest and we have to pray daily for our strength. Continued strength of our people and our land – our very existence.[39]

First Nation languages tell the story of the sacred laws, how we are to live and our purpose as a people. The way we speak comes from the teachings of the four directions. To honour these teachings is essentially to have an awareness and connection with the Creator and all of creation. The Medicine Wheel is used for various purposes including ceremonial, astrological and symbolic teachings. One of the uses of the Medicine Wheel is to assist in understanding Indigenous philosophy and beliefs:

> This is an ancient symbol used by almost all the Native people of North and South America. There are many different ways that this basic concept is expressed: the four grandfathers, the four winds, the four cardinal directions and many other relationships that can be expressed in sets of four. Just like a mirror can be used to see things not normally visible (e.g. behind us or around a corner), the medicine wheel can be used to help us see or understand things we can't quite see or understand because they are ideas and not physical objects.[40]

The teachings of the Medicine Wheel are completely holistic; you cannot see the elements as separate parts but must seek to understand the relationship between all parts.[41] Bent Arrow helpers illuminate the interconnection between the natural laws expressed through their work: 'We approach every person we meet with love/kindness which opens the door to honesty, through that comes the ability to share, allowing us to seek determination, building on strengths which results in maintaining a safe environment and success for both participants and the program'.[42] The four-directions teachings found in the Medicine Wheel and the principles of *miyo wicehtowin* (good relationship) provide the philosophy that guides Bent Arrow.

miyo wicehtowin

At Bent Arrow there is awareness of the need for balance within the self as well as in relation to others. Figure 1 shows how the relationships practised by Bent Arrow are represented in the Medicine Wheel teachings and the key elements of *miyo wicehtowin*: *îyinewiwin* (being human), *ayamihewâtsowin* (spirituality), *kitimâkeyimowin* (feeling passionate about a subject) and *cikâstepekisin* (her/his reflection can be seen in the water). Co-Founder Shauna Seneca developed this model to convey some of the teachings that informs Bent Arrow's practice.

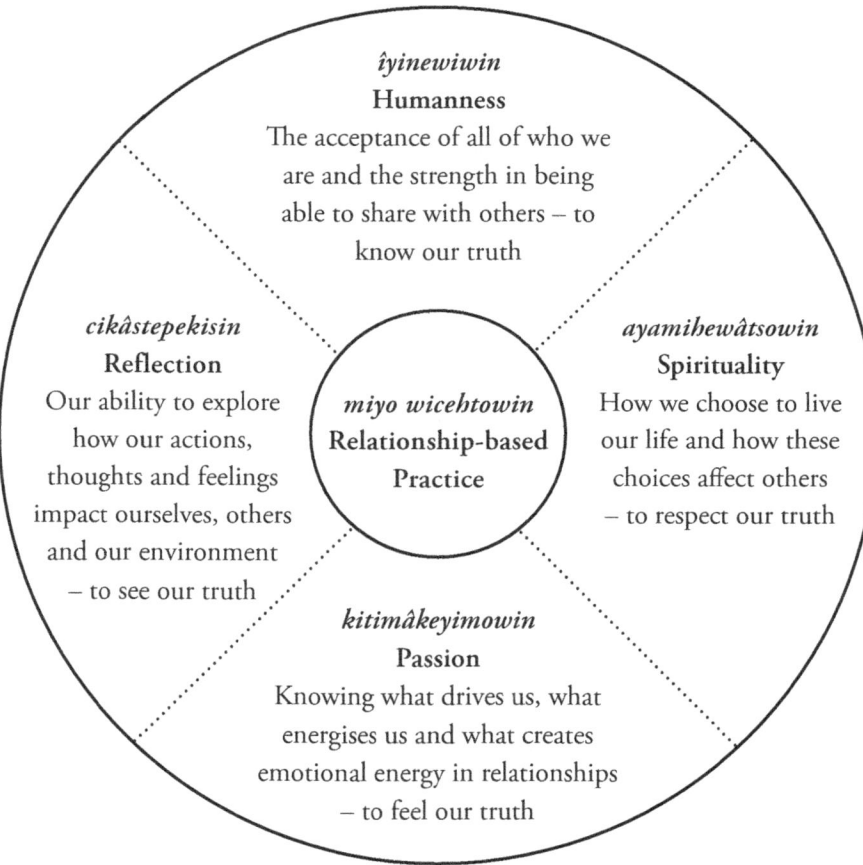

Figure 1. *Relationship-based Practice.*[43]

Bent Arrow advocates the understanding of the need to reflect on one's own values and how these beliefs affect others: 'Values are the way human beings pattern and use their energy. If there is not a balance between our values concerning ourselves and our values concerning others, we cannot continue to develop our true potential as human beings. Indeed, if there is an imbalance, individuals and whole communities suffer and even die'.⁴⁴ This understanding and the founders' opinions that this type of reflective practice is severely lacking in many Western-based support services motivated the founders of Bent Arrow to look at the teachings of the Medicine Wheel and to articulate the values and beliefs of Bent Arrow through Relationship-based Practice. *Miyo wicehtowin,* or Relationship-based Practice, is a philosophy allowing helpers to achieve balance between their own values as well as their values concerning others. *Miyo wicehtowin* can also refer to having a partnership, being in unity or living in harmony with each other. The root of *wicehtowin* is *wiceht*, which means to come along side or to support. At Bent Arrow the focus on the four practices of humanness, spirituality, passion and reflection nurtures balance, creating an environment where the helpers can be in *miyo wicehtowin* with each other as well as to come alongside and support others.

îyinewiwin

> *Humanness: The acceptance of all of who we are and the strength in being able to share with others – to know our truth.*

When examining Western social service practices, the first observation Shauna Seneca had was how inhuman the system can be.⁴⁵ She explained that 'there seems to be this misconception in mainstream practice that to somehow be professional in your work means that you cannot be human, that you cannot connect with your families on a human level'.⁴⁶ People who received help from Bent Arrow stated that they experienced something different because they felt equality and were not being judged; no one put them down. In the interviews, research participants focused on the word 'humanness, they were treating me as a human being'. One of the teachings that the founders of Bent Arrow often hear from Aboriginal Elders is that the one thing that connects everyone is that we are all human beings. At one level we are the same. There are many other things that are different but one thing keeps us connected no matter who we are and that is our humanness. This understanding made the helpers realise that in this profession sometimes you must deliberately find ways for people to be human, to naturally share with each other and build the connections so important in relationships. At Bent Arrow they use the term 'helpers' to describe the role of staff in their relationships to families. Shauna Seneca explains the importance of humanness at Bent Arrow:

> One of the things we do at Bent Arrow is that we encourage people to be able to connect from their humanness. When people come we suggest they sit at the kitchen table and simply talk to people, to know who's here – to have that opportunity to engage. In some cases we really had to teach people how to be human in their ability to be helpers. This is because the institutions have taken the humanness out of them; the institutions' focus is always on doing it right, doing it better, being smarter, knowing all the answers. Of course that doesn't fix people; nobody does that, that's the Creator's job.[47]

At Bent Arrow, humanity leads to humbleness, humility and being grateful. It leads people to a place of being able to talk about their values and their beliefs, which is often how they get to know each other and why they trust each other.

Orenda House Family Housing Project provides transitional housing for young Aboriginal homeless families, with the necessary support services to assist in moving to independence. Cheryl Bridges is a helper who lives at Orenda House. She explains that everyone at Orenda was homeless and that they share that as families: 'That is humbling … they say that you have to be kind to be humble'.[48] The importance of trust and sharing in strengthening the community has been well articulated by the Healthy Families helpers. Healthy Families is Bent Arrow's long-term, intensive, voluntary home-visitation programme, which provides services to pregnant women and first-time parenting families. The helpers in this programme explain the importance of sharing and being human in creating an environment that fosters positive change:

> The mothers that we work with have never had an honest relationship with anyone, some not even with their own mothers. This is why they don't trust and they don't share. Some of these moms also carry shame. In our approach with families and in using the natural laws, the moms begin to talk with us and we begin to share and a trusting relationship begins to form. The moms realize there are people out there that can help them heal. The women get strength from who they are and then they become more gentler and kinder to themselves and others. That effects who you are, but in using and living the natural laws these families make a full circle within the natural laws. The natural laws all closely tie into each other.[49]

This quotation is an example of how the Medicine Wheel teachings are practised. By focusing on humanness, the helpers and the families try to develop *miyo wicehtowin* to support their healing journey.

The other aspect of *iyinewiwin* is knowing what your personal truth is. In social work, Shauna Seneca experienced that it is common to judge a circumstance based on personal experiences or a person's own truth.[50] At Bent Arrow the helpers say that they need to know their own truth and how this impacts others. This approach is about being in tune with yourself physically, emotionally, mentally and spiritually and being able to be truthful without fear of judgement – this is about being *human*. Shauna Seneca explains:

> I get better as a helper when I'm more conscious of what the truth is from my perspective. I think sometimes the Creator works through us and it's our ability to take those risks and to be open and honest about that. Sometimes the truth isn't what people want to hear. How do we think about that from our own perspective in our role as a helper? Why can someone tell you a story and you figure it out differently; you see a different truth in it, you see a different insight. Truth isn't about judgement, it just is.[51]

Being reflective and understanding personal truth and how that truth affects relationships is an important part of the philosophy of Bent Arrow. Sacred Circle provides support and aid to families involved with the child welfare system. As a strengths-based programme, Sacred Circle workers develop skills in recognising the positive qualities within a family while also showing humanness and honesty:

> It is our belief that as we approach our families with a non-judgmental attitude we will be able to have them share their experiences and they will accept our support. We may also have the opportunity to share our own journey of growth and change. Our support and experiences of sharing is to give encouragement and insights into self-empowerment.[52]

The helpers in this programme take a risk in revealing their own personal stories to community members. Through this honesty, families not only see examples of Aboriginal role models but also feel more comfortable sharing their own struggles.

ayamihewâtsowin

> *Spirituality: How we choose to live our life and how these choices affect others – to respect our truth.*

In the Medicine Wheel, the East refers to the spiritual sphere. At Bent Arrow helpers see the importance of spirituality in healing. This is not solely about a certain cultural or spiritual practice but involves incorporating those teachings and values in daily interactions and the way you exist in the world. During the interviews staff explained how important it is to include spirituality for themselves and to find ways to encourage that in other people. Looking at how people are living their lives, what their values and beliefs are, being able to talk, explore and be honest about this, is all part of their job as helpers. Shauna Seneca explains that at Bent Arrow, 'our experience has often been that when we go through a spiritual moment with someone, whether that's in ceremony or when we're just that open and vulnerable to each other, that often binds us in a way that all the therapy and work would never do'.[53]

Spirituality is embraced at Bent Arrow in a very holistic and practical way. Every morning people from Bent Arrow come together to smudge and pray. During interviews, people explained how this practice fosters *miyo wicehtowin*, acknowledges the Creator and their spiritual selves and is done in a way to respect their own truth and the truth of others. With these teachings there is a focus on the need to be respectful of other practices and beliefs, while also having others reciprocate this respect. At Bent Arrow not everyone smudges but people still feel comfortable to come and pray in their own way. The view is that they do not all have to share the same beliefs or do things in the same way but they can value each other's beliefs and learn from each other – this is a way of developing humanness as well as connecting on a deeper level.

kitimâkeyimowin

> *Passion: Knowing what drives us, what energises us and what creates emotional energy in relationships – to feel our truth.*

The South is where we contemplate the importance of passion. In the South, the Medicine Wheel refers to the emotional aspect of self; this is a place of innocence – the pureness of energy that creates passion. The teachers in the book *The Sacred Tree* explain that 'the focused concentration learned in the East ... becomes in the South, a passionate involvement with the world. In the South, the traveller learns the idealism that makes all causes possible'.⁵⁴ In the work that Bent Arrow does, it is essential that the helpers have something that drives and energises them. If you are going to be healthy you have to feel good about what you are doing; passion is the energy driver in the work that they do. In the Circle of Hope programme, the helpers draw upon the strength of this teaching. Through sharing circles with Elders and other programmes, residential school survivors are supported in a safe environment. The Circle of Hope programme helpers articulate the importance of having passion in caring for people:

> In order to properly work with our people, we as outreach workers must be able to love the work and the families that we provide the service to. In showing our love the people will know and feel that our intentions to assist them are truly from the heart. Our kindness and understanding towards our people paves the way to a better and more open relationship with the people we serve.⁵⁵

Through Bent Arrow's passion for people, the community responds by allowing the helpers into their lives to see their pain, hear their stories and share in the road to healing. Passionate people are often good listeners because they are emotionally engaged in the conversation. At Bent Arrow, when a person shares a story and the listener is affected, it is all right to show that they are emotionally impacted, therefore affirming that person and building *miyo wicehtowin*.

Bent Arrow helpers encourage people to understand themselves, what motivates them and what their passions are. In Bent Arrow's training and development with staff, time is spent exploring those elements that get their blood moving and see how they can take that passion and apply it in other areas. There is the understanding that you will not be passionate in everything you do, but you are encouraged to nurture the passion that you do have. In relationships with the community, Bent Arrow helpers try to see the passions that the family has, what gets them going, makes them feel good and motivates them to take that next risk. This teaching is really about giving people permission to be passionate and then helping them give this gift to others. Cheryl Bridges from the Orenda House programme explains that 'healing needs to be inspired, inspired by something they realize they want, maybe a quality they see in someone else'.⁵⁶ Another principle in the direction of the South is that when you are passionately engaged in a relationship you need to acknowledge how you are feeling, honour where you are at and be able to feel your truth. It is said that the most difficult and valuable gift of the South of the Medicine Wheel is 'the capacity to express feelings openly and freely in ways that do not hurt other beings'.[57] When working with families in *miyo wicehtowin* it is natural that a helper might at times feel disappointed. This is healthy and the important part is to be able to acknowledge this feeling and be able to move past it without having it interfere in the work.

cikâstepekisin

> *Reflection: Our ability to explore how our actions, thoughts and feelings impact on ourselves, others and our environment – to see our truth.*

The Medicine Wheel teaches that the West is the place of introspection, where we have the ability to truly know ourselves. It is said that the greatest lesson from the West is to be able to accept ourselves as we really are. One of the things Bent Arrow noticed was that people began to blame others in the work they were doing without consideration of their own role in the relationship. People were not able to reflect, they could only look at feedback as judgement. Shauna Seneca explains that they realised that in their work they 'needed to teach people how to be reflective. Reflective practice is like a mirror in being able to look at something and being able to see what is reflected back to us based on our own values and beliefs'.[58] There was the realisation that to be reflective in the work with families they first had to be reflective with themselves. According to *The Sacred Tree*, 'no two people will see exactly the same things when they look into the mirror of the medicine wheel. Yet everyone who looks deeply will see the tree of their unique lives with its roots buried deep in the soil of universal truths'.[59]

To begin to teach this practice, Bent Arrow developed an exercise where participants would take a mirror and stare at themselves for three minutes without talking. At the end of that time the facilitator would ask them to write down what they saw when they looked in the mirror – which could be physical attributes, resemblances to family or other observances. The second element asked participants to picture someone looking over their shoulder into their mirror – what would the participant hope was observed? The third element, which delves even deeper, is to have them write down what they hope no one ever sees in the mirror. The intention is to start to be reflective about yourself without judgement. It is not right or wrong, it just is. Reflection is reflection. This exercise has been very powerful in allowing people to be introspective about themselves and the work they do and how that impacts the world around them and their relationships. This type of training has enabled the helpers in the Circle of Hope programme to support residential school survivors and their families:

> In the *Circle of Hope* program we are here to provide a safe environment to help the families learn how to live a healthy lifestyle. Our participants are the direct and indirect results of the residential school era; through the sharing circles and teaching the people acquire the determination and strength to enhance their lives. The Elders and the residential school survivors share their experiences and bring forth how they coped and survived the effects of residential schools.[60]

The helpers try to live out the behaviour they are asking from the community. It seems from the interviews that this personal reflexive process demonstrates authenticity and creates an environment where survivors are able to be reflective about their personal journeys. The teachings of the Wheel are about becoming a balanced human being who is grounded in his or her own self and, therefore, able to be in a healthy *miyo wicehtowin* with others. The intention of Bent Arrow is to increasingly foster this growth in all of the members.

Mary initially became part of Bent Arrow as a participant in the Four Arrows Adult Employment programme. After this programme she eventually came to work at Bent Arrow, starting as a part-time dishwasher in the kitchen. From this position, Mary was nurtured into a clerical role. Mary noticed that people were passionate about their work and helping others: 'my supervisor is really good to work with and she is supportive. The people I work with are tremendous, soft-spoken and easy to get along with'.[61] Mary was given the opportunity to reflect on her skills and abilities and then encouraged to apply them at Bent Arrow. Mary noticed a big difference in that people were treated as human beings and respected: 'Everyone's equal here, they don't judge people here. Things are also confidential, they are professional. They don't turn people away here, no one is turned away. Everyone does their job. No one is discriminated against here'.[62] By practising the principle of humanness, the community at Bent Arrow is able to receive support and services in a safe, caring environment. The practise of humanness, spirituality, passion and reflection create an environment of *miyo wicehtowin*, where community strengthening is achieved:

> Everyone knows everyone here. People are friendly and introduce themselves. The more you find out [about Bent Arrow] the easier it is. Everyone is close. We'll joke around with each other, people say good-morning. There isn't a feeling of tension here. When I come here even if I had a hard day the night before, I get here and it's a big relief – it is peaceful here.[63]

Bent Arrow staff and community members believe that this relationship-based practice makes their organisation unique:

> Although this agency has over ninety staff in different programs we are still all connected. This is different then the non-Native agency I worked for where everything was separate. Here it is all about families. Bent Arrow is a family and very welcoming. Here you get ten hellos when walking through the building. The atmosphere is amazing, you feel like family here.[64]

Bent Arrow has been able to create a community of Aboriginal people living in an urban area where people feel safe to embrace their cultures and traditional practices while also focusing on building healthy people and families. Culturally appropriate community-based organisations like this one are key building blocks in creating self-determination in urban areas.

oyakihcikewin
The act of analysing

Bent Arrow provides an example of one way in which Aboriginals are providing services and claiming space in urban environments. Commonalities across Aboriginal cultures and traditions are drawn on for the purpose of creating governance structures and community in cities. For Bent Arrow, the Medicine Wheel teachings and the development of the Relationship-based Practice model have functioned to provide a unifying set of values and principles that enable many different Indigenous cultures to come together and develop a community space. This analysis is supported by research done by David Newhouse, Evelyn Peters and others, which explains that Aboriginal peoples are 'reformulating western institutions and practices'[65] in unique ways to support Aboriginal peoples and cultures.[66]

There are challenges that Bent Arrow and other Aboriginal organisations face in this process. Many Aboriginal organisations began through the vision of a small group of committed people. For Bent Arrow, this included the two founders with the support of Aboriginal Elders in the community. With rapid growth in a short period of time, one concern voiced by the founders was how to ensure the true intent and spirit of the organisation was kept intact and how to ensure the organisation would continue for more than one generation. To address these issues,

Bent Arrow has focused on developing leadership throughout the organisation and empowering its staff to take an active role in communicating and sharing its values.[67] Another strategy the founders have engaged in is to begin documenting their philosophy to share with new staff and others in the community.

To achieve a level of Aboriginal self-determination in an urban area requires a focus not only on organisational governance but collective actions towards community governance:

> The priorities of the vast majority of urban Aboriginal organizations surveyed for this study seemed to be focused inward on the operations and development of their organizations and on the improvement of services to their clients, rather than on the achievement of collective forms of self-government. They receive resources and are governed according to their service functions rather than in keeping with a broader self-government role.[68]

This quotation identifies two key issues facing urban Aboriginal organisations. The first is the constraints surrounding financing a non-profit agency and the second is the need for individual organisations to become part of a collective movement working on the development of self-government initiatives. Many community-based organisations currently receive project-specific funding that can revolve around municipal, provincial and federal priorities that do not necessarily match the needs that the grassroots organisations see in their community.[69] The current fiscal situation can result in Aboriginal organisations competing against each other for limited project dollars. This system can split a larger Aboriginal collective, creating division and distrust among Aboriginal organisations. An alternative approach is being called for that would give Aboriginal peoples authority to control the allocation of resources based on community needs that they identify.[70] Facilitating this type of fundamental change would require mobilisation of Aboriginal peoples, communities and organisations and an agreement to unite in working cooperatively on common goals. Often this requires a process of relationship-building where a common set of guiding principles can be established. Community-based organisations would need to focus not only insularly on their own organisational priorities, community needs and financial and human resources but also towards a larger collective project, unifying many peoples and organisations. The Wicihitowin: Circle of Shared Responsibility and Stewardship is one such collective mobilisation initiative. The success of this project and others like it will require new ways of moving beyond the current funding constraints, while creating a common vision and strategy based on an agreed-upon set of collective principles.

It is clear that with increasing numbers of Aboriginal peoples in urban environments, innovative organisations and communities are being developed to meet the unique needs of this population. From Aboriginal-specific community-based organisations founded on traditional teachings and values, to new urban communal governance structures that connect numerous organisations, nations and peoples, Aboriginal peoples are asserting their rights to remain Indigenous in urban spaces. Although Indigenous peoples in Edmonton are diverse and come from different nations and areas, they often have a desire to come together to share their commonalities and their struggle for recognition, and to claim a rightful place in the land that their ancestors called their own.

CHAPTER TEN

The Nationalist Gaze of an Aboriginal Artist

Nathalie Kermoal

Average Canadians all too frequently perceive Aboriginal art as a collection of utilitarian objects or artefacts exposed in museums.[1] People have expressed annoyance and disappointment when viewing the work of contemporary Aboriginal artists, qualifying the art work as 'not real Aboriginal Art', 'as though a real Aboriginal would only ever paint traditional works – though it is unlikely that they would insist white artists should all still paint like Michelangelo or, indeed, the cave painters of Lascaux'.[2] Authenticity, or more specifically its myth (that which is free of European influence), has therefore been at the centre of the struggle of contemporary Aboriginal artists. If the art is not deemed 'Indian' enough, it is criticised and rejected by the dominant society. The ideological gap that exists between the artist and his or her critics exacerbates misunderstandings and rejection. For instance, famous Ojibwa painter Daphne Odjig, 'in those early years of establishing Native art in Canada, faced such a rejection as a Native/female artist when art critic Jay Scott from the *Globe and Mail* wrote that she was puréeing everything from Picasso to Walt Disney into a blandly decorative pictorial pulp'.[3]

Nonetheless, in the last twenty years, contemporary Aboriginal art has seen considerable expansion and has played a central role in challenging stereotypical images of Aboriginal people. It has had a major influence in the reconsideration 'of the socio-political forces affecting the lives of First Nations peoples'.[4] Many contemporary Aboriginal artists share a common desire to question history, to revisit the past, to reveal to the world what has been kept invisible or what has been cut out of the history books.[5] Notions of objectivity, of absolute truth, so important to conventional historians,[6] have given way to the complexities of subjectivities, to multiple ways of knowing the world. In order to know and to understand Aboriginal realities, it is important to look into the diversity of texts no matter what their form. Aboriginal writers and artists have actively tried to affirm their vision of the world: they never ceased to resist and to reformulate the perceptions that others have had of them.

According to feminist writer bell hooks, challenging colonial representations allows a critique of the representation of the 'Other' to emerge:

> Looking at the work [of an artist] from a Eurocentric perspective, one sees and values only those aspects that mimic familiar white Western artistic traditions. Looking at the work from a more inclusive standpoint, we are able to see the dynamism springing from the convergence, contact and conflict of varied traditions.[7]

It is these points of 'convergence, contact and conflict of varied traditions' that are of interest to me. As historian Olive Dickason notes: 'Canada's first nations, far from being interesting relics of the past, are a vital part of Canada's persona, both present and future'.[8] One can therefore ask: How is this vitality expressed when one is an Aboriginal female artist?

In this chapter, I argue that women's contemporary Aboriginal art is part of a movement to rewrite history, born from the desire to correct misrepresentation and stereotypes and the necessity to re-establish an aboriginal female knowledge. The sculpture's aesthetic value is of no concern to me here: my intention is to position this art textually for what it tells us about the past, the present and the future, as well as for what it tells us about identity and representation. I am interested in the social voice or discourse, speaking through the image to highlight the displaced and dormant voices. I seek to highlight the expression of the female voice, one that has been muffled first by the colonial history of Canada and then by the androcentric discourses of political leaders. For this purpose, a work by the Mi'kmaq artist Teresa Marshall, *Elitekey*, is examined.[9] I have used interviews given by the artist during the exhibition *Land, Spirit, Power*, to illustrate my analysis.

The rewriting of history

> *Along with all other peoples variously designated as backward, degenerate, uncivilised and retarded, the Orientals were viewed in a framework constructed out of biological determinism and moral-political admonishment. The Oriental was linked thus to elements in Western society (delinquents, the insane, women, the poor) having in common an identity best described as lamentably alien.*[10]

What Edward Said describes about the 'Orientals' is applicable to the colonial discourse that has developed in North America. The standard view of Aboriginal people in Canadian history has been as backward and uncivilised. Their laws, customs or cultures have been scrutinised and categorised by successive colonial powers. Though colonialists sometimes portrayed the Aboriginal people in a positive light (positioning them as part of the 'exotic'), more often this portrayal has been negative. Close scrutiny also placed Aboriginal people under a 'veil of homogeneity' that was detrimental to understanding them fully. Throughout the nineteenth century, detailed knowledge of the 'Other' was gathered by the State – in Canada, this was particularly true after the Dominion was created in 1867 – in an effort to better control the population. As philosopher Michel Foucault has shown in his writings, such gathering of knowledge was not done simply out of curiosity. It was also to collect concrete, specific, measurable data that could be used by the State to better exercise its power.[11] Whether or not Aboriginal people would be allowed to flourish became a matter of political choice made by and for the State.

Europe and its colonies were therefore perceived as the only motor for progress and the world was seen through the eyes of the colonisers. This concept of European superiority has had a devastating impact on Aboriginal people around the world and been the main justification for territorial dispossession. Since the 1960s, Indigenous scholars, feminists, historians, critical race theorists as well as artists have challenged this historical essentialism. Important questions have been and continue to be raised about who produces knowledge, what constitutes knowledge and how Aboriginal people have been historically represented. As Smith points out, 'Research [is] a significant site of struggle between the interests and ways of knowing the West and the interests and ways of resisting the Other'.[12]

Of course, as Said articulated in his writings, our formulation and representation of the past has an impact on our perceptions and conceptions of the present. It is, therefore, important not only to remember, but also to 're-member' since people have been fragmented or 'dis-membered'.[13] Moreover, it is necessary to question the chronological breakdown of history since 'fragmentation has been the consequence of imperialism'.[14] Promoting ideas such as that North America was 'discovered' has allowed Euro-Canadian meta-narratives of history to hide its conquest. 'When the dominant narrative focuses on the populating of Canada, the depopulation of Canada through diseases and other means is automatically silenced. Also, an emphasis on growth and progress mutes the process of putting people on reserves.'[15]

It is through questioning, exposing and exploiting these exclusions and silencings and by questioning facts that Aboriginal artists are contesting Canadian history's meta-narrative. According to Cornel West, artists play a very important role since they can 'cast their nets widely, flex their muscles broadly and thereby refuse to limit their visions, their analyses and praxis to their particular terrains'.[16]

Their ultimate goal is to redefine and to revise the notions of modernity, of dominance, of marginality and of difference in order to 'look toward the future and vow to make it different and better'.[17]

During the rise of Aboriginal nationalism in the 1960s in Canada, an artist like Alex Janvier would sign his work using only his treaty number. For him, this was an expression of his identity, of his difference and was, in fact, an act of resistance. By telling their stories, Aboriginal artists show the Canadian public that active resistance is everywhere, since '[n]ever was it the case that the imperial encounter pitted an active Western intruder against a supine or inert non-Western native'.[18] The works of artists such as Janvier have challenged the official history of Canada by infusing it with a different perspective: the 'Other'. 'To hold alternative histories is to hold alternative knowledges'[19] and a 'contrapuntal' reading is necessary in order to describe not only what is in the text but also what is invisible. This is what Said terms 'writing back' to the Orientalists. In *Culture and Imperialism*, he states that 'contrapuntal reading must take account of both processes, that of imperialism and that of resistance to it, which can be done by extending our reading of the texts to include what was once forcibly excluded …'.[20] It is this active resistance that I find most interesting. As Emma Larocque suggests, 'to appreciate Native resistance we need to understand their "long walk" as they have experienced it and as they have told it and now as they are recording it'.[21] Aboriginal women have been particularly affected by colonial legislation and other colonial processes. For example, under the Indian Act of 1876, status Indian women lost their status upon marriage to non-status men and with it, the ability to live on their reserves. As an illustration of understanding the 'long walk', I will now turn my attention to Teresa Marshall's *Elitekey*.

Teresa Marshall's *Elitekey*

Teresa Marshall is a Mi'kmaq artist born in Truro, Nova Scotia, in 1962. She studied at Dalhousie University and at the Nova Scotia College of Art and Design in Halifax. Her multimedia sculptures and installations are particularly important since they 'address the ellipses and absences in the dominant Eurocentric version of North American history'.[22] During the exhibition *Land, Spirit, Power* at the National Gallery in Ottawa in 1992, she presented an installation entitled *Elitekey*. Created in 1990, this artwork is made of cement, washed in pale ochre. It has three important features: the Canadian flag, a canoe and a female figure.

The Canadian flag

If one looks closely at the artwork, one can see that the maple leaf has been cut out and the flag is at half-mast. The adoption of the Canadian flag in 1965 was the first of a series of measures by the federal government to give Canada a distinctive symbol to consolidate a sense of national identity. The nationalist movements of the Quebecers and of Aboriginal people have repeatedly threatened a unified vision of Canada. According to philosopher Will Kymlicka, Canada cannot be referred to as a nation-state in the traditional sense of the word because these national minorities have their own agenda of self-determination.[23] Since the 1960s, Aboriginal people have clearly indicated that self-government and Aboriginal rights, rather than allegiance to Canada, is their primary concern.

By flying the flag at half-mast, the artist mourns First Nations in light of the hypocrisy of the national discourse. On the international scene, Canada is represented as a democratic country *par excellence*, concerned for the freedom of oppressed people and for justice in the world. But on national soil, this discourse loses its strength. From the nineteenth century onwards, the federal government put in place an array of policies to assimilate Aboriginal people into the dominant society. Duncan Campbell Scott, head of the Department of Indian Affairs (1913–32), pursued this agenda and made it clear that it was necessary to 'continue until there is not a single Indian left in Canada that has not been absorbed into the body politic and there is no Indian question and no Indian Department'.[24]

The most famous piece of legislation to affect First Nations across Canada has been the Indian Act. Passed in 1876, this law – and its numerous amendments – has had an impact on every economic, social and cultural aspect of Native life. It reaches not only the private sphere but the public sphere as well since, for example, it can determine the content of a will, political rights and freedoms. As underlined by the Report on the Royal Commission on Aboriginal Peoples (1996), these interdictions and penalties would have been deemed illegal and anti-constitutional had they been applied to other Canadians. 'The Indian Act continues to be the only federal statute administering to Indians generally … despite the fact that, as of 1982, the constitution recognizes and affirms the Aboriginal and treaty rights of the Aboriginal people of Canada'.[25] Throughout this history of domination, the Crown broke promises and adopted new legislation in their attempt to more efficiently and 'totally' control Aboriginal people.

In *Elitekey*, it is quite clear that the artist does not place herself under the flag; it is the flag of the coloniser. This flag, without the maple leaf, was created out of rage and despair. According to the artist herself:

I've also borrowed from the 'Canadian symbol,' the flag, which serves as the symbolic umbrella of what it means to be a Canadian. As a First Nations citizen I don't stand under that umbrella. It serves as an icon of oppression, assimilation, injustice and racism that intends to deny First Nations people the inherent right to self-identify and human rights.[26]

At the time of the creation of *Elitekey*, the political context included major constitutional talks that excluded Aboriginal people, and tensions between Aboriginal people and governments (the Municipality of Oka, the provincial government of Quebec and the federal government). From 1983 to 1987, the First Ministers' Conferences were organised to determine and define Aboriginal rights as recognised in the 1982 Constitution of Canada: including that of self-government. Provincial premiers were so unwilling to question the status quo that these conferences failed miserably. In 1987, Prime Minister Brian Mulroney and the provincial premiers signed the Meech Lake Accord, to be ratified within three years by the provincial legislatures. Canada was ready to recognise Quebec as a distinct society, but it refused such recognition for Aboriginal people across the country. Faced with an Accord that had been made behind closed doors, Aboriginal people rallied and decided to kill it: 'Elijah Harper, an Oji-Cree from Red Sucker Lake and the only Native member of the Manitoba legislature, withheld his vote on the grounds that procedural rules were not being followed'.[27] Since the deadline was not met, the Accord died on 23 June 1990. This political impasse reminded Canadians and their representatives that Aboriginal people could not be ignored.

That same summer, the Mohawks in the Montreal area were involved in armed stand-offs with provincial police. This incident, known as the 'Oka crisis', culminated in the intervention of the Canadian armed forces. For the Mohawks of Kanesatake, at the heart of the conflict was a backlog of unfinished business relating to their land claim in the area.[28] The Oka crisis not only illustrated what the consequences can be when negotiations break down between several parties, but also revealed that the rhetoric used by Canadians and the federal government to give Aboriginal people more control over their own affairs was just that: rhetoric. Indeed, the concept of self-determination, sovereignty and control needed to be clarified and negotiated in ways meaningful to the diversity of Aboriginal peoples in Canada.

Constitutional debates and the Oka crisis formed the context within which Teresa Marshall created *Elitekey*. She chose a flag recognised by the general public as Canadian. Yet this same flag also reflects her separateness from Canada. The artist believes that by taking out the maple leaf she gave space to the individual: 'With a leaf-shaped void in the flag, a person can stand in its place as an autonomous being, free to celebrate their individual or collective identity'.[29] As an artist and as a woman, she asserts her individual, local and singular voice through the transcription of her own forms of knowledge.

The canoe

The canoe is Mi'kmaq, as shown by the curved, raised sides. It represents a traditional means of transportation but also conveys the transmission of knowledge. According to the artist, the canoe comes directly from a Mi'kmaq oral account:

> There's a story about a ... hero figure, Glooscap, who, at a time of great need, was to come to the aid of the people in a great stone canoe. The properties of cement, with its limestone/shell base, made it seem like an appropriate material to construct a canoe with. As I was making it, the Oka crisis raged, the time of need seemed to be at hand. While I had originally set out to produce a vessel of hope, the tides changed and so, too, did my intent. The canoe became ... a crypt rather than a cradle.[30]

Glooscap is a central figure in Mi'kmaq cosmogony. In Mi'kmaq creation stories, Glooscap is an extremely important hero who left traces of his story for his people scattered in the Maritimes provinces' landscape. According to Anne-Christine Hornborg, Glooscap did not create the landscape, but transformed it while hunting beaver, going from place to place and eating. He left something behind with each interaction he had with animals, people and other types of creatures.[31] Glooscap created the animals and humans and taught the Mi'kmaq to create tools and weapons. When the time came for Glooscap to leave the earth:

> A great feast was organized and it was attended by all the animals and when it drew to a close Glooscap entered his great canoe and slowly drifted out of sight. When they couldn't see him no longer [sic] they still heard his beautiful singing growing fainter and fainter in the distance, until at last it died away altogether. Then a strange thing happened. The beasts, who up to this time had spoken but one language, could no longer understand each other and in confusion fled away, never again to meet in friendly converse until Glooscap shall return.[32]

In light of this story, one can understand the importance of this canoe made of cement, which represents the misunderstandings that exist between the dominant political discourse and the discourse of Aboriginal people. By incorporating the Oka crisis in her work, the artist is doing what her ancestors have done before her: she is enriching the story with her own reality. Glooscap's story emerges in a hybrid space between the traditional and the new, as an expression of assimilation but also of resistance.[33] Only the return of Glooscap can change the (political) landscape again.

The female figure

Teresa Marshall's Mi'kmaq community named her female figure Eta Joe. The artist herself identifies the figure as her grandmother. She is dressed in traditional Mi'kmaq clothing, recognisable at a glance by the peaked pointed hat. This figure has no face, no hands and looks towards the Canadian flag without its maple leaf; her gaze travels with the canoe. According to Marshall: 'Elitekey in Micmac means I fashion things, these are the things that I make, things that my people, my ancestors make …'.[34] The artist emphasises the importance of Mi'kmaq material culture, matching what she was able to gather through oral history and academic research. As Joan Acland has shown in 'Elitekey: The Artistic Production of Mi'kmaq Women', clothes were a site of colonisation for the Mi'kmaq. The clothed body is important here, not only because it replicates the artist's grandmother's traditional clothing, but also because 'it provides a valuable site for reading race and gender issues within colonizing parameters'.[35]

The shrinking of traditional territories into tiny reserves, the restrictions imposed by the state on hunting and fishing, the forced farming as well as the ravages of diseases (particularly tuberculosis), all greatly reduced the economic position of the Mi'kmaq during the nineteenth century. Baskets and fibre art created by women became the only means of survival for communities.[36] Their clothing was in demand by non-Natives and thus its production became a valuable source of income. According to Acland, 'Fibre arts produced by the women were world-renowned and could be found in the Smithsonian and Musée de l'Homme in Paris. They consist of intricately woven birch bark objects adorned with delicate quillwork designs, embroidery of fine moose hair, splendid floral beadwork and appliqué on elaborate traditional garments'.[37]

While this type of production was revered and romanticised by the dominant culture, the actual life experiences of Native women living under colonialism was rendered invisible.[38] As Gerdine Van Woudenberg has shown, the colonial dispossession became so great that it forced Mi'kmaq people to find new bases for negotiations between themselves.[39] Because they were losing their hunting grounds, men were forced to undertake certain economic activities, like basketry, which had previously been exclusively feminine. Ironically, by the middle of the twentieth century, men were teaching basketry to women, since the latter's access to natural resources had been restricted. The former relationship that enjoined women to the land was now negotiated through men.[40]

Women's invisibility was further accentuated by discriminatory measures, particularly the impact of the Indian Act on Aboriginal women.[41] Women were deprived of status when they married a non-status man, therefore losing their connection to their community as well as some of their prestige and respect. Their voices were muffled not only by the dominant society, but also over time by the official discourse of Aboriginal leaders as well. Van Woudenberg argues that inaccurate colonial representations of women as landless and domestically bound contributed to the placing of the female category under the male.[42]

One can, therefore, better understand why the canoe became a crypt. The word crypt comes from the Latin *crypta* and the Greek *kruptos*, which means 'hidden'. The word evokes a chapel, usually underground below a church, which housed the corpses and relics of martyrs and saints. Here, it is the Aboriginal woman's knowledge that has gone underground, labelled a relic by dominant society. Nevertheless, it resurfaces through oral history. By preserving this knowledge, the woman is no longer simply a victim. She becomes a symbol of resistance as well. Her traditional costume evokes the spirit of the ancestors and a profound sense of personal and collective history. For the artist, Eta Joe symbolises the discovery of a past – a past that was denied because the dominant society had attempted to limit representation of her people's identity and, thus, of herself. Marshall tells: 'When I went to the reserve for summer vacation I didn't understand why my grandparents and my family were not decked out in fluff and feathers, why they weren't running around scalping folks and why they didn't compare to the drunken savage image that I'd learned about in school'.[43]

The featureless woman also eliminates any discourse on eroticisation and helps to move away from the colonial gaze that 'objectifies and eroticizes that which it captures'.[44] The generic depiction of Aboriginal women has wobbled from the nubile 'princess' to the 'prostitute'. These historic misrepresentations have also kept women silent and invisible. According to French critic Hélène Cixous in an essay entitled 'Castration or Decapitation?', when her body is eroticised, a woman is kept at a distance and when she speaks, she doesn't really speak – she lives in a place of silence and she remains beyond the reach of knowledge. In order to exist, 'she would have to start speaking, stop saying that she has nothing to say! Stop learning in school that women are created to listen, to believe, to make no discoveries. Dare to speak her piece about giving, the possibility of a giving that doesn't take away, but *gives*'.[45] By challenging conventional Canadian history, the artist is re-empowering the female voices and constructing Aboriginal women as agents of history. The artist is also reinvesting the historical images with her own history and the history of her people. Teresa Marshall is revisiting the past but she is also including these voices with an eye towards a better future.

Conclusion

In *The Wretched of the Earth*, Frantz Fanon called 'for the Indigenous intellectual and artist to create a new literature [or art], to work in the cause of a national culture after liberation'.[46] As shown in this analysis, the challenge still stands and is being answered by artists like Teresa Marshall. *Elitekey* clearly demonstrates that 'we cannot simply collapse contemporary aboriginal art into the western discourses; we need to learn a second language, a new visual vocabulary, to deal with these works and the practices and traditions that inform and underpin them'.[47] It is, therefore, important to pay close attention to the political and philosophical aspects of the artwork. As Jolene Rickard wrote: 'If [these aspects] are merely footnotes, everyone will be deprived of an opportunity to rethink the Americas not only as an indigenous space, but also as a continuously colonizing Canadian … space'.[48] By presenting an artwork that includes several pieces (a flag, a canoe and a woman in traditional costume), Teresa Marshall is not creating a linear narrative but a fractured one that addresses her dislocation and her marginalisation, 'expressive of substantive moments of cultural/communal specificity'.[49] Marshall articulates her reflection of the past, her representation of contemporary realities and her vision of the future. She draws in her subjectivity to focus on the notion of discovery; not discovery in the modernist sense of the word, but a blend of contradictions that includes the loss of her identity, the joy of finding it again and rediscovering her Aboriginal heritage. In finding her language, she identifies an infinity of interpenetration, but it is at the same time a way to resist dissolution into the dominant society. This art is not the art of marginalisation but the art of the resistance to marginalisation: a form of agency' aimed at telling us a different story and making us aware of the fallacy of colonial meta-narratives.

CHAPTER ELEVEN

The Fiction of Post-Colonial Pacific Writers

Sina Vaai

This chapter will focus on the role of the creative writer in the South Pacific in the contemporary era of post-colonialism. In this era, Empire and its consequences have not only been addressed but also aggressively assaulted in the fiction emanating from this region. One of the key motifs in such a literature of resistance, reassertion and reclaiming is *the quest for identity*, often connected to and grounded in land or place. The quest for identity, however defined, has often boiled down to the 'telling of our own story/stories' to affirm a sense of self erased during the process of colonisation. In many respects, the writer becomes a historical witness, setting down for the record, even in a fictional form, the key events vital for rebuilding and sustaining the identities of individuals and communities to ensure their growth and development at all levels. In this chapter, I examine several recent fictional works that explore the many layers of identity experienced by the people who inhabit Pacific societies, such as those of Fiji and Sāmoa, in particular Sudesh Mishra's play *Ferringhi* and Sia Figiel's performance poem, *The Centre*.

I begin with a story about a recent key event in the Pacific which succinctly illustrates the complexity of identities and the ways individuals successfully combine different elements of custom with aspects of the colonial European culture. On 19 January 2006, Sāmoa mourned the passing of one of her greatest contemporary leaders, Cardinal Pio Taofinuu. The story of Taofinuu's life is one of great inspiration and courage. In 1968 he was made Bishop in the Catholic Church and in 1973 was elevated to the College of Cardinals, the first and only Pacific Islander to be so honoured. As a Prince of the Catholic Church, he initiated many visionary post-Vatican II reforms and renewals for the Archdiocese; they were pioneering and sometimes controversial, but are fundamental to liturgical practice in Sāmoa today. Many testimonies given during the week before Cardinal Pio's burial pointed to the fact that the enculturation of liturgy which he installed and promoted demonstrated what he himself defined as his two guiding principles:

his Christian faith and his patriotism, based on a deep understanding of custom and tradition. Teresia Teaiwa, in her 2004 article titled 'Lomani Viti: Reflections on Patriotic Literature from Post-Coups Fiji', makes a distinction between the definition of patriotism and nationalism which is relevant to the story of Cardinal Pio's life. She states: 'Patriotism is based on the desire to contribute, to build a nation, nationalism on the other hand is undergirded by a sense of entitlement, a desire to assert the legitimacy of one's claim on an identity or resources over the claims of others'.[1]

Polynesians will attest to their belief that their ancient cultures prefigured Christianity with a strong emphasis on hospitality, generosity and the family spirit. In the case of modern Sāmoa, many Sāmoans claim that Christianity and Sāmoan culture are synonymous. These values were sorely tested in late 1975 when an American Sāmoan Senator was murdered in Savaii.[2] No Western Sāmoan could be guaranteed a safe arrival at Tafuna Airport in Tutuila, such was the rage and hatred that erupted when the American Sāmoans learnt about the murder of Senator Lualemana, a guest and relative visiting in Savaii at the time. The official word from American Sāmoan Governor Ruth to the Secretary to the Western Sāmoan government at the time, Maiava Iulai Toma, was that it was best to cancel any visit by Western Sāmoans wishing to escort the body back with the Senator's widow. The civility, diplomacy and modernity of Western democracy as a means of attaining peace were considered inappropriate for the occasion.

Cardinal Pio offered to go, the lone representative of a nation shamed and remorseful for the tragic murder of their honoured guest. When he arrived at Tafuna, he faced a crowd armed with guns, ready for vengeance. In his appeal for forgiveness, the Cardinal unfolded a large fine mat, the *ie toga*, a *measina* (treasure) of Sāmoan culture by which most important events on life's journey are marked. Appealing for peace and reconciliation in the name of Christ, he reminisced, 'I unfolded a big fine mat and said to them that I was not there to approach them in the traditional culture but was there to speak for the people of Western Sāmoa, crying from the cross of shame and humiliation'.[3] Using a fine mat in a gesture of humility according to Sāmoan custom is a sign which cultural players recognise as a real indication of remorse that invariably triggers responses of facilitation and compassion. The *matais* (chiefs) immediately responded by siding for peace with the Cardinal – the messenger of peace, and those who had guns lowered them. The crisis was averted, forgiveness and reconciliation won the day and a sense of peace and restoration of the *va* (relationships) returned.

Whilst the colonial Pacific story highlighted oppression and erasure of Indigenous histories, knowledges and identities, this narrative about Cardinal Pio reflects an excellent example of the post-colonial story. He was a Sāmoan church leader, who had a strong commitment to employing and integrating foundational cultural values and practices into Christian liturgy, and his extensive knowledge of custom underpinned the courage he showed in his actions that fateful day.

In early 1976, in the first independent issue of *Mana Review*, Albert Wendt wrote of the collective creative movement seen in the renaissance of Pacific creative arts and in the flowering of literary and artistic productions as a movement 'towards a new Oceania',[4] redefining and reconstructing the cultures of the region into newness, free from the 'wounds of colonialism'[5] and 'based firmly on their own pasts'.[6] Furthermore, the '*aitu*' (ghost/spirit) of racism is according to Wendt, '... most evil [and] ... the symbol of all repression',[7] which continues to transform and humiliate Pacific Islanders and their cultures and the only way to exorcise this '*aitu*' was to understand colonialism and 'what it did and is still doing to us'.[8]

Two years later in 1978 Satendra Nandan's address, 'The Indian-Fijian: A Complex Fate',[9] described how Fijian-Indians, the main migrant group in Fiji, were becoming aware of their fate as Pacific Islanders. This would require a sea-change of seeking, establishing and fostering new relationships with Pacific neighbours, both big and small, leading to a time when Fijian-Indians could say unselfconsciously 'these are our people, this sea of islands make up our country'.[10] The multicultural islands of Fiji would then stand as beacons of light in a world of encircling gloom. This statement was made before the 1987 military coups and was echoed in late 1993, when Epeli Hau'ofa published his theoretical essay 'Our Sea of Islands'[11] in a book titled *A New Oceania: Rediscovering Our Sea of Islands*. Hau'ofa called for a liberation of the mind, especially amongst Pacific Islanders, in the way that Pacific island nations and their inhabitants were seen and represented. This new way of seeing involved a reclaiming or rediscovery of the 'ancient truth' of the vastness and richness of the Oceanian 'pasts', in which Islanders interacted in large exchange communities across this great 'sea of islands'. In 2000, in his follow-up essay 'Pasts to Remember', Hau'ofa added, 'we must, in addition to other measures, be able to define and construct our pasts and present in our own ways'.[12] Across four decades, the cry from Pacific writers/theorists is still basically about the same struggle for recognition and reassertion of cultural identity and selfhood. Wendt stated emphatically: 'We must not consent to our own abasement'[13] and Hau'ofa echoed the same sentiment: 'we must not let anyone belittle us again'.[14]

Ngugi wa Thiong'o, in a similar call for the decolonisation of the African mind, described the legacy of empire very succinctly as a 'cultural bomb',[15] the effect of which is to 'annihilate a peoples' belief in their names, in their languages, in their environment, in their heritage of struggle, in their unity, in their capacities and ultimately in themselves'.[16] Even more telling is the effect of imperialism on their past, which is then viewed as 'one wasteland of non-achievement'.[17] Thus the wounds of colonialism cut back through the heritage of the past, into the present and reach over the horizon into the future. In this context, creative writing for Pacific Islanders and migrants like the Fijian-Indians who have been transplanted to an island home in the Pacific, can be seen as Pio Manoa puts it, as an attempt 'to harmonise the split in themselves and the splits in their changing cultural environments,'[18] to feel complete in a new world order that maps out for colonised and decolonised peoples experiences that emphasise their fragility and interdependence.

After colonisation comes the desire to be liberated, to write out the resilience of Pacific peoples and their ability to survive the impact of imperial domination, blending the 'received goods' from the West with those of their own Indigenous homelands. There is a need to celebrate and to make sense of the many facets of the Pacific self which is made up of many voices and shifting identities – to externalise, to put outside what was previously held captive, often in turmoil, inside. This process of turning the inside out, creatively speaking, leads to a process that brings healing and forgiveness, as 'the (Pacific) other', the coloniser, is allowed to see the inside view, the emotional and cultural terrain/s of the decolonised writer and his/her experiences, to enter imaginatively into previously silenced/silent cultural spaces and stories.[19] The language and style in which the story is woven is also significant, as words and phrases from tongues other than the global language of the coloniser (English, in this case) open up and are incorporated into the post-colonial literary landscape.

The writer in this corpus of creative writing plays a vital role in facilitating and promoting cross-cultural understanding and in building bridges across cultural divides that previously seemed impossible to negotiate. In this time of great social, environmental and political upheaval and the reality of another wave of Imperialism, in the dominance of rich nations over poor nations within the framework of accession to the World Trade Organisation, such literary/cultural texts sound many warnings that Pacific communities ignore at their own peril.

Sudesh Mishra

Ferringhi, Sudesh Mishra's play performed in Suva in 1993 and finally published in 2001, is a play about neocolonialism that focuses on the importance of cultural identity and survival.[20] It fits Teaiwa's definition of 'patriotic literature', where the writer is at 'the forefront of a battle over the imaginative terrain of Fiji's society…'.[21]

The play focuses on memory, forgetting, history, lies and all those things that add to an explosive situation. The play 'looks at life from the grog (kava) bowl',[22] a traditional ritualistic site signifying a shared humanity, where a common *bilo* (coconut shell-cup) is served to each participant involved in the meeting. Five main characters are trapped in a spotlight and each character has his own particular fear that prevents him from going out beyond or approaching the circumference of this illuminated zone. Paradoxically, the spotlight, symbolising its opposite, the darkness, points to the many reversals of positive expectations of enlightenment that have, since colonial times, been a reality for Pacific peoples, particularly the citizens of Fiji, living in a multicultural and multiracial reality introduced by British colonial administrators who 'constructed the nation and its aristocracy … to accord with their [own] ideas of governance'.[23] *Ferringhi* thus becomes a play about self-discovery at several levels: personal, political and historical. It is also a play that demonstrates the importance of Indigenous knowledge, which is acquired in a communal context of sharing and fellowship, building relationships that are enduring and liberating.

It is important to note that the play was written and performed after the first two military coups in Fiji in 1987 and published after the third coup in 2000. All three coups were aimed at removing what many Indigenous Fijians perceived as a threat: Indo-Fijian-dominated governments voted into power. The negotiation of identity in Fiji, as in other post-colonial societies in the Pacific, is often complex and intriguing, pertaining more to place than to race even though the politics of race still play a prominent role in the national arena of Fiji. The Fiji Islands Bureau of Statistics noted that in the lead-up to the May 2006 General Elections, more and more Indians were leaving Fiji. The Indian population of Fiji, which was once 49 per cent in 1986, dropped to an estimated 38 per cent by 2004.[24]

Mishra commented about his conceptualising of the play,

> Each individual in that pool of light has some kind of memory lapse or amnesia and every scene (*lila*) is based on identifying this particular amnesia and then actually trying to make these characters remember what it was they had forgotten or had actually repressed. And the agent for this kind of remembering is Ferringhi, [which means] … the outsider (in Arabic, Urdu and Hindi as well).[25]

In the play, Ferringhi, also known as Tusitala (the Sāmoan name meaning 'teller of tales', that was given to Robert Louis Stevenson who lived for a few years in Sāmoa before his death in 1894) unpacks his collection of stories, each one applying in some way to the life of one of the individuals around the kava bowl. As the story is told, the relevant individual identifies himself in that particular story and learns something in the process. The storyteller's revealing narratives liberate each character sitting around the kava bowl as they discover the truth about themselves and leave the area of darkness that symbolises the light. Puglu (meaning 'mad person' in Hindi), another storyteller who plays roles of both a male and female nature, is also an outsider and ultimately acts to save Ferringhi.[26]

In the opening *lila* of the play, the group of five (Mooves, Aslam, Pumpkin, Chan and Seru) lament their present dilemma of being caged by their various fears in this perimeter and remaining in ignorance of outside events. Aslam states 'Man, we need another storyteller. Chan don't know what happening out there anymore'.[27] Of equal importance is the fact that they are out of *waka* (kava roots) to keep the grog flowing and all five men refuse to risk going outside of their circle to obtain some more. Very early into this first scene it is revealed that there is a misunderstanding about Chan's storytelling; while the other four thought he went outside the circle of light to obtain his stories, he very quickly assures them that they are 'reconditioned stories'[28] that he borrowed (*choro*(ed)) from others as he sat on the edge listening to their *talanoa* (telling stories and talking). The vital role of story as history or narrative defining the self is shown by Seru at the end of the first *lila*, when he tries to cross the 'rubicon of light'[29] and baulks saying '*Sega*, man. I'm too afraid of stories. What if a story get me? You gang never come save me!'[30]

Puglu makes his initial appearance early in this scene, alluding to the Hindu epics, his monologic outbursts considered lunatic by those around the kava bowl. He moves agitatedly out into the audience, searching for answers to questions that are not clear to anyone but him, before making his exit. Ferringhi is unable to see anything in the light of the circle around the kava bowl, but enunciates for the group what he sees out there in the dark, off-stage where the audience is sitting. His identity becomes a moot point of discussion for the kava-drinkers. His initial narratives are spoken in the Standard English of empire but when he answers Mooves' questions about himself, he speaks in their idiom. This code-switching makes him an ambivalent figure and casts doubts upon his identity and his stories; 'Aslam: But this fallah's no *kavalagi*, he jus like us only he different … Seru: *Io*, he speak like us gang and he speak like the *kavalagi*. Only he's better; he's *gusu macamaca*. My *bete* say that the devil go speak in many tongues'.[31] After offering to go outside to get them some *waka*, Ferringhi returns to narrate his experience in the local market where 'tongues broke on or overlapped with each other, so that a drone of sound like that of locusts in the season of harmattan, hung above the utterances of vendors and accountants, plumbers and teachers …

bodies ... grailing for food in a pursuit that dissolves differences'.[32] This 'tapestry of noise ... and colours'[33] is disturbed by an Indigenous mob wearing balaclavas destroying property and bashing up imaginary foes. Seru then becomes the focus of interrogation as he remembers a dockworkers' meeting that erupted into violence but his guilt blocks any memory of his role in the incident. When Aslam suddenly remembers that his grandfather was the old 'markit [sic] vendor'[34] beaten up by the gang and tearfully accuses Seru of being one of the attackers, Seru is put on the defensive, declaring 'You must remember your place here. We *taukei*, you *vulagi*. You breathe when we say you breathe. Otherwise we drive you into the sea. We are the indigenous people, you just an immigrant race'.[35]

This interchange provides a dramatic opening for the issue of race where Puglu, impersonating a colonial official of mixed descent questions himself acting as an anonymous citizen:

> *Puglu (impersonating an irritated official)*:
> Sir, it is imperative that you indicate your
> race in the relevant column of the yellow
> form. Nothing personal, just government
> statistics. Put a tick in one of the boxes.
> Here let me do it for you. What are you:
> Fijian, Rotuman, European, part-European,
> Chinese, Indian or Other?
> (*Acting the role of the addressee*): Other.
> *Official*: What other?
> *Addressee*: Just other.
> *Official (losing his temper)*: This woman
> here is Chinese, that man there is Fijian and
> I here am part-European. What are you?
> *Addressee*: Your others.[36]

The scene ends with Mooves serving Puglu a *bilo* of kava, which he then takes out into the audience and offers to several people, reciting before each offering; 'Drink deeply my friend,/For your personal thirst/Is but a national thirst,/What you sip in solitude,/Sips the noisy multitude./Drink deeply, my friend'.[37] The group notes and Chan makes the observation to Ferringhi that Puglu takes the spotlight away from them when he moves back and forth into the audience. And while this is a technical necessity, it is also symbolic of his agency in illuminating the narratives of colonialism.

In *lilas* three to seven, each of the five characters, beginning with Mooves then Aslam, Pumpkin, Chan and finally Seru (now called Ratu Seru), are freed as they remember fundamental chunks of history, which then make sense of their own contemporary situations. For instance, the sixth *lila* liberates Chan by helping him to remember his Chinese motherland, paralleled by the actions of Puglu (now attired as an Arab woman) as she searches for her long-lost mother, only to end up seeing her own image in the mirror with which Ferringhi blocks her path. Chan replies to Seru's question about the *lewa* ('girl' in Fijian) finding herself with 'Sega, the fallah say that all gang search for themselves, but cos we think the thing outside us, we can't find the real thing inside and when we do, it jus like a Naboro cell'.[38] Chan exits shortly after to follow a dragonfly, a symbol of his Chinese past. Just as his uncle Lum followed the same flighty creatures down the Yangtze River, eventually making the passage to Fiji, Chan's journey will involve the reverse movement in order to find his own identity.

The seventh and final *lila* concerns Ratu Seru's enlightenment about the impact of the colonial mindset upon his own Indigenous people. His unthinking acceptance of Sir Hen Crusher's schemes for economic development has led to an existence 'in a lazar-house among blind men'.[39] So Ferringhi (whose stories Crusher warned the group against) is able to tell the neocolonial businessman with satisfaction that the local workers needed for the project have left: 'They don't want to act in your *meke*'.[40] When Crusher threatens Seru with breaking a written contract, Seru's answer is passionate: 'Your papers, your deal, your company. You expect us to respect your system as if it come to us from god. That colonial trick as old as indenture, Sir Hen. It don't work anymore'.[41] Back in his natural *vanua*, he has realised the bond he has with the land, saying, 'Once again, I was worm of soil and crab of ocean floor and the *vanua* was in me and I was in the *vanua*'. Sir Hen is then accosted by Puglu dressed as a Fijian warrior, who first announces, 'I'm the Spirit of the Pacific Way gone remarkably wrong'[42] and then manages to drive Sir Hen off the stage. Seru informs Ferringhi before he exits the stage into the darkness that he is going to consult his *yavusa* in the hills, to appease the forgotten gods because he admits 'that instead of changing what we had, we borrowed from others without reflection'.[43] He is the last of the characters to enter the darkness, experiencing similar surprise at the new visions in the dark, calling back to Ferringhi, 'Tusitala, you right about another thing. It's light here'.[44]

Ferringhi has now lost his audience and is left without a purpose; his role as a teller of stories is now in doubt as he reveals,

> Like a pupa tearing through its drapery;
> Like an imago imagining itself a universe.
> Caught in a slipstream between vista and vista,
> Slowly become both teller and listener,
> He negotiates these roles like a paradox,
> His own double in a place of confinement:
> The teller listens, the listener tells the tale.[45]

It is left to Puglu (now dressed as a weary woman-traveller) to rescue him, in a sense, from his shadows and illusions and to lead him forward on a road, stretching toward endless possibilities, epitomising the growth of moral consciousness. As she says,

> You are at a junction, you are never not at a junction, so you take a road, any road you care to take or any that cares to take you, then you take a road crossing that road and another crossing the second one and so on ad infinitum. There are no departures or arrivals; but there are resting places like this one and time leads you on from one to the next.[46]

The play ends with Ferringhi accompanying Puglu as she walks down the aisle towards the theatre entrance, where both stop at the threshold. Puglu begins a story and as the playwright intended, 'Ferringhi becomes a listener and discovers himself as they walk across and also leave the zone of darkness … actually the scene on the stage, one spotlight which traps them into this demonic darkness which is actually light'. The last word is left to Puglu when she is asked her name as she begins her story. Her reply, 'Maya' ('Illusion' in Hindi) ties the seven *lilas* thematically together.

Pat Craddock, who directed the Suva production of the play in 1993 observed, 'Mishra has done a remarkable thing. He has created a picture of his country in images of satire and tragedy … sometimes it is a dream world, other times it is stark reality … This gives the cast an opportunity to look at themselves as actors on a stage but also as people who live in the community and are part of what Mishra is saying'.[47] Given the recent uneasy relationship between the military and the government in Fiji in 2005–6 leading up to the May 2006 General Elections,[48] it is evident that the tensions and uncertainties surrounding ethnic and national identity in a post-coup Fiji which emanate from Mishra's play still have relevance and resonance in the current times.

Sia Figiel

Like Mishra, Sia Figiel is a Pacific writer who focuses on the vexed issue of multiple post-colonial identities in the contemporary era of porous national borders and is typical of those writers 'who want not only to resist the new empire [of globalisation] but also to change, unambiguously, the representation of the oppressed'.[49] She initially won recognition by winning the inaugural Polynesian Literary Competition in 1994 with her long poetic song in Sāmoan and English, 'O Le Solo La Lupe Ma Le I'a' or 'Poem Of Lupe And The Fish' and since then, with her publication of *The Centre*, written in the same style. *Where We Once Belonged*, her first novel, won acclaim, receiving the 1997 Commonwealth Writers Prize for the Best First Book for the South-East Asia/South Pacific Region.[50] Figiel names the style of her writing as a composition in '*su'ifefiloi*', defined as:

> ... a sewing together (or stringing together) of different songs. Different ideas. Events. Flowers. One to another to form one long *ula*. One long song. One that comes to life on a *poula*. Or *fiafia* night. When we feast. Perform our dance. Our songs. The *taualuga* dance or closing item being the climax of the night. When the songs of *su'ifefiloi* come to life'.[51]

Figiel's compositions in this style so far have experimented with the persona of a young adolescent Sāmoan girl, initially named Sila, then Alofa and now Sāmoana. Figiel attempts with Sāmoana's language to 'portray in English the aesthetics of her mother tongue. One full of metaphors. Analogies. And rhythm'.[52] Her use of fragments, phrases and repetition attempt to mirror the cadences of the spoken word and in this respect, she follows the recited and oratory tradition of the *fa'amatai* (Sāmoan chiefly system). If the Sāmoan thought cannot be translated into English, it is left in the original Sāmoan (using the colloquial 'k' instead of the formal 't' version), signifying to the reader literally 'a different world'.[53]

Her long poem 'Of Lupe and the Fish', recounts a time before Lupe's people were Christianised by the 'Messenger(s) of Forgetting' (MOF).[54] During this time, birds, trees, lizards and winds as well as fish were considered gods and oaths were taken before them: '*Kauko i luma o le I'a*/We swear in the presence of the Fish!'[55] If these oaths were false, retribution was immediate and visible for all to see, with red marks all over their faces – 'marks which are called/*fasia*'.[56] With the introduction of Christianity, the one God became the only God: 'Everyone runs around worshipping *Le Akua/Kauko i luma o le Akua!/Kauko i luma o le Akua!*'[57] and a European representation of the Christian God is imprisoned in plastic frames and hung with shell-necklaces in Sāmoan homes. Figiel's satire of the wholesale adoption of Christianity by Sāmoans is bitter:

> An image carried all the way from the
> Cold wintery Europe. – From London in the
> saliva of Imagesellers
> (Men and women) Who spat it unto the faces of 'savages' – chiefs and
> Chieftains – *aualuma* and *aumaga* – *fafine ma tamaitai-*
> *Taulealea-teine ma tama-tamaiti*
> Who were living without wax – without candles.
> This is the light! said they
> This is your new image!⁵⁸

The erasure of the memory of the past and the introduction of a new Western framework begins the sense of disintegration for Lupe and is the cause of her lament before she dies. This new world of plastic products, Coca-Cola cans, video games from Europe and America, clocks, money, cars, European houses and nuclear bombs and the new language of English reinforces the 'forgetting' of many ancient beliefs. 'Lupe's Lament', which makes up the last third of the poem, is a search for past creeds, with Lupe asking Oh beautiful fish – Where are you?'⁵⁹ At the end of her life, she feels helpless, alone and surrounded by 'madness'.

In contrast to this bitter, nostalgic poem, *The Centre* encapsulates the polyphony of voices and stories of Sāmoans living in Apia and celebrates difference in the post-colonial capital. Covering forty-four pages, it opens with a definition of the city – 'Apia./Capital of the independent state./Of Samoa./Centre of government agencies./Tourism./And trade'⁶⁰ – and then examines from the perspectives of twenty various individuals and groups, what the essence of the centre is: 'There's no consensus as to what the centre of Apia is./Everyone has their own versions./Their own definitions./Which vary in degree. From one person to another'.⁶¹ Figiel traces this *su'ifefiloi* of voices and stories physically, by beginning at the Apia landmark of the Ioane Viliamu building (the highest building in Apia at six storeys) at the western end of Beach Road and coming down towards what was the New Market until 1995. (The market has since been relocated further inland.) Each perspective claims a different centre for various reasons, be they religious, political, personal or economic, ranging from Fesili So'o (Asking Too Many Questions), a Protestant deacon at the western end of the town who insists that the Viliamu Building is the centre of Apia, to Mataolepo (Eye of the Night) at the eastern end of town, a vendor at the New Market who claims her site of work at the Maketi Fou (New Market) is the centre.

Between these two points on Beach Road, the voices track an *ula* (garland) of stories. There is Soia, the 75-year-old Catholic mother of twins who claims the Catholic Cathedral as her centre. Her only boys, twins Derek (Keleki) and Freeman (Pagoka-ua-faasaolokoiga), named after a European anthropologist, are both homosexuals. Here, Figiel is obviously mocking the Mead–Freeman debate which depicted contrary, European images of Sāmoans from Mead's free-loving, promiscuous noble savages to Freeman's interpretation which focused on the dark side of Sāmoan nature, seeing them as volatile.

Alaisa Fiaola-Confusion (Rice Want-to-live-Confusion) is Chinese-Sāmoan, as his name might suggest. He hangs out at the Fale Kifaga o Saiga (House of Movies of the Chinese) at Taufusi. Twenty-seven-year-old part-Solomon Islander Tu Lou sits with her baby Si-mea and sells her locally made cricket balls outside Bartley's Store. She is the descendant of a Solomon Island indentured labourer brought in the late nineteenth century by European settlers[62] to work on plantations and build roads. Her grandmother, from Vaiala, became pregnant to her *meauli* (black thing) grandfather, causing great family distress. Her grandmother was ostracised, indicating the racism directed to migrant colonial workers of the time. The elevator man who 'helps everything go/Up and down'[63] at the National Provident Fund (NPF) Building, Alu E-Su'e-Gi-Fafie-O-Le-Saka (Go-and-Look-for-Firewood-for-the-Saka), opposite Le Fale o Pipi (Burns Philips, now Chan Mow Limited) is certain that these two buildings are the centre of influence. Losa Fiaaulelei or Roseline Vain, waits at the corner of the Nelson Public Library and the RSA for her boyfriend (Alu's son), for 'Him',[64] a rugby player in the Manu Sāmoa Sevens team. The animals of Apia – cats, dog, pigs – don't care about centres since all they know is the location of the rubbish bins at the Maketi Fou. The bus depot at the same place, where the buses from all over Upolu discharge and pick up passengers, their animals and belongings, becomes the next focal point for crowds of people, including the policeman and the newspaper boy.

Midway through the *su'ifefiloi* narrative, Figiel places the story of the naming of Sāmoa (or one version of it). Moa, the mid or centre, is the son of Salevao, 'god of the rocks' and everything the child needed is 'sa ia Moa' (sacred to Moa).[65] The time of the story is noon, the mid-point of the day, usually a time of oppressive heat. The last half of the *ula* weaves fourteen sites connected to individuals or groups around the Maketi Fou, from Sione Sione, an owner of a stall at the food section of the market, to the schoolchildren at the pancake section, to Iole, the fisherman at the live animal section, to Ludwig Spinoza aka Luki Sipinosa, a taxi-driver of mixed-race descent whose father Heinrich fell in love with his Sāmoan wife Fayawayaway ('Fayaway' is a Polynesian dreamgirl in Melville's fiction *Typee*), and La Goto (Setting Sun or Sunset), the derelict scholar sitting under the clock tower. This sequence is followed by the public toilet which everyone sees as a centre at some time or another, to the comedy and storytelling or gossip sections found all over the market, then returns to Pule Pule, head of personnel at Le Fale o Molesi (Morris Hedstroms), who is having his lunch-break at the food section, thinking: 'It's the only place where a Samoan can still eat like a Samoan./Without paying *papalagi* prices',[66] and the final character, Su'ekage (Looking for a Man), who is looking for the male who has fathered her illegitimate child. The winding narrative threading all these stories and voices together, ends 'In the moa./Of that place./ They each call./... The Centre'.[67]

The humour in *The Centre* derives from the untranslated colloquial expressions used as well as the names of the characters, both European and Sāmoan, which reflect their personalities or actions. Significantly too, the repetition of words and phrases, some onomatopoeic in nature, reflect the orality of Sāmoan society and the emphasis on the spoken word. For example, in order to convey the business of congested traffic outside the Maketi Fou in the hot sun: 'Taxis zoom zoom./Vans zoom zoom./Lorries zoom zoom./Bicycles zoom zoom./Motor-cycles zoom zoom./ Tour-buses zoom zoom./A limousine zoom zoom./Everyone owns a car./Everyone wants to own a car'.[68] Also, the use of unglossed lines from Sāmoan songs and other discourses (such as *Filemuepeiolelupeuatulelauolivemalueleolonaonafaauoi-Aue!* the first line of a well-known Sāmoan song, running the words together without any punctuation to signify how it is sung) adds to the unique nature of this long poem. The poem reveals the manifold nature of a post-colonial Pacific setting. The capital of Apia, as represented in this poetic chain, reflects different interpretations of the one physical reality and is saluted for its richness and diversity.

The dynamic nature of Figiel's performance poem often strikes an obvious chord with many Pacific audiences, who respond with enthusiasm and laughter at this witty representation of the poet's homeland.[69] Along with Mishra's *Ferringhi*, her poem illustrates that identities and insider perceptions of identities are not static, that in the globalised Pacific of the New Millennium, they are influenced by a 'continual process of transcultural interaction, appropriation and transformation'.[70]

Conclusion

I conclude with reference to a poem by Tongan poet, Konai Helu Thaman. Modern cross-cultural perspectives are a way of seeing the world for many Pacific islanders who, like Mishra, Figiel and Thaman, are well educated in the Western context and live the lives of migrant pan-Pacific people, crossing the boundaries of several cultural worlds. This provides the essence of Thaman's 1993 poem, 'Different Eyes'.[71] The ambivalence in the first stanza is extreme, the images striking: the 'global life' is seen as a state between life and death, the feeling of being smothered very real, all the traditional softness of the fruits of the earth, like the *heilala*, are 'hidden' and 'lost', rationality 'drown(ing)' out the 'soft fragrance' of the *salusalu* (a garland of flowers symbolising the unity of a common humanity which binds us all together). The middle stanza, addressed directly to the 'you' to whom the poem is dedicated (in this instance Ron Crocombe),[72] looks at the sensitive outsider's contribution, who asks questions, notices what Islanders 'took for granted' and empathises with the pain felt by Pacific peoples 'of not being able to go back'. In Crocombe's case, this includes his own efforts in the post-colonial struggle in the Pacific for self-respect and paving new ways forward. In his role in the formation of the Institute of Pacific Studies at the University of the South Pacific, Professor Crocombe and his wife Marjorie encouraged many Pacific Islanders, both Indigenous and migrant, to 'write their own stories/histories' for publication and to 'write for the record as historical witnesses, important narratives of identity'.

Coming to a new awareness brings a burden all of its own, allowing Pacific peoples to realistically envision the future with 'different eyes'.

> this global life
> gives us light
> and love
> but it also gives us death
> because living inside a dream
> is like being buried alive
> like turning into grass
> a *heilala* hidden
> amidst the exotic flowers
> of our lost *salusalu*
> its soft fragrance drowned
> in the strenuous sounds
> of our rational minds[73]

The poem ends: 'now we look at tomorrow with different eyes, the truths about us weigh us down'.[74] It is in this spirit of a sincere, sometimes painful, quest to uncover all the many discomfiting layers of identity that creative writers in the South Pacific continue to play a vital role in the post-colonial literature of resistance, reassertion and reclamation.

CHAPTER TWELVE

Neoliberalism, Racialised Gender and Indigeneity

Isabel Altamirano-Jiménez

The past decade has witnessed the growth of an extensive literature aimed at understanding the ways in which globalisation has negatively impacted the lives of people. What is often neglected is how economic globalisation affects women differently, particularly those located at the margins. Aboriginal women are not only among the hardest hit by economic globalisation both in the global north and south, but they are also exposed to a complex system of oppression involving race, colonisation, rules and institutions. Although under neo-liberalism this system of oppression is often constructed as inherent to the margins, it is rather a creature of neo-liberal governance and colonial discourses whose relationship to men and women is complex, uneven and contradictory.

In this chapter, I explore the main connections between neo-liberalism, racialised gender and indigeneity. I argue that neo-liberal ideology and the discourse of human rights perpetuate a hierarchy and a global codification of peoples and places that are within and outside of global progress. From this perspective, violence and gender discrimination against Aboriginal women are constructed as cultural problems, rather than as a result of the multiple social markers and power relations that structure social, economic and political systems. Thus, systematic gender differences and uneven access to property rights, resources and the legal system are inextricably linked to a mode of governance that symbolically empowers Aboriginal women, yet disqualifies them as subjects.

Contemporary global, national and local processes signal markedly different contexts in normalising postcolonial relations among Indigenous peoples. Academic and political discourses have emphasised the increasingly complex forms of social interactions associated with global capital flow, neo-liberalism, technology, information, labour and new forms of economic integration. The variety of economic globalisation landscapes is not limited to the global north versus the south, for difference and geographic constructions continue to subsume the uneven and contradictory impacts of economic development among actors, social groups, institutions and regions, suggesting the existence of a racialised, gendered geography of development even within rich countries such as Canada.

Aboriginal peoples and neo-liberal governance

Neo-liberal globalisation is an extremely complex and multi-dimensional phenomenon. Globalisation is not a new process, it has occurred for centuries. In the early colonial periods, many Indigenous peoples in the Americas were viewed by European settlers as 'nations' and accorded some degree of autonomy and rights. As European settlers became dominant, they transformed Indigenous nationhood into a minority status granted by the state. Thus, Indigenous sovereignty, political autonomy and resource appropriation have been a major concern within national states.[1] As a historically contingent phenomenon, globalisation has evolved and maintained continuities.[2] Scholars have emphasised the increasingly complex forms of social interactions associated with global capital flow, neo-liberal governance, technology, information, new forms of economic integration, liberalisation, privatisation, reduction of the welfare state and individualism.

From the 1970s the scope and pace of global integration increased, as did linkages among countries and social actors, creating a new trend towards the globalisation of business and dissemination of information. Renewed pressure for energy resources, mining and hydroelectric resources sparked interest in untapped frontiers/territories. At the same time, decolonising movements created numerous small independent states around the world. Liberalisation movements and struggles for the expansion of citizen's rights, such as the Black Power and Red Power movements, encouraged an explosion of rights-consciousness partially sustained by the United Nations and other organisations, which contributed to the emergence of new rights-based discourses and legal tools that Indigenous peoples have since used.

The Organisation of American States (OAS) and the United Nations Education Science and Culture Organisation (UNESCO) recommended that states promoted the revival of Indigenous cultures in the early seventies. Also, the International Labour Organisation (ILO) study of Indigenous peoples made public the exclusion of Indigenous peoples and their status as 'internal colonies' in most countries and prompted the adoption of Convention 107 (now 169) and Recommendation 104 for the protection and integration of Indigenous populations. After a long journey, the Universal Declaration of the Rights of Indigenous Peoples was finally passed in 2007. According to Ronald Niezen, the evolution of this rights regime has been part of a translocal attempt to address Indigenous grievances such as the siege of Wounded Knee in 1973, the Maya genocide in Guatemala in 1980 and the Mohawk insurrection in Canada in 1991.[3]

While some of these translocal efforts were taking place, neo-liberalism as a doctrine of governance was altering power relationships between the global economy and the local, sponsoring the idea that the world was made up of individuals who increasingly related to each other only as consumers. This situation opened up spaces for complex changes involving new loci of power, complex interrelations, new opportunities and new forms of vulnerability for people, as well as increasing social inequality not only among countries but also within countries.[4]

Neoliberal governance and the international human rights discourse are embedded in cultural assumptions that challenge and discipline other forms of diversity and innovation. The fact that neo-liberalism emphasises the role of the market results in the adoption of peculiar views on the question of human rights, and often champions the freedom of individual action and the right to own and dispose of property while excluding subsistence rights such as housing and healthcare.[5] Thus, Indigenous peoples' struggles aimed at recovering control over their future are often limited to the local construction of human rights' 'universals', ignoring other place-situated ways of resolving conflict and conferring social responsibilities.

Consequently, Indigenous peoples' relationship with the State is redefined and new forms of governance are negotiated along the lines of decentralisation, devolution, development, the affirmation of basic human rights, social capital and individual freedom and responsibility. However, history and collective land tenure, which are constituents of Indigenous identity, are redefined. From this point of view, the connection between land and political power is not only about accessing land as a means of production, but also about constituting community.

Thus neo-liberal governance and human rights in many instances works as a way to neutralise, disqualify and discipline Indigenous collective rights in a way that does not challenge the neo-liberal economic project itself.[6] Because many of the territories, environments and cultural artefacts Indigenous peoples seek to control are of national and global interest, Indigenous struggles confront a tension between the local needs and the extra-local wants.[7] Thus, under neo-liberal governance the dichotomy is not between individual/collective rights, nor between cultural and material local needs. Rather the imperative is about how to frame Indigenous empowerment in such a way that the market continues to be politically possible.

Neo-liberalism and racialised gender

Neo-liberal understanding of power relies on specific erasure of history and memory, privileging Western ideals, norms and values. Whereas neo-liberal globalisation privileges and exacerbates these hierarchies of value, nation-states are crucial in perpetuating difference and marginalisation through ideological and institutionalised forms of sexism, racism, patriarchy and class privilege. The neo-liberal transformation of social reproduction has enabled the accumulation of capital but deepened differences in wealth, poverty and gender relations. While social reproduction is basically about the biological production of the labour force at differentiated levels of expertise, this differentiation is socially constituted. The impact of economic globalisation is resented by the many who struggle to secure the material goods and social practices associated with social reproduction. However, some groups, specifically women, are more negatively affected than men.

Gender inequality is constructed both through society's formal laws and statutes and through unwritten norms and shared understandings. Gender inequality is not only pervasive across all societies but is also one of the most pervasive forms of social disadvantage, particularly when it intersects with race. Eileen Boris notes that race 'is an arena of power, deriving its meaning from political struggle and in turn offering a language through which politics operates and people comprehend their lives'.[8] Historically, colonial discourse and laws defined the status of Aboriginal peoples by differentiating them from white settlers, while dispossessing the former from their lands.

As a central category of analysis, race does not imply that racialised males and females face the same experience. As a legacy of colonialism, bodies, particularly those of Indigenous women, were objectified. They not only took the form of property, but were also considered 'ugly', 'impure', 'savage' and 'sexual'. What results from this process is the all-inclusive and omnipresent division of the world into the familiar places of inside and outside, sacred and profane, public and private, economic and domestic, urban and rural, city and suburb, as well as specific places marked by race and gender. For instance, justification for policies affecting women's reproductive rights fit pre-existing images of racialised, poor women as being sexually undisciplined. Equally appealing, Aboriginal women who challenge gender discrimination and violence within their communities confront ostracism and other forms of disapproval for not being loyal to their communities. Thus racialised gender marks distinctions between men and women and impacts on Aboriginal women's identity formation and experiences of well-being.

Colonial governance and the Indian Act, the statute that concerns registered 'Indians', their bands and the reserve system, was enacted in 1876 and provided

Canada's federal government exclusive authority to legislate in relation to these peoples and their lands. This legislation was amended numerous times, further limiting First Nations peoples' mobility and expanding federal government's control over them. Women have experienced the harmful consequences of the Indian Act. In paternalistically defining who was and was not 'Indian', the government took away First Nations women and their children's birthrights. Colonial definition and governance have affected the construction of social provision and the boundaries of inclusion and exclusion within Indigenous communities.

Institutions set up the rules by which society and people's relationships are governed. These rules may be written or unwritten, explicit or implicit, codified in laws, mandated by policy, upheld by religion, tradition or convention, or embodied in the standards of family, community and society. Institutions take concrete form in organisations and groups such as the state, the market, civil society/community and kinship/family. As such, racial and gender differences are institutionally legitimised through ideologies of difference and inequality embodying assumptions about white privileges and about the nature of femininity and masculinity.

Gendered and racialised inequalities are not a consequence of neo-liberalism but an integral component of wealth accumulation; nevertheless, neo-liberalism depoliticises and decontextualises those inequalities, thus transforming racialised gender discrimination into a problem that only happens in certain places and in certain cultures. Thus state intervention is considered essential in order to rectify such anomalies. The free market and the human rights regime work together to codify people and places that are within and outside of a modernist notion of progress. According to Newdick, the treatment of Indigenous women becomes a measure of a political society's placement on the scale of democracy and development.[9] Violence against women and gender discrimination are cast as a cultural problem, as distinctive marks of regional or national otherness to the 'universal' standard of gender relations. This construction, however, conceals the many marks of colonial, racial and gender-based structural marginalisation that have historically made Aboriginal women more vulnerable than other groups within Canadian society.

Neoliberal government cuts to social services and programmes have deepened Aboriginal women's structural inequality by making them even more vulnerable to violence from non-Aboriginal men and, related to this, vulnerable to involvement in the sex trade. At least three-quarters of Aboriginal women have been victims of family violence and the overall mortality rate due to violence is three times higher for Indigenous women than non-Indigenous women.[10] Government responses tend not to rectify these structural problems. Rather, efforts are oriented to policing, security and criminal-justice approaches, which target poor people, youth, sex-trade workers and substance users among others. In other words, efforts are aimed at targeting those living at the margins without questioning how these people came to live in that marginal space in the first place. Thus, rather than being 'impersonal', the state and the market become bearers of gender, race and class privileges.

The Canadian racialised gendered geography of development

As a settler society, Canada's political economy has been historically linked to the political economy of Aboriginal peoples. As Stephen Clarkson suggests, Canada's political, social and economic reality was part of globalisation trends even before they were noticeable elsewhere.[11] Although the internationalisation of Canada's economy has a long tradition, neo-liberal globalisation has changed rural landscapes, produced new regional discrepancies and reinforced old and new patterns of urbanisation and resource appropriation.

Canada's resource-based economy and international trade have depended upon the dispossession of Aboriginal land and resources. In the late nineteenth century, the government promoted a free-entry or open-access system, emphasising developers' and prospectors' rights and privileges. This system was characterised by its unrestrictive access to Crown minerals, free acquisition of title, the right to develop and mine and its disregard of other land-use priorities.[12] The timing, context and way in which Canada developed during its origins resulted in the establishment of treaties between some First Nations peoples and Euro-Canadians and, later, in the transformation of treaty relations into a relationship of domination. The free-entry system first appeared in British Columbia, where treaties were not generally established, and spread eastward.[13]

Since that time, the free-entry system took precedent over Aboriginal land claims and conservation planning. Through the 1960s and beyond, the scope and pace of global economic integration and the development of new technologies placed a renewed pressure on the search for energy and mining resources, a search which targeted untapped Aboriginal territories.[14] The federal and provincial governments supported these global economic trends by encouraging stake claims, surveys and occupation of Aboriginal lands for mineral and energy exploration and development. Since most Aboriginal lands were considered hinterland, much of this economic activity gave Indigenous peoples little or no benefit, thus contributing to a fundamental conflict between laws granting unrestricted access to land and the government's obligation to honour Aboriginal peoples' relationships to their lands. At both the national and international levels, the Inuit of the Arctic, the Dene of the Northwest Territories, the Indigenous peoples in the Yukon, the peoples of the northwest coast and the Cree of Quebec, among others, began to assert their territorial sovereignty and their right to self-determination by drawing attention to the negative impact of economic development on their traditional way of life. By the 1970s, Aboriginal territorial claims were one of the major political challenges confronting Canada's economic strategies.[15]

Pierre Elliott Trudeau's attempt to solve Aboriginal claims (1968–84) was shaped by a liberal conception of equality and individual rights.[16] From this perspective, Aboriginal poverty and marginalisation were considered to be the main issues, requiring a combination of economic development and inclusion into a citizenship regime. The 'Statement on Indian Policy', commonly known as the 'White Paper' 1969, was one of the cornerstones of this policy. It recommended parcelling out reserve lands on the basis of individual ownership and eliminating 'Indian status'. At the same time, the White Paper sought to eliminate obstacles to development and exploration of resources within Aboriginal regions, particularly the north. However, strong Indigenous mobilisation contributed to the withdrawal of this initiative. Aboriginal peoples mobilised on different fronts, such as the United Nations Working Group on Indigenous rights, the Supreme Court of Canada and the political arena, to claim nationhood and collective rights.

Starting in the early 1970s, various judicial decisions confirmed the existence of Aboriginal land title in Canada and helped to legitimise Aboriginal demands for self-determination and sovereignty. This newfound legitimacy, however, threatened Canada's right to access and develop Aboriginal lands and the 'right to explore' for minerals in much of this country's territory without Native consent.[17] Accordingly, developers and investors played a significant role in pressuring the government to seek a solution through the implementation of land-claim negotiations guaranteeing that economic development operations would be carried out with certainty and confidence within Aboriginal territories.[18] As a result, the Canadian government redefined its relationship with Aboriginal peoples by reproducing colonising practices within a decolonising framework. According to Bird Rose, complex and contradictory practices are included in land-claim processes.[19] On the one hand, land claims have the potential to reverse colonisation by recognising Aboriginal land title. On the other, by connecting land to development, land claims continue to legitimise resource appropriation and undermine Aboriginal land uses. Furthermore, by ignoring Aboriginal women's contribution to the local economies, land claims reproduce colonising practices and colonial constructions of women as being landless and domestically placed.

From this perspective, the most basic aspect of the land-claim negotiation has been the embrace of 'finality' or 'once and for all' settlements where claims are renounced in favour of a workable relationship between Aboriginal communities and the federal government. Certainly the principle of 'finality' responded to developers' needs but, at the same time, it positioned some Aboriginal leaders as economic players in the global market. Arguably, developers have influenced not only the Canadian government's decision to solve Aboriginal territorial claims but also how these claims have been addressed. In fact, Robert McPherson argues that whenever the government has become visibly motivated and more inclined to negotiate Aboriginal land claims, it has done so because development has been threatened or delayed.[20] Thus, a direct relationship exists between signing modern agreements and opening Aboriginal lands to development.

In the early 1990s, the Jean Chrétien government formalised this 'certainty policy' by openly linking the negotiation of modern agreements finalising land claims with the promotion of economic development. The implementation of this policy coincided with neo-liberal reform emphasising deregulation and devolution, as well as with the negotiation of economic agreements such as the North American Free Trade Agreement (NAFTA). The basic assumption behind this government policy was that development would provide new opportunities and jobs for Aboriginal peoples while removing their dependence on state programmes.[21] Accordingly, the self-sufficiency of Aboriginal peoples, as advanced through land-claim agreements, is dependent on the major commercial exploitation of natural resources and on emphasising self-government as a means of transmitting capitalist values to this population.[22]

Canada has invested major financial resources in the signing of these modern agreements with the intention of compensating Aboriginal peoples for the surrender of their lands and encouraging Aboriginal participation in the global economy. Nonetheless, the implementation of this particular certainty policy has neither benefited all Aboriginal peoples nor all members of Aboriginal communities. In fact, class stratification and social differentiation are adding tensions within Aboriginal communities. Because the scope of each agreement is determined, to a large extent, by the type of natural resources found within Indigenous territories and by investors' interests, these types of arrangements have been completed on a case-by-case basis, producing very different substantive outcomes.[23] Moreover, since government institutions tend to prioritise men's concerns and male-oriented large-scale natural-resource development activities, whenever treaties are negotiated women often get lesser benefits.

Although some Aboriginal peoples have entered into modern land claim negotiations, others are either still confronting Canadian ownership over what they consider to be their traditional lands or refusing to sign the agreement offered by the government. This situation continues to subsume the uneven and contradictory impacts of economic development among the different Aboriginal regions and to produce socially and spatially uneven processes. In many poor Aboriginal communities where the primary income comes from inadequate government transfers or the welfare state, any alternative offering an increased standard of living is likely to be welcome.

Under these circumstances, Aboriginal–state relations in Canada are based upon a hegemonic strategy replacing the Indian Act's coercive paternalistic relation with forms of neo-liberal Aboriginal self-governance aimed at inserting Indigenous peoples into the global economy. This model has exacerbated poverty, social and regional disparities, violence, internal migration and deepened the experience of racialised gender. With the Aboriginal elite controlling the economic benefits and the political agenda, little attention has been paid to pressing social issues such as alcoholism, domestic violence and the creation of mechanisms to provide Aboriginal women with the space and funding to create safety networks and articulate their concerns and knowledge.[24]

Aboriginal women and Harper's third way

In his final years as Prime Minister, Chrétien put forward an initiative that would further shape Aboriginal governance. The First Nations Governance Act (FNAG) focused on making Indigenous governance more accountable to both the community and the federal government. Once again, the chiefs opposed this policy because it violated the Aboriginal right to self-government. Their opposition was strong enough that Prime Minister Paul Martin was forced to withdraw the draft legislation. Instead he initiated high-profile meetings with Aboriginal organisations and provincial and territorial governments, which culminated in the First Ministers and National Aboriginal Leaders meeting in Kelowna in November 2005.

In the document entitled *First Ministers and National Aboriginal Leaders Strengthening Relations and Closing the Gap*, also known as the Kelowna Accord, all the negotiating parties agreed on the need to close the socio-economic gaps between Aboriginal and non-Aboriginal Canadians and to address discrimination against Aboriginal women. These parties acknowledged that in Canadian cities, half of all Aboriginal children are members of one-parent families, living in poverty and that some of the most devastating obstacles that have for far too long afflicted the lives of Aboriginal women, the lives of their children and the health of their communities, had to be addressed. The historical Kelowna Accord committed $5.1 billion dollars to Canada's Aboriginal population. The federal, provincial and Aboriginal organisations agreed on targeting areas such as education, health, housing, infrastructure and economic opportunities, which are critical to Indigenous peoples. In general, the agreement envisioned a large-scale investment in education targeted at Indigenous peoples and tailored to their specific linguistic and cultural characteristics. The Accord's ultimate goal was to combat poverty by increasing investment in human and social capital and promoting Aboriginal peoples' productive success in both market and non-market activities.[25] However, Prime Minister Martin was not in power long enough to implement the Accord.

While the neo-liberal model still positions the free market as the primary and most effective organising principle in society, it is now assumed that government intervention is necessary to direct the market forces to improve both economic and social outcomes.[26] In this new phase, duties are emphasised over rights assuming that all individuals must take responsibility in order to transform and enhance their economic competitiveness.[27]

During his campaign, Conservative Party candidate Stephen Harper noted that Aboriginal issues would become a priority for his government. Once elected, Harper has followed a path different from that of the Kelowna Accord. According to this government, the Kelowna Accord's emphasis on on-reserve Indigenous peoples does not make sense because half of the one million Canadians identified as Aboriginal in the 2001 Census live in urban settings. The Harper government has insisted on the need to realign federal Aboriginal expenditure and development and has moved away from gender and equality issues.

The election of the Conservative government in 2006 significantly shifted the terms of the Aboriginal policy debate in Canada. The Harper government represents not only a continuation of the market-based neo-liberal trajectory, but also a shift that will likely alter both the framework and nature of social policy discussions.[28] The Conservative agenda promotes a new type of social and economic order that implies not only the continuation of privatisation and market-oriented solutions, but also the promotion of certain ways of intruding into the lives of families and women. In terms of the Aboriginal policy, the two pillars of the Conservative government are economic development and human rights, while self-government has a lower profile.

The Conservative government Aboriginal policy focuses on strategies and programmes to alleviate Aboriginal poverty. Such strategies are grounded in 'common sense' and the acceptance of everyone's responsibility. Under this policy, *everyone* involved must accept responsibility and get equally involved. Unlike other governments, the Harper government has stated that a new relationship between Aboriginal peoples and the government is unnecessary, for all that is needed is to make the existing relationship work. The government's commitment to Aboriginal peoples focuses on empowering Indigenous citizens while protecting the vulnerable.[29] To the Harper government, the extension of the Human Rights Act to the Indian Act aims at protecting Aboriginal Canadians, particularly women. However, extending the Human Rights Act to Aboriginal peoples has been extremely controversial. While it has been acknowledged that the Act has a role to play in the advancement of the human rights of Aboriginal women, this Act should not be constructed as abrogating Aboriginal collective rights.[30]

Ironically, under the Harper government, the word 'equality' has become obsolete. This government decided that organisations would no longer be eligible for funding for advocacy, government lobbying or research projects. As part of the new terms and conditions, the Status of Women Canada eliminated 'equality' from its mandate. These decisions have important implications for all women but particularly for Aboriginal women. Pay inequity is still the rule. Women still make only 71 cents for every dollar earned by a man and Aboriginal women only 46 cents. While 0.67 per cent of non-Aboriginal children need child welfare, 3.31 of Métis children and 10.23 per cent of status Indian children receive welfare.[31]

Government cuts to programmes have also limited women's resources. For close to twenty years, First Nations women have fought to reverse sex discrimination in the Indian Act and to restore equal Indian status to First Nations women and their descendants. In 2007, in a case brought forward by Sharon McIvor dealing with gender discrimination, the Court ordered the federal government to remove any trace of gender discrimination from the Indian Act. The government decided to appeal this ruling and eliminated funding for the Court Challenges programme, which would have financially assisted McIvor in taking her case forward once again.[32] This government's actions seem to contradict the arguments used to advance the Human Rights Act. While the Human Rights Act is envisioned to enable Aboriginal women to challenge Aboriginal governments, the elimination of funding for the Court Challenges programme prevents these same women from challenging federal government legislation and policies. In other words, the government promotes equality at the Aboriginal nation level but undermines equality at the national state level suggesting once again that gender discrimination and inequalities exist within Aboriginal communities.

This situation not only exarcerbates the challenges Indigenous women face within their communities, but also perpetuates the widespread mistreatment of Aboriginal women, who seek to secure the same rights as those of other women. Since 1986, matrimonial property rights have been another important yet controversial issue in what has been constructed as 'Indigenous gender war', when the Supreme

Court of Canada ruled that provincial and territorial laws on matrimonial real property (MRP) do not apply to reserve land. This decision created a gap in the law that has had serious consequences for Aboriginal women.

The Native Women Association of Canada report on matrimonial property rights showed that women do experience greater disadvantages and are allocated less property title than men. The study also showed that a greater percentage of Aboriginal women live off-reserve and that the differences between on- and off-reserve suggest that matrimonial real property has an uneven impact on where a child resides. While the report acknowledged that matrimonial property rights would greatly benefit women, the report was careful to emphasise a more holistic approach for dealing with women's rights.[33] The document also stated that solutions must be found that are based on Indigenous peoples' traditions, that accommodate human rights and that acknowledge the traditionally strong role of First Nations women in their communities.

The federal government's goal of privatising property on reserves, so that valuable property can be sold, mortgaged or be used to fight poverty, is implicitly linked to the issue of matrimonial state property.[34] Similarly, the government response to the Seventh Report of the Standing Committee on Aboriginal Affairs and Northern Development on Aboriginal Housing was that structural reforms are needed to address the housing needs of Aboriginal peoples through the promotion of market-based housing including individual ownership and private rental housing.[35]

This suggestion seems to take the Land Use Management Act a step forward by transforming land into commodity property and questioning Indigenous peoples' connections to the land in the name of a better future. Battles for individual land ownership and matrimonial property rights are seen as strategies women have adopted to claim rights to land. Because Indigenous women's ties to land have been mediated by the Canadian state and women's relationship with men in patriarchal society, Indigenous women's attempts to assert their rights are often internally perceived as an attempt to disrupt gender relations. Ironically, Aboriginal women's actions are externally perceived as a liberating battle against the backwardness of their cultures. Thus, state intervention into Aboriginal affairs aims at rescuing the Aboriginal woman from her people. Like race, culture can also be used to conceal the structural sources of discrimination against Indigenous women.

The tensions around collective/individual rights/women's rights/self-government show that Aboriginal women's rights are still far from being realised and that gender discrimination within Indigenous communities, while real, is constructed as an anomaly inherent to Aboriginal cultures. Therefore, human rights discourses disguise the role that the state has played in creating and perpetuating the exclusion of Aboriginal women from both national state and Indigenous citizenship. Government policies aimed at reversing these discriminatory conditions justify interfering with self-government, on the grounds of rescuing women from their own culture and people. The manipulation of semantics erases the historical and structural marginalisation of Aboriginal peoples, which arose from colonial power relations and continues to favour the dominant society.[36]

Several studies have shown that despite the implementation of different partial Aboriginal policies, the conditions of life within Indigenous communities have not changed and will not change without a long-term policy.[37] Indigenous organisations have produced their own reports emphasising the urgent need for action. The Solving Poverty Report 2007 advises the federal government on the cornerstones of a workable, national strategy for solving poverty, a strategy that should be connected to larger economic, social and political issues. In particular, the report warns that factors such as racism and gender discrimination, which put Aboriginal women, men and children at greater risk than others, must be addressed. The elimination of the equality mandate and cuts to housing and health care have worsened the conditions of life of Aboriginal women overall. The First Nations campaign to make poverty history and to create new opportunities demands that the government act to remedy the disadvantages, discrimination and poverty facing Aboriginal women beyond Indigenous communities.

This campaign also emphasised that Aboriginal peoples are diverse, so policies aimed at addressing barriers must also be diverse. Despite racial prejudice, off-reserve Aboriginals have significantly higher employment rates, incomes and education levels than on-reserve Aboriginals. The urban population is increasing, posing a challenge to the delivery of social services. Currently, Aboriginal people are receiving services from three orders of governments: federal, provincial and band-based. The tensions between the commitment to Aboriginal self-government and the rhetoric of constrained spending imply that Canadians perceive that culturally-based Aboriginal services are beneficial but also a financial burden, particularly when Aboriginal populations are described as growing at twice the rate of the Canadian population,[38] and Aboriginal women are constructed as empowered citizens and yet as victim subjects. These racialised constructions have shaped a contradictory dynamic where recognition of Aboriginal women's rights is articulated only at the Indigenous-nation level while their citizenship rights at the nation-state level remains limited.

Conclusions

Government policies are inextricably linked to the dominant ideology. The assumed neutrality of white Canadian values has led to the implementation of neo-liberal Aboriginal policies and modes of service delivery that have praised efficiency and accountability, but have been of limited effectiveness for Aboriginal peoples, particularly women. Intertwined with explicit resistance to Indigenous entitlements, Aboriginal policies construct Indigenous peoples as a policy issue, not as knowing subjects, Indigenous women as victim subjects and not as agents, and their socio-economic, racial and political conditions as social cultural problems to be solved. From this perspective, neo-liberal Aboriginal policies reproduce colonial racialised constructions of the victim subject, who remains on the margins of citizenship and waits for the state to rescue her. Furthermore, while these policies are constructed as a way to reverse colonialism and gender discrimination, they are pillars of a neo-liberal economic project that rest on racial and gender inequalities.

CHAPTER THIRTEEN

A Genealogy of Indigenous Resistance

Brendan Hokowhitu

> *We have, as a people, never felt more let down, more insecure and more economically and socially deprived ... we will no longer tolerate policies which take no account of our language, customs and lifestyles, nor will we accept being governed or administered by anyone who does not understand the way we think.*
> Matiu Rata, 1979[1]

This chapter asks how do we explain the continued subjugation of Indigenous peoples given their ubiquitous relationship to resistance? Is the colonial condition perpetual or, reframed, have the commonly held modes of Indigenous resistance become futile? I also seek to problematise the common discourses underpinning Indigenous resistance and, therefore, the basic tenets by which Indigenous identity has come to be marked. For instance, according to Gerald Alfred, 'It has been said that being born Indian is being born into politics. I believe this to be true; because being born a Mohawk of Kahnawake, I do not remember a time free from the impact of political conflict'.[2] Perhaps the 'facticity' of the matter (i.e., the situation colonised Indigenous peoples face) imposes the colonial condition upon us, but certainly I desire for myself and my children a future where entry into political conflict is a choice, not a pre-ordainment.

Thirty years prior to the publication of this collection, due to his disenchantment with his party's Indigenous policies, Matiu Rata delivered the impassioned speech that begins this chapter upon resignation from the New Zealand Labour Party. Subsequently, Rata formed a breakaway political party named 'Mana Motuhake'. Twenty-five years after Rata's resignation, New Zealand Labour Party Minister Tariana Turia resigned from her party in protest over the legalisation of an act that further debilitated Indigenous rights. Subsequently, Turia led the largest ever *hīkoi* (political protest march) in New Zealand history, culminating with her formation of the Māori Party on 7 July 2004 on the steps of Parliament Buildings in Wellington.

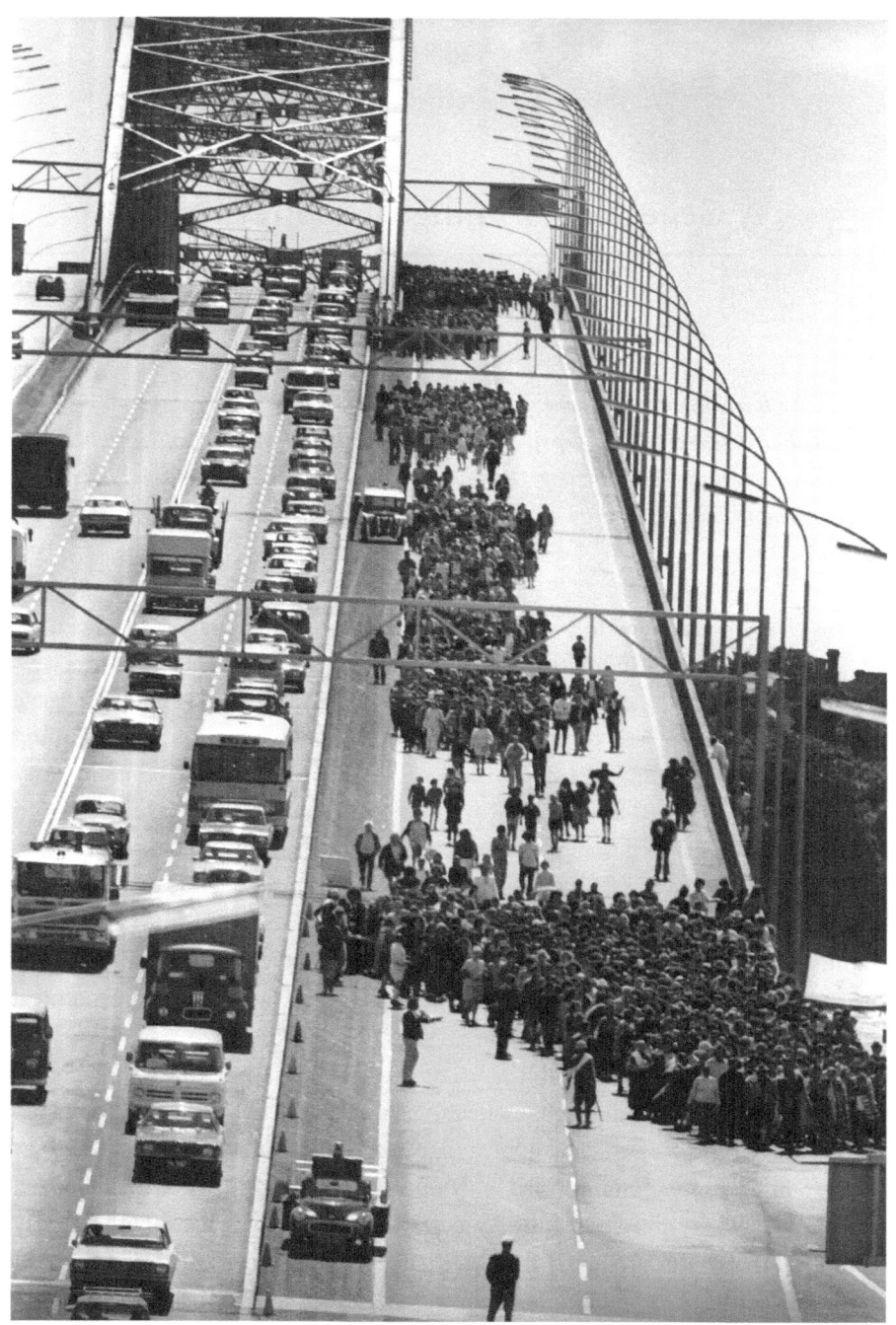

Land march 1975. New Zealand Herald, March 1975

Nearly three decades prior to the 2004 *hīkoi*, the '1975 Land March' began on 13 September 1975 at Spirits Bay, and it has since become the enduring face of Indigenous resistance in New Zealand. The 1975 Land March, like the 2004 *hīkoi*, eventuated in the 'far north' (top of New Zealand's North Island), marched the length of the North Island to Parliament Buildings in Wellington and was led by a prominent Māori woman activist, Whina Cooper. The Land March acted as a buttress to Māori resistance, under the banner 'Not one more acre of Māori land to be surrendered to the Pākehā'.[3] The banner originated seventy years prior in 1905, as a reaction to what Indigenous peoples referred to as 'Ture Kōhuru-tangata' or 'Confiscatory Act'. Officially named the Māori Land Settlement Act, it prompted the Reverend Rewiti Kohere to state in an editorial of the Māori language newspaper *Te Pipiwharauroa*: 'The Act for the compulsory taking of [Indigenous] lands has been passed into law; but before a single acre has been confiscated under this Act, let the voice of the conference of tribes be heard. Let the Government hear, so that they may be afraid to forcibly lay hands on the land'.[4]

This brief account of the historical connections between salient moments of Indigenous resistance in New Zealand should not bring comfort that the oppositional will of a people has temporal continuance. It seems to me that whilst the Indigenous peoples of New Zealand have constantly resisted colonisation, employing and re-employing the same tactics like 'land marches' and 'occupations', the colonial power structures are in constant mutation. Accordingly, methods of resistance must also change and anticipate change. Take, for instance, the iconisation of the 1975 Land March and its subsequent re-enactments in 1984, 2004 (following the Foreshore and Seabed travesty) and 2007 (following the 15 October 'Terror Raids'). The month-long march in 1975 gained significant media coverage, rupturing the narrative of an abiding Indigenous citizenry, whilst mobilising and giving a united voice to Māori resistance. Yet the most recent marches were void of such resonance, appearing at times as if resistance had become like 'a Sunday walk in the park', where the liberally politically inclined rallied, not in radical resistance, but in 'chic opposition', seen in the symbols of stylised counterculture such as the hip 'Che Guevara t-shirt'. In Hawai'i, 'Da Hui' was formed by a group of surfers in resistance to the neo-colonisation of their famous North Shore surf-breaks and lack of respect shown by surfers from Australia, South Africa and mainland United States, especially. At one time the Da Hui symbol of a simple stick figure riding a surfboard represented a threat to neocolonialism, yet today it can be seen on the t-shirts of tourists on Waikiki Beach. Over the past forty to fifty years, neocolonial power has come to recognise, commodify and thus capture forms and icons of resistance, rendering them meaningless and impotent, smothering their original radical intent.

Beyond its commodification, the mere fact that Indigenous resistance is in repetition (i.e., its intergenerational duplication) should not be cause for celebration under the latest banner of the most recent *hīkoi*; it should be of deep concern. Yet, seemingly unproblematically, the title of Ranginui Walker's seminal text, *Ka Whawhai Tonu Matou: Struggle Without End*, frames Indigenous resistance in relation to an eternal defiance to an omnipresent coloniser. As this chapter will point out, since the advent of the revolution against the dominant culture of white heterosexual patriarchy in the late 1960s, Indigenous people have taken part in the global social movement by largely writing on the history of oppression, ostensibly at the expense of theorising their existentiality.

This chapter conceptually traces a genealogy of Indigenous resistance in relation to the formation of Indigenous identity, especially as it has played out in New Zealand. It does not, however, pretend to provide an exhaustive account of Indigenous resistance, for that account would be too diverse and extensive. Employing an existentialist lens, it theorises and problematises the very concept of 'Indigenous resistance' and why 'being born Indian', for instance, has come to signify 'being born into politics'. The tethering of Indigenous identities to a colonised/coloniser dialectic of resistance becomes dubious when Indigenous forms of self-governance are produced only in relation to liberation from colonisation (i.e., 'decolonisation'). In other words, Indigenous existentialism has become bound by its relationship to an (imaginary or otherwise) oppressive other.

As this chapter points out, Indigenous resistance has internalised the colonial and neocolonial state, the past and continued trauma of colonisation and, hence, the 'psychology' of colonisation, leading to the commonly heard idiom on the Indigenous academic circuit, 'decolonising the mind'. Such analyses are alluring within a mentality of guilt where responsibility for one's own condition is passed to another. Yet, as I argue, recourses based on such *ressentiment* are no longer effective. The assertion of Indigenous self-determination in constant referral to the colonising other merely serves to re-establish the neo-imperial colonial power structures themselves.

Resistance

> *Be swift to act; should you delay you will fall beneath the blows of the Pakeha. The cautious war party first builds its entrenchments.*
> Reverend Rewiti Kohere[5]

The quote above encourages swift caution. In the context of contemporary resistance, I take it to mean diligence in understanding the Indigenous condition, as opposed to repeating action for action's sake. Most pressingly, I am wary that Indigenous peoples are yet to take responsibility for their facticity. Indeed, I contend that the way Indigenous people have approached the colonial past, the present neocolonial condition and the future, has lacked the responsibility needed to transcend self-imposed limitations. The following genealogy argues that the formation of the coloniser-as-oppressor should not and cannot constitute an organic precursor to Indigenous resistance itself. We should recognise instead that the vilification of the coloniser resulted from historically contingent circumstance and although it served the useful function of mobilising Indigenous activist movements it has superseded its intent and thus its teleological function. As a consequence, Indigenous resistance can be seen in the commodified voice of 'chic opposition', which only serves to inhibit Indigenous responsibility, freedom and choice.

In this chapter, the term 'genealogy' is understood through a Foucauldian sense. Like Michel Foucault, I am interested in the historical relationship between power, knowledge and truth. In much of Foucault's writings he follows Nietzsche's methodology of genealogy, examining how knowledge and truth emerge as universal and objective, whereas in fact they merely reflect the product of the struggles between ideas, typically claimed and disclaimed within institutions. I am interested, then, in analysing how Indigenous people have framed resistance, how such resistance has come to be thought of as 'natural', how such framing of Indigenous resistance enables it to fall prey to the very power structures it is attempting to resist and, indeed, how resistance has come to be naturalised as fundamental to Indigenous identity and how Indigenous methods of resistance are re-established as 'truthful'. The notions 'Nationalism', 'Traditions and Cultural Authenticity', 'Rights' and 'Occupation' I use to create this genealogy cannot be read as exhaustive. Yet, to me at least, they stand out as indicative of how Indigenous people have come to frame their resistance and, in doing so, have limited the conditions of possibility through which 'freedom' can be recognised.

Nationalism

To paraphrase Benedict Anderson, in the colonised world every indigene 'can, should, will, "have" a nationality, as he or she "has" a gender'.[6] And, indeed Anderson was correct in intimating that while nationalism is not 'natural' per se, discrete groups (including Indigenous peoples) increasingly thought of 'the nation' as a natural progression in resistance to the colonial state. According to Manuel Castells, a distinction is to be made between 'the nation' and 'the state': 'the nation is a group of people who share a collective identity, centered on language and culture, rather than territorial groupings within a geographic location bounded by recognised borders'.[7] Yet such conglomerations are inauthentic prepositions to resistance, especially where 'nation', 'tradition' and 'resistance' intertwine to form an Indigenous national identity, that is, where identity is tethered to exclusion, duality, hierarchy and opposition.

While Māori, for example, seldom speak of a 'Māori nation', culturally identifying as 'Māori' in itself refers to an allegiance to a centralised national identity (as opposed to allegiances organised around familial hierarchies). Whilst pragmatic, such self-definition was/is 'inauthentic', meaning the decision to self-identify with a developing sense of Māori nationalism reflected weight of circumstance and the growing cultural power of the colonial state as opposed to an authentic choice. That is, Māori solidarity arose because of an encroaching imperialism. Walker argues in this context that 'Māori opposition to the endless stream of settlers crystallised around an emerging sense of Māori nationalism'.[8]

Forms of Māori nationalism had been discussed since the 1830s (e.g. 'Kīngitanga' [Māori King movement] in the 1850s and 'Kotahitanga' [one-people, unity] in the 1890s), resurfacing into prominence three quarters of a century later in April 1907 when 3,000 Indigenous people assembled at Waahi (Huntly), to discuss 'the sufferings through injustices of the people of the Island of Aotearoa and Waipounamu'.[9] The meeting resolved:

> We, the representative rangatiras [sic] [chief, leader] and delegates of all the tribes scattered throughout the length and breadth of Aotearoa and Waipounamu, do hereby agree to unite in one confederated body, so that this union will include all members of the native race; and that we pledge ourselves to maintain and uphold all the rights and privileges enjoyed by our race in the year 1834, signalised by the flag of 1836 and maintained until the enactment of the New Zealand Constitution Act of 1852.[10]

Although couched in different discourses, the already mentioned breakaway political parties, Mana Motuhake and the Māori Party, had similar nationalistic intent, namely, to unify Indigenous peoples in order to gain political credence.

Future permutations of Indigenous resistance bound Indigenous identity through nation and political resistance to colonial threat and neocolonial power. The burgeoning nationalistic Māori identity came to view itself as 'one culture' in resistance to and in dual consciousness with its other, the Pākehā colonist and oppressor. Thenceforth, when Māori (as a political polity) have been mobilised they have done so in resistance to that other who lies both outside and within their colonial consciousness. For instance, Walker contends that as a consequence of the 1975 Land March, 'Māori people throughout the land were politicised in a unity of purpose to a level unprecedented in modern times, in the endless struggle against colonisation'.[11] Nearly a decade later, 'the political significance' of the 1984 *hīkoi* 'lay in its deep, spiritual sense of unity … it brought together a wide spectrum of people under a common cause, to stop the celebration of a treaty [the Treaty of Waitangi] that had been dishonoured by the coloniser'.[12] As a caveat, it must be pointed out that the inauthenticity of Indigenous nationalistic solidarity has been criticised by Māori since its inception. In New Zealand, the 1850s Kīngitanga movement was resisted by many *iwi* who chose, even under the pressure of imperialism, distinct *iwi* identity over amalgamation.

Today, the omnipresence of 'Māori' as a marker of identity and thus its epistemic acceptance has become so conventional that Indigenous people of New Zealand seldom conceptualise its inauthenticity. One challenger, Evan Poata-Smith, framed by a Marxist critique, demystifies the unifying project:

> There has been a tendency to present the interests of Māori in contemporary capitalist society as essentially unitary. The notion that all Māori share an overpowering and innate attachment based on blood, culture and language has underpinned cultural nationalist political ideology and practice, which emphasises the fundamental commonality of Māori interests in contemporary capitalist society.[13]

She further argues that 'Despite the fact that all Māori clearly do not share the same experiences of inequality, the existence of antagonistic class interests within Māori communities is routinely disregarded or ignored'.[14] First and foremost then, the term 'Māori' and its implication of nationalistic culture and identity must be problematised, *especially* in relation to resistance.

Tradition and cultural authenticity

Tied to the duality of consciousness briefly introduced above is the inauthentic repatriation of pre-colonised culture. In *The Genealogy of Morals*,[15] Friedrich Nietzsche discussed how Christian slaves in *ressentiment* of the power the Romans held over them manufactured the Christian religion to gain power over their Roman captors by repositioning the tenets of Roman power as 'evil', creating a morality in opposition to this power as 'good', thus gaining the 'moral high-ground'. While situationally effective, ultimately the morality created was birthed out of fear and hatred and, consequently, was 'inauthentic'. This led Nietzsche to announce the teleological 'Death of God', arguing that religion had outlived its use and had become a hindering custom.

A similar process has, I suggest, taken place in the renaissance of Indigenous cultures, where the tyranny of the coloniser has been positioned in opposition to the purity and authenticity of Indigenous culture in order to gain the moral high ground. Again, this is a useful strategy but an inauthentic one and, ultimately, a will to power that Indigenous people must declare and discard so as to effect their existential being. In saying this, the facticity of the matter should not be treated insipidly. The search for Indigenous cultural security eventuated out of extreme structural oppression. Indeed, like Christianity, the search and desire for classical Indigenous culture was necessitated by the cultural insecurity, the unprincipled, immoral, unethical, anarchical cultural void left in colonisation's wake. Unmistakably then, a sense of loss and a desire for origin was colonisation's etching on the Indigenous psyche.

The glue of Indigenous identity markers such as land, language and culture has, as a consequence, bound Indigenous resistance movements: 'For Maori people ... the cultural institutions which encouraged oral debate and the sense of injustice which fuelled the debates made politics the basis of everyday life'.[16] Movements based on Indigenous peoples' inimitable rights to land and civil liberties such as the right to speak Indigenous languages and perform Indigenous cultures are/were inherently intermixed with Indigenous identities and opposition. Accordingly, postcolonial Indigenous identities are/were made distinct by their constitutional opposition to the annexation and subjugation of their unique lands and cultures. As Clea Te Kawehau Hoskins critically points out:

> Te Reo and tikanga are understood by Māori as central to any meaningful reclamation and reconstruction of a distinct and *authentic* identity ... they are recognised (especially Te Reo) as a largely unpolluted source of insight

and knowledge into the thinking/worldview of our tupuna [forebears] and, therefore, to a time and knowledge base understood by the forces of colonialism. [From here] we can retrieve and reconstruct an *authentic* Māori identity/ies and cultural life. [*Emphasis added*] [17]

In other words, the renaissance of classical (i.e., 'pre-colonial') Indigenous culture involved the inauthentic search for a pre-colonial authentic culture and reconstruction of pre-colonial Indigenous language and culture as 'unpolluted', as 'pure', as 'traditional'.

This is not to criticise the practising of Indigenous culture, merely rather to argue that when contemporary culture is reframed in terms of the renaissance of classical practices lost due to colonisation and where this supposed cultural renaissance is underpinned by an inherent resistance to the dominant colonial ideology, then Indigenous people lose their existential self: the immediacy of just being, of living, of doing. In the search for a 'pure' past, Indigenous peoples devalue the possibility of living in and for the present. In this search, Indigenous peoples' reactions to colonisation have disfigured the complexity of Indigenous existentialism. Indigenous people must position their 'being' from a more authentic source, in cognisance that Indigenous cultures were never in stasis.

The ontological blunder of divorcing what it means to be Indigenous from the present and the idealism we locate in the 'pure past' limits how we conceive of ourselves experiencing and determining the immediacy of culture. Likewise, the production of decolonial theory in its very nomenclature demands an understanding of the philosophies and history of the colonists in order to understand the genealogy of power in the colonial context. Accordingly, decolonial theory has developed as *re*-scholarship where alternative knowledges are *re*-inserted into text so that Indigenous people can deconstruct occidental history to produce alternative histories. For instance, Linda Tuhiwai Smith argues, 'Transforming our colonised views of our own history (as written by the West) ... requires us to revisit, site by site, our history under Western eyes. This in turn requires a theory or approach, which helps us to engage with, understand and then act upon history'.[18] A worthy project, yet we must at least question the semantics of the project of 'decolonisation'; what does that actually mean and, if we could ever define it, is it actually possible? I suggest a more worthy project is one of Indigenous existentialism, including discussions surrounding the immediacy of Indigenous culture and the stirring forms of cultural expression that occur at cultural borders.

Essential to the promotion of Indigenous existentialism will be the customary incorporation of cultural critique, so that the commonly held discourses surrounding Indigenous culture, such as 'tradition' and 'authenticity' can be dislodged. Below, Hoskins challenges the status quo:

> Because this knowledge is sourced in a world and time we know little about, we feel almost completely unable to be critical of it. Rather we tend to accept and take up uncritically such discourses, placing our trust in those keepers and interpreters of what is promoted as 'authentic' genuine Māori knowledge, practice and thought.[19]

Moreover, the repositioning of Indigenous culture as morally superior creates a hierarchical discourse within Indigenous cultures, where some Indigenous people are positioned as more 'authentic' than others. Here we need to be mindful of Cornell West's words: 'One crucial lesson ... remains the manner in which most Third World authoritarian bureaucratic elites deploy essentialist rhetoric about "homogenous national communities" and "positive images" in order to repress and regiment their diverse and heterogeneous populations'.[20] And here I am reminded of Nietzsche's reproach to religion. Seemingly at times the *de rigueur* of neocolonial Indigenous cultures is advocated with religious, dogmatic and moralistic zeal based on an inauthentic tradition that now serves to limit and exclude.

Resistance through 'rights'

> *The attitudes of the Maori mind towards the new conceptions of sovereignty, personified by the Queen, Government, as embodied in the Governor and his officials, the ownership of land according to custom and usage as guaranteed by the Treaty and finally, towards the abstract idea of legal equality with the representatives of the new culture, is a subject well worth the attention of the ethnologist.*
> Sir Apirana Ngata[21]

Critical analyses of how Indigenous people take up notions of resistance from general discourses are essential in terms of teleological function. The above quote is telling because it speaks of a context (in the early twentieth century) where power remained personified for Indigenous people, where sovereign power materialised locally in colonial representatives and Indigenous leaders themselves, where from an Indigenous New Zealander's perspective, power remained interpreted in terms of personal *mana*. Conversely, today the same nominal notion of 'sovereignty' has transformed to mean 'rights based on group membership' or 'a society of individuals who collectively constitute a de facto sovereign authority'.[22] For Indigenous New Zealanders, argues Aroha Harris, 'tino rangatiratanga' (the sovereignty of chiefs, used now to describe autonomy or self-government for Māori in Aotearoa) has become the catch-cry for Māori rights, which embraced 'both positive action towards a shared goal and active resistance to State goals'.[23]

Indigenous resistance, therefore, has not been immune to global discourses. In the 1970s New Zealand context, Walker refers to the 'new wave' of Indigenous resistors as 'Neo-Maori Activists' who formed, in overlapping collections, groups such as Ngā Tamatoa, Waitangi Action Committee (WAC), He Taua, Māori People's Liberation Movement of Aotearoa and Black Women. 'The political ethos of the groups was based on the liberation struggle against racism, sexism, capitalism and government oppression' [24] In other words, Indigenous resistance movements aligned with the 'equal-rights' and/or 'consciousness-raising' discourses of the 1960s and 70s. Here it is important to note that the face of the vanguard of Indigenous politics had changed in New Zealand. As Harris points out, 'Ngā Tamatoa was the progenitor of a Māori movement that would eventually comprise a potent collection of Māori protest groups and individuals: politically conscious, radical and unwaveringly committed to the pursuit of tino rangatiratanga'.[25]

> Members were young, educated and urbanised ... They were leaders and social commentators recently come-of-age, the new face of Māori activism ... Ngā Tamatoa also heralded a new analysis of the Māori experience of colonisation; one that understood racism and how it worked ... [challenging but not replacing the old-guard] to face new choices and strategies for articulating Māori grievances and engaging with State. The things that distinguished the modern activists from the conservatives of old were more a matter of means than ends.[26]

It is important to note the paradigmatic shift: the concept of Indigenous resistance was no longer epistemically driven by Indigenous worldviews, but rather driven by the concept of 'individual rights', which at its nucleus is/was occidental, as explained by David Theo Goldberg:

> ... fundamental to the self-conception of the emergent possessive individualism of bourgeois culture, the concepts of rights has come to assume central importance in moral, political and legal vocabulary ... we have come this century to conceive all human beings as bearing the inalienable – the natural or human – right to choose individually and equally how to lead

A Genealogy of Indigenous Resistance : 217

their own atomic lives without disadvantaging anyone else (and so violating their rights). A right, then, is understood minimally as the conjunction of the freedom to do whatever one chooses and the claim to be protected from interference by others ... each individual is taken equally as occupying a domain of sovereign autonomy free from trespass or transgression by others.[27]

As with women's, sexual and race-based liberation movements, Indigenous groups have rallied around the cry for 'equal rights'. These social movements, according to Kate Nash, challenged 'the grounds that only those who conform to the norm of the white, heterosexual male head of household actually enjoy full citizenship rights'.[28] Although this broader challenge was important and necessary, arguably the only real significant power shift it effected was for upper middle-class white women and gay white men who, after all, were sons and daughters of colonists and slave-owners. Of more relevance is the apparent void that lies between authentic Indigenous resistance and Western 'rights' discourses. In other words, why would Indigenous groups even need to claim equal rights if the Western democratic colonial state was actually achieving its basic tenets?

Through colonisation many Indigenous peoples have come to understand 'equal rights' as the morals they live by, as the code that governs their lives and, thus, as the rules that underpin their resistance. Yet, these morals do not reside beyond good and evil, they have clearly not transcended the power structures maintained beyond their perimeters. Equal rights discourses are subjectively constructed moral structures maintained by the powerful to preserve their power. That is, as Goldberg argues, the democratic process of equal rights has been constructed as inalienably 'natural or human' and beyond power, beyond the very constructs that underpin dictums of power such as gender, sexuality, class, race and indigeneity. Goldberg conceives of the notion of 'rights' as a value-laden social contract, only acting in accordance to predetermined denominations based on group membership located within the power structures themselves, which lie 'outside the law':

> Rights assertion, accordingly, has come to refract these social identities, delimiting certain others as "extrinsic" to rights entitlement. The objects of the contractual arrangement, those excluded from this contract or from contracting as such, have no rights. Subjects assume value, then, only in so far as they are bearers of rights; and they are properly vested with rights only in so far as they are imbued with value. The rights others as a matter of course

enjoy are yet denied people of colour because black, brown, red and yellow subjectivities continue to be disvalued ... In literally being outside the law, the rights to which one might appeal are erased.[29]

Goldberg highlights that the construction of rights discourses 'effectively excludes only explicit and intentional discrimination. It fails to recognize structural forms of discrimination or (unintended) patterns of exclusion'.[30]

For Indigenous peoples however, deconstructing resistance through rights (i.e., the 'fight for rights') is a more relevant concept than the idea of 'discrimination'. In arguing for 'Indigenous rights', Indigenous activists set off three processes that serve to perpetuate oppression. First, 'rights' reifies that the moral code will actually provide what it says it provides – that it is indeed transcendental – when in truth the moral code of equal rights is a will to power. The formation of Indigenous resistance through recourses to 'rights' adheres to their construction as objective and unsullied by power and to their construction as morals that reside beyond good and evil. Second, the location of Indigenous resistance within the conceptual space of 'rights', that is, within the natural, blind law of all humans, means transgressions can be processed 'objectively', with no sense of privilege. Indigenous resistance based on epistemic claims to difference through rights discourses can be claimed to be 'unnatural' and thus, illegal, especially where claims are reconstructed as 'interference' upon the rights of others. Indigenous rights are permitted as long as they do not interfere with the privileged rights of the powerful, if not, such claims are easily reconstituted as 'greedy' and 'separatist'.

Thirdly, Indigenous rights entrust the concealed room of 'blind justice', enabling the shadow puppet judge to report 'yes', when in truth beyond this room, power's discursiveness constantly says 'no'. Pursuing Indigenous resistance through rights is ultimately un-transformative, whilst colonial power remains unscathed. The Western conception of individual 'man' interprets the self-determination of others (i.e., Indigenous peoples) to be an encroachment upon the rights of the Western individual, where rights are conceived of as finite; the gaining of Indigenous rights thus necessarily produces a trespass upon non-Indigenous rights. For, in the end, the alignment with a human rights discourse precedes the denial of epistemic difference and, accordingly, reinstates the dominant belief of a universal worldview; a will to power that reasserts power's status quo. In this context, Foucault's 'death of man', where he claims the very concept 'man' was the creation of a unique set of historical contingencies, is important to reconsider when reformulating Indigenous resistance.[31] Within rights discourses, Man, to paraphrase Foucault, as a self-contained rational agent who maintains an autonomous sovereign space free from trespass or transgression by others, needs to be properly understood as a subjective construction if Indigenous peoples are to move beyond good and evil, that is, to find paths beyond rights discourses where epistemic difference becomes a choice.

'Occupation'

> ... *hostile to the past, impatient of the present and cheated of the future, we were much like those whom men's justice or hatred forces to live behind prison bars.*
> *The Plague*, Albert Camus[32]

Albert Camus' *The Plague* metaphorically describes the people of Paris under German occupation as located within a plague-ridden quarantined city. Camus' existential critique points out, first, that peoples' consciousness and beliefs surrounding the situation they find themselves in determines how they conceptualise the past, present and future and, second, that it is a choice to view one's facticity in such limited terms. Camus refers to occupation in terms of peoples' perceptions of possibility as opposed to the enforced plague upon the city itself. In the colonial context, Camus' existentialism lends a lens for how we can interpret colonised 'consciousness'. How have colonised Indigenous peoples come to locate their past, present and future in terms of an identity tethered to the colonial context and, more specifically, colonial resistance? Have we romanticised a past of pure origins temporally located by the rupture of colonial invasion? Are we anxiety-ridden about our present in seeking a pure past and in comparison with our invading Other? And do we feel cheated or resigned to a future that ties our identities infinitely to 'a struggle without end'?

In deciphering what occupies the mind of the colonised, it is important to note that one prevalent form of Indigenous resistance is 'occupation' itself. For New Zealand's Indigenous populations, whilst there have been many 'occupations', the one that remains enduring to modern consciousness, the one that occupies our thoughts, is 'Bastion Point', where after a prolonged period of political stasis and 'being occupied', Ngāti Whatua o Orakei and others led by Joe Hawke repossessed their lands: 'On 25 May 1978, after 506 days of *occupation*, 600 police officers, supported by the New Zealand Army, arrested 222 protesters for willful trespass on Crown land. The use of army and police ordered by Prime Minister Robert Muldoon received dramatic media attention, which reverberated through the country [*emphasis added*].'[33] Interestingly, in a book called *The Waitangi Tribunal: The Conscience of a Nation*, Paul Temm notes: 'The "occupation" of Bastion Point by the protesters, from 1976 to 1978, was the first time any part of the tribe had stepped outside the law'.[34]

The case of Bastion Point engenders three ideas. First, the actions of the 1975 land march protesters and the rebel occupants of Bastion Point were contemporaneously necessary to rupture the colonial narrative. Second, nomenclature such as 'occupation' and 'attack' framed the resistance. Third and in relation to this last point, the lasting image of Bastion Point is of Māori versus Pākehā-as-state. In short, the consciousness of New Zealand's modern Indigenous peoples re-insisted on a dual consciousness initiated by colonisation itself, as pointed out by Tuhiwai Smith:

> Under European imperialism indigenous peoples were positioned within new political formations which ruptured previous relations, strategic alliances, trade routes and ways of communicating with other indigenous nations. The assertion of European sovereignty over indigenous peoples effectively shifted the focus of indigenous international relations to a colonizer/colonized relationship.[35]

The conscious displacement from a largely genealogically defined episteme to one initially conceived in racially dichotomous terms led New Zealand's Indigenous population to view themselves as Māori in opposition to their Other, Pākehā. At a *hui* of chiefs in 1857, Māori disgust with early settler behaviour led the famous chief Te Heuheu of Ngāti Tuwharetoa to suggest 'reason for separation of the races'.[36]

The duality of Indigenous post-colonised consciousness, as analysed by theorists such as Franz Fanon and Paulo Freire, recalls Hegel's *Phenomenology of Spirit*[37] where the fundamental duality, the dialectic of self and other, is ruled by the 'logic of negation', when the consciousness of the self meets the consciousness of the other. In this context, where Indigenous post-colonised consciousness is defined 'in terms of the dependence/independence of "lordship" and "bondage"',[38]

> First, it has lost itself, for it finds itself as an other being; secondly in doing so it has superseded the other, for it does not see the other as an essential being, but in the other sees its own self ... It must supersede this otherness of itself. This is the supersession of the first ambiguity and is, therefore, itself a second ambiguity. First, it must proceed to supersede the other independent being in order thereby to become certain of itself as the essential being; secondly, in so doing it proceeds to supersede its own self, for this other is itself.[39]

In terms of Indigenous resistance to colonial power, Hegel's 'power of negation' explains the omnipresent duality of consciousness underpinning such notions as 'struggle without end', in which colonised Indigenous populations come to define themselves through resistance to the coloniser where the colonised and the coloniser, as Hegel puts it, 'prove themselves and each other through a life-and-death struggle'.[40] According to Albert Memmi: 'the bond between colonizer and colonized is thus destructive and creative. It destroys and re-creates the two partners of colonization into colonizer and colonized. One is disfigured into an oppressor … the other into an oppressed creature'.[41]

Here then, I refer to occupation as the continued inhabitance of the Indigenous consciousness by a will to resist the coloniser, whether imaginary or not. Such a dialectic is not a healthy state of mind; constant referral to the power another holds over oneself, in my view, only reproduces that power. Indigenous people locked in a decolonial mindset thus romanticise a pure pre-colonial past, remain anxiety-ridden in the present and resign themselves to a future where their identities will be forever tied to 'a struggle without end'. As witness to the current academic discourses surrounding Indigenous resistance (underpinned by the notion of 'decolonisation'), it seems to me that the oppressed creature, in its evolution, has developed a 'holier-than-thou' self-righteousness, personified by 'the 70s Indian' who, instead of theorising and articulating their subjectivity, reverts to tears and self-pity. As articulated by Audra Simpson:

> Here we have mental distress as an etiology of colonialism itself, whereby the category of Indian, already established as one … of being a problem, but then in these analyses being a problem that 'has problems' that now have to be dealt with … [that is, to] fetishize and pathologize this categorical construction as some scholars of 'urban native communities' were wont to do in the 1970s …[42]

Here, in briefly turning back to Nietzsche, it is possible that the notion of *ressentiment* can inform the condition of the colonised Indigenous academic. As explained above, in formulating the 'Death of God', Nietzsche locates the morality of Judeo-Christian ethics as merely subjective 'will to power', as opposed to an ubiquitous human morality. In relation to the offensive self-righteousness of some Indigenous academics, the comparison between the Christian slave/Roman master dialectic and the colonised/coloniser dialectic cannot be entirely made because of the obvious ideological importation of Christianity throughout colonisation. Yet the secularisation of modern colonial societies and the imbrication of Christianity with what has come to be thought of as 'traditional' Indigenous cultures allows for some comparison. Thus motivated by *ressentiment* against the power of the coloniser, has the ignobility of the secular coloniser become the colonised virtues of Indigenous peoples – such as selflessness, humility and pity? Have the actions of the coloniser been categorised as 'evil' in relation to the 'good', the purity of the virtues of the pre-colonial indigene? Like the Christian slave, has the colonised indigene repositioned a morality in the hope that the coloniser acquiesces to the moral conduct of the colonised? Nietzsche points out that the Christian slave via moral inversion was tactically successful and, thus, teleologically prudent. Yet, by the nineteenth century, Christianity had exceeded its teleological function and hence the 'Death of God' was foretold.

It seems to me that the inversion of colonised morality has underpinned the decolonial movement since the late 1960s and that, similarly, its teleological capacity is now floundering. The pity sought by such Indigenous academic discourses not only falls on deaf ears, it limits us to a 'plague-ridden city' (i.e., the neocolonial state). While, in the parlance of our times, 'crying is healthy', nevertheless the amount of tears that flow at Indigenous academic conferences never ceases to amaze. The physiological reaction of tears to colonial occupation is not surprising if our past, present and future appears limited to a 'struggle without end'. I do not have the space here to fully explore the notion of 'Indigenous existentialism', suffice to say that colonised Indigenous *ressentiment* must be replaced by an Indigenous mindset that takes 'responsibility' for colonisation, not to release the coloniser from responsibility but to re-claim freedom of choice beyond a 'struggle without end'. Self-determination is key, not based on guilt and pity, but on freedom and choice.

It is false to argue that Indigenous peoples have in unison attempted to position their political will beyond the coloniser/colonised dialectic; indeed, we have captured much of our reactionary post-colonised power within this dialectic. A definite (but ultimately limiting) will to power exists within this symbiotic relationship. The polarity feeds us, for if we are not *not* the coloniser – then who are we? If we are not the pure pre-colonial self, then how do we *relocate* ourselves? What does such de-centering afford Indigenous people? Without the colonising other, how do we configure our political subjectivities? If we cannot march under the banner of the 'Māori Party' or 'tino rangatiratanga', can we march at all? These are the questions Indigenous peoples must now confront, for any vision outside this dialectic implies fragmentation and uncertainty, which should be reframed as useful. In terms of Indigenous existentialism, the 'struggle without end' state of mind forecloses our capacity to 'be' in the present, to enjoy the materiality of our situation, to live free of the consciousness of the will to power of another, to live free of occupation – an occupation underscored by *ressentiment*.

Conclusion

> *Everyone has the war he deserves.*
> *We were never so free as under the occupation.*
> Jean-Paul Sartre[43]

According to Smith, the 'modern indigenous peoples' project' 'has been defined by over 500 years of contact with the West ... [with] one major priority: survival'.[44] Again, neither our colonial histories of suffering nor the continued oppressive situations many Indigenous people find ourselves in today can be treated insipidly. We may nevertheless note, however, that Indigenous peoples should seriously critique and analyse *how* we have resisted, recalling Reverend Rewiti Kohere's quote above advocating cautious haste. The very idea that Indigenous resistance has occurred in reaction to the facticity of 'survival' should itself point to a paradigmatic reconceptualisation of how resistance could be framed.

As asked by Pierre Bourdieu in another context, the question remains: how do Indigenous peoples in the neocolonial context 'revolt against a socially imposed categorization except by organizing themselves as a category constructed according to that categorization and so implementing the classifications and restrictions that it seeks to resist'?[45] That is, when drawing upon a colonised/coloniser duality, Indigenous peoples inherently reinstate the very framework of power they are attempting to overcome. Since the late 1960s, Indigenous resistance has largely been understood through derivatives of Gramscian thought: 'hegemony' and 'false consciousness'. This chapter challenges these foundational concepts in suggesting that no greater ideological control exists than the etching of an eternal coloniser/colonised dual consciousness on the Indigenous psyche. Scott Lash writes that there has been 'a shift in power from the hegemonic mode of "power over" to an intensive notion of power from within (including domination from within) and power as a generative force'.[46] Here power is not conceived of as hierarchical, rather as internalised within the subject and, consequently, it is the existentialism of the Indigenous subject, the immediacy of indigeneity that lies beyond the limiting recourse to the pre-colonial or colonial past, which becomes fundamentally important.

In realisation of this condition, Indigenous choice, responsibility and freedom is a worthier project than 'decolonisation', a project that suggests self-righteousness and pity are inauthentic virtues by which to improve the Indigenous state of being, for 'what is there, ultimately?' Blaming the individual colonist, that is, the coloniser's drive or will to power merely asserts the colonist's right to choose, while disowning Indigenous responsibility. Be mindful of Nietzsche's 'error of free will' where he explains in *Human, All Too Human* that 'the evil acts at which we are most indignant rest on the error that he who perpetrates them against us possesses free will, that is to say, that he could have chosen not to cause us this harm'.[47] There is error in affording the colonist 'choice' beyond those limitations of imperialist power s/he found themselves in and, in so doing, Indigenous peoples should remain mindful of their own choices and responsibilities they possessed yesterday and possess today and tomorrow; Indigenous peoples need be reminded of our capacity to choose. *Per* Sartre, if, in even the most desperate situations we acknowledge choice and responsibility, then we enable the possibility of moving beyond them. *Choice and responsibility* are never so apparent and realisable as in a state of occupation.

Notes

Introduction: Indigenous Studies – Research, Identity and Resistance

1. L.T. Smith, *Decolonising Methodologies: Research and Indigenous Peoples*, Zed Books, London, 1999, p. 110.
2. A. Nandy, *The Intimate Enemy*, Oxford University, Oxford, 1983, pp. 48–9.
3. I. Colgan McCarthy, 1991, cited in G. Moane, *Gender and Colonialism: A Psychological Analysis of Oppression and Liberation*, St Martin's, New York, 1999, p. 104.
4. Smith, p. 110.
5. R. Young, *Postcolonialism: An Historical Introduction*, Blackwell, Oxford 2001, p. 338.

Chapter 1: Mixed Ancestry or Métis?

My thanks to the anonymous reviewers and to Nathalie Kermoal for their careful readings of earlier drafts. This chapter was supported by a Social Sciences and Humanities Council grant #410-2006-2419

1. Although critical legal and feminist scholars tend to legitimise an unproblematic relationship between 'law' and the creation of identity (see generally K. Crenshaw et al. (eds), *Critical Race Theory: The Key Writings that Formed the Movement*, New Press, New York, 1995; L. Gotell, 'Queering Law: Not by Vriend', *Canadian Journal of Law and Society*, vol. 17, no. 1 (2003), pp. 39–113), the relationship is not so straightforward. Being Métis – like any identity – involves numerable practices, behaviours, values and traditions that sit squarely outside 'law's majesty'. Indeed, the court itself speaks not of 'Métis identity' but more narrowly of the constitutional protection for selected practices.
2. *R. v. Powley*, Supreme Court of Canada, 2003, file no. 28533, para. 11.
3. See, for example, C. Denis, *We Are Not You: First Nations and Canadian Modernity*, Broadview, Peterborough, 1997.
4. W. Wicken, *Mi'kmaq Treaties on Trial: History, Land and Donald Marshall Junior*, University of Toronto, Toronto, 2002; W. Wicken, 'Encounters with Tall Sails and Tall Tales: Mi'kmaq Society from 1500–1760', PhD thesis, McGill University, 1994.
5. See O. Dickason, *Canada's First Nations: A History of Founding Peoples from Earliest Times*, McClelland & Stewart Inc., Toronto, 1992, pp. 106–7.
6. W. Wicken, 'Mi'kmaq Decisions: Antoine Tecouenemac, the Conquest and the Treaty of Utrecht', in J. Reid et al. (eds), *The 'Conquest' of Acadia: Imperial, Colonial and Aboriginal Constructions*, University of Toronto, Toronto, 2004, p. 93.
7. The Treaty of Utrecht involved France's formal succession of 'its' colonies (including the Maritimes) to Britain (see Dickason, passim; T. Isaac, *Aboriginal and Treaty Rights in the Maritimes: The Marshall Decision and Beyond*, Purich Ltd, Saskatoon, 2001; Wicken, *Mi'kmaq Treaties on Trial*, passim; Reid et al. (eds), *The 'Conquest' of Acadia: Imperial, Colonial and Aboriginal Constructions*, University of Toronto, Toronto, 2004, for an overview of this era).
8. Wicken, 'Mi'kmac Decisions', p. 95.
9. O. Dickason, 'Amerindians Between French and English in Nova Scotia, 1713–1763', in J.R. Miller (ed), *Sweet Promises: A Reader on Indian–White Relations in Canada*, University of Toronto, Toronto, 1991, pp. 45–6.
10. The so-called era of 'protection' was most prominent in the eighteenth century and culminated in the British government's Royal Proclamation of 1763. Tobias notes that this document set out various policies around trade and land encroachment and alienation and, he argues, formed the basis of Britain's Indian policy for the next fifty years. John Tobias, 'Protection, Civilization, Assimilation: An Outline History of Canada's Indian Policy', in A.L. Getty and A. Lussier (eds), *As Long as the Sun Shines and Water Flows: A Reader in Canadian Native Studies*, University of British Columbia (UBC), Vancouver, 1983.
11. Tobias, pp. 43–4.
12. J. Milloy, 'The Early Indian Acts: Development Strategy and Constitutional Change', in J.R. Miller (ed.), *Sweet Promises: A Reader on Indian–White Relations in Canada*, University of Toronto, Toronto, 1983, p. 57.

13. Royal Commission on Aboriginal Peoples Report, vol. 1, Stage Three: Displacement and Assimilation, Ottawa, 1996. Online. Available: http://www.ainc-inac.gc.ca/ch/rcap/sg/cg6_e.pdf, p. 6 of 74 (accessed 8 March 2007).
14. Tobias, passim.
15. Enfranchisement removed the status of those designated as Indians (and any accompanying rights and privileges) and, rhetorically at least, made them 'Canadians as all other Canadians'.
16. B. Lawrence, *'Real' Indians and Others: Mixed-Blood Urban Native Peoples and Indigenous Nationhood*, UBC, Vancouver, 2004, p. 31.
17. See K. Jamieson, *Indian Women and the Law: Citizen Minus*, Minister of Supply and Services Canada for Canadian Advisory Council on the Status of Women and Equal Rights for Indian Women, Ottawa, 1978; M.E. Turpel, 'Patriarchy and Paternalism: The Legacy of the Canadian State for First Nations Women', *Canadian Journal of Women and the Law*, vol. 6 (1993), pp. 174–92.
18. J. Borrows and L. Rotman, *Aboriginal Legal Issues: Cases, Materials & Commentary*, 2nd edition, Butterworths, Vancouver, 2003, p. 597.
19. Ibid.
20. Lawrence, passim.
21. Bill C-31 constitutes the attempt by the Canadian state to formally rectify the patriarchal Indian Act of 1876. Status Indian women endured numerous forms of discrimination under this legislation, not the least of which was their removal from their reserve communities as their status was removed. See Borrows and Rotman, chapter 8, for an extended legal discussion of the issues surrounding the eventual creation of Bill C-31 as well as its subsequent effects on First Nations communities. One of the bittersweet elements of Bill C-31 was to recognise the right for status Indian communities (i.e., Indian 'bands') to control their own membership.
22. Turpel, p. 181.
23. See generally J. Green, 'Constitutionalizing the Patriarchy: Aboriginal women and Aboriginal Government', in R. Laliberte et al. (eds), *Expressions in Canadian Native Studies*, University of Saskatchewan, University Extension, Saskatoon, 1993, pp. 328–54; Jamieson, passim; J. Silman (ed), *Enough is Enough: Aboriginal Women Speak Out*, The Women's Press, Toronto, 1987.
24. See, for example, J. Peterson, 'Many Roads to Red River: Métis Genesis in the Great Lakes Region, 1680–1815', in J. Peterson and J. Brown (eds), *The New Peoples: Being and Becoming Métis in North America*, University of Manitoba, Winnipeg, 1985; J. Peterson, 'Prelude to Red River: A Social Portrait of the Great Lakes Métis', *Ethnohistory*, vol. 25, no. 1 (1978), pp. 41–67; A. Ray, 'An Economic History of the Robinson Treaties Area Before 1860', Expert Report, *R. v. Powley*, 17 March 1998.
25. See F. Tough, *'As Their Natural Resources Fail': Native Peoples and the Economic History of Northern Manitoba, 1870–1930*, UBC, Vancouver, 1996.
26. N. St-Onge, 'Uncertain Margins: Métis and Saulteaux Indians in St-Paul de Saulteaux, Red River 1821–1870', *Manitoba History*, vol. 53 (October 2006), p. 1.
27. Ibid.
28. The 'official voice' of the Métis Nation and the organisation with which most government agencies interact in their official relations with Métis.
29. J. Peterson and J. Brown, 'Introduction', in J. Peterson and J. Brown (eds), *The New Peoples: Being and Becoming Métis in North America*, University of Manitoba, Winnipeg, 1985.
30. P. Bourdieu and L. Wacquant, *An Invitation to a Reflexive Sociology*, University of Chicago, Chicago, 1992, p. 168.
31. P. Bourdieu, *Language and Symbolic Power*, trans. by G. Raymond and M. Adamson, Harvard University, Cambridge, 1991, p. 164.
32. Categorisation as a 6(1) or a 6(2) is based on whether both or just one of the parents were eligible to receive (or possess) 'Indian status' under the Indian Act. Section 6(1) means both parents are eligible; 6(2) means just one parent is eligible. The mathematics goes something like this: 6(1) + 6(1) (parents) = 6(1) (child); 6(1) + 6(2) = 6(1) (child); 6(2) + 6(2) = 6(1) (child); 6(1) + non-status = 6(2) (child); 6(2) + non-status = non-status (child). Thus, generally speaking, a status Indian marrying a non-status Indian over two subsequent generations leads to the loss of status for a second-generation child.

33. See E. Dickson-Gilmore, 'Iati-Onkwehonwe: Blood Quantum, Membership and the Politics of Exclusion in Kahnawake', *Citizenship Studies*, vol 3, no. 1 (1997), pp. 27–44. 'As the Kahnawake situation brings into stark relief, often what is at stake [in these debates] is tribal membership, along with the treaty rights and benefits, such as health care or shares of the proceeds of tribal enterprises, that come along with membership … At a deeper and more significant level, however, the debate is about who is an Indian from the point of view of Indian people.' J. Hamill, 'Show me your CDIB: Blood Quantum and Indian Identity among Indian People of Oklahoma', *American Behavioral Scientist*, vol. 47, no. 3 (2003), pp. 267–82. Interestingly, Kahnawake has been excoriated for their imposition of a blood quantum rule (an imposition that has more recently been attenuated) despite the fact that 'status' and its conferral under 6(1) and 6(2) operates according to exactly the same logic yet receives little of the vitriol they endure. Moreover, in his legal factum presented before the *Powley* court, the Attorney General Representative for Saskatchewan, M. McAdam, notes that forty-six of the more than 600 Indian bands in Canada possess a blood quantum stipulation in their membership code (see Attorney General for Saskatchewan Factum, *R.* v. *Powley*, Supreme Court of Canada, 2002, file no. 28533).
34. Statistics Canada, *Aboriginal Peoples in Canada in 2006: Inuit, Métis and First Nations, 2006 Census* Ottawa, Minister of Industry, 2008.
35. See A. Siggner, 'Impact of "Ethnic Mobility" on Socio-economic Conditions of Aboriginal Peoples', *Canadian Studies in Population*, vol. 30, no. 1, pp. 137–58. A. Siggner and R. Costa, *Aboriginal Conditions in Census Metropolitan Areas*, 1981–2001, Statistics Canada, Ottawa, 2005.
36. C. Jaenen, *The French Relationship with the Native Peoples of New France and Acadia*, Indian and Northern Affairs, Canada, 1984, p. 72.
37. O. Dickason, 'From "One Nation" in the Northeast to "New Nation" in the Northwest: A Look at the Emergence of the Métis', in J. Peterson and J. Brown (eds), *The New Peoples: Being and Becoming Métis in North America*, University of Manitoba, Winnipeg, 1985, p. 19.
38. Dickason, *Canada's First Nations*, pp. 167–70.
39. Jaenen, p. 73.
40. No websites or academic writings about New Brunswick Métis were available at the time of this writing.
41. 'Métis Culture in Nova Scotia' – emphasis added. Online. Available: http://www.geocities.com/nsmetis/culture.html (accessed 8 March 2007).
42. Jaenan, passim; Dickason, 'From "One Nation"', passim; Dickason, *Canada's First Nations*, passim.
43. See Reid et al., passim and N. Griffiths, *From Migrant to Acadian: A North American Border People, 1604–1755*, McGill-Queen's University, Montreal/Kingston, 2005 for a discussion of the birth, rise and disbandment of Acadia.
44. Dickason, *Canada's First Nations*, p. 170.
45. *Ibid.*
46. R. Francis et al., *Origins: Canadian History to Confederation*, Holt, Rinehart and Winston of Canada Ltd, Toronto, 1988, p. 128.
47. Griffiths, p. xv.
48. Ironically, the Acadian associations do not emphasise their Indigenous ancestry: 'Yvon Samson, chairman of the Conseil Scolaire Acadien Provincial, said some Acadians have established Mi'kmaq ancestry, but it's a minority … "There are some. They do exist, whether you call them Métis or anything else." he said'. 'Announcements: Confederacy of Nova Scotia Métis'. Online. Available: http://www.geocities.com/nsmetis/culture.html (accessed 8 March 2007).
49. 'Métis claims in Maritimes leap by thousands'. Online. Available: http://www.cbc.ca/canada/nova-scotia/story/2006/09/07/metis-maritimes.html (accessed 8 March 2007).
50. 'Métis Culture in Nova Scotia'. Online. Available: http://www.geocities.com/nsmetis/culture.html (accessed 8 March 2007).
51. *Ibid.*
52. 'Who We Are' Online. Available: http://www.geocities.com/nsmetis/member.html (accessed 8 March 2007).
53. 'Application Information'. Online. Available: http://www.geocities.com/nsmetis/member.html (accessed 8 March 2007).

54. P. Bourdieu, 'The Force of Law: Toward a Sociology of the Juridical Field', *Hastings Law Journal*, 38 (July 1987), p. 838.
55. Bourdieu, p. 844.
56. M. McCann, 'How the Supreme Court Matters in American Politics: New Institutionalist Perspectives', in H. Gillman and C. Clayton (eds), *The Supreme Court In American Politics: New Institutionalist Interpretations*, University Press of Kansas, Kansas, 1999, p. 80.
57. *R. v. Powley*, 2003, para. 10.
58. *R. v. Powley*, para. 11 – emphasis added.
59. *Halifax Daily News*, 17 July 2004, p. 3.
60. P. Bourdieu, *The Logic of Practice*, trans. by R. Nice, Stanford University, Stanford, 1980, pp. 112–21.
61. Métis National Council Factum, *R. v. Powley*, Supreme Court of Canada, 2003, file no. 28533.

Chapter 2: 'My Poetry is a Fire'

Ngā mihi ki ngā kaimahi me ngā kaitautoko. Thanks as always to the people who have supported me in my thinking about this topic: especially AnnaMarie Christiansen and Hokulani Aikau in Hawai'i. Special thanks to the editors and anonymous reviewer for your support and feedback. Massive acknowledgement to Robert and Vernice for your fabulous poetry, kind support and great *kōrero*.

1. R. Sullivan, *Voice Carried My Family*, Auckland University, Auckland, 2005, p. 58.
2. Sullivan, p. 60. I have reflected on this poem in depth elsewhere but re-engage it here in order to derive a metaphor for the effect of this Māori writing from Hawai'i. See A. Te Punga Somerville, 'If I Close my Mouth I will Die: Writing, Resisting, Centring', in M. Bargh, *Resistance: An Indigenous Response to Neoliberalism*, Huia, Wellington, 2007, pp. 85–111.
3. Sullivan, p. 36.
4. I say this with acknowledgement, of course, that some Māori people claim that their ancestors are from earlier migrations/'pre-migrations'.
5. Lapita is a type of pottery that archaeologists have identified as having a unique style that is traceable through the islands of the Pacific. The various innovations and styles in Lapita are examined in order to provide some sense of the direction and timing of early Pacific migrations.
6. Sullivan, p. 36.
7. V. Wineera Pere, *Mahanga*, Institute for Pacific Studies, Laie, Brigham Young University, Hawai'i, 1978.
8. E. Patuawa-Nathan, *Opening Doors: A Collection of Poems*, Mana Publications, Suva, 1979.
9. W. Ihimaera, *The Whale Rider*, Heinemann, Auckland, 1987.
10. H. Tuwhare, *Sapwood and Milk*, Caveman, Dunedin, 1972.
11. A. Taylor's 1986 short story 'Pa Mai' uses the recognition of linguistic similarities between Māori and Sāmoan as an entry point for a conversation between two men drinking at a bar (one of whom is Māori and one Sāmoan) about cultural parallels that come from genealogical relationship. A. Taylor, *He Rau Aroha = A Hundred Leaves of Love*, Penguin, Auckland, 1986.
12. In C. Dunsford's *Manawa Toa = Heart Warrior*, Cowrie, a Māori/Hawaiian/Pākehā woman completes her previous travels of the first two novels of the trilogy (to Hawai'i and Berkeley respectively) by protesting French nuclear testing at Moruroa and French colonisation in Tahiti. C. Dunsford, *Manawa Toa = Heart Warrior*, Spinifex, North Melbourne, 2000.
13. Also, an extension of these intersections between Māori and Hawaiian people which should surely at some point gain the attention of those of us who work at these cusps of the 'Indigenous' and the 'Pacific'. We need one day to look at prejudice: when will we be ready to start to honestly and carefully critique the issue of prejudice on the part of some discourse located in the Māori and Hawaiian communities towards migrants from around the Pacific and the role this has in mediating our identification as Pacific peoples?
14. H. Tuwhare, *No Ordinary Sun*, Blackwood and Janet Paul, Auckland, 1964.
15. R. Kohere, *The Autobiography of a Maori*, A.H. & A.W. Reed, Wellington, 1951.
16. W. Ihimaera, *Pounamu Pounamu*, Heinemann, Auckland, 1972.
17. P. Grace, *Waiariki*, Longman Paul, Auckland, 1975.
18. In the 1990s at the University of Auckland I received the best possible training in

Māori literature in English that one could get in this country up to Masters level, and it was not until I was finishing up my PhD that I bumped into Vernice's book on the open stack shelves in a library in Hawai'i for the first time!
19. Indeed, several writers who do not live in New Zealand or do not hold New Zealand citizenship are celebrated as 'New Zealand' writers more than Wineera: eg Sia Figiel and Paula Morris.
20. This collection was published with the name Vernice Wineera Pere, although the poet now uses the name Vernice Wineera. When referring to this specific collection, I will use the publication name and when I refer to later poetry or make more general statements about the poet I will use 'Wineera'.
21. The preface is written by R.D. Craig, Publications Editor, Institute for Polynesian Studies (this was later renamed 'Pacific Studies'), Brigham Young University, Hawai'i. For an exploration of the relationship between Polynesianness and the Mormon church, look for Hokulani Aikau's work.
22. 'Introduction' in V. Wineera Pere, *Mahanga: Pacific Poems*, Brigham Young University, Hawai'i, 1978.
23. Pere, p. 31.
24. *Ibid*.
25. *Ibid*.
26. E. Hau'ofa, 'Our Sea of Islands', *A New Oceania: Rediscovering our Sea of Islands*, USP/SEED, Suva, 1993, pp. 2–16.
27. D. Walcott, 'The Sea is History', *The Starapple Kingdom*, Farrar, Straus and Giroux, New York, 1979.
28. Pere, p. 31.
29. A more explicitly Māori position is asserted in Wineera's poem 'Heritage', in which the poet explores various 'markers' of being Māori and – significantly, for this chapter – this exploration, that focuses the very individualised and personal carving of the face, takes her not to a specific 'home' geographic location of Aotearoa (as one might expect from a Māori writer based in Aotearoa), but instead to a 'vast *marae*', 'the Pacific/we call home'. My own copy of this poem is stained, torn and faded after literally years of being stuck to the fridge doors of my various homes. I look forward to working with this text in more depth in a separate project. Wineera has written more writing since the publication of *Mahanga*; she gave me copies of several poems set in Aotearoa, Hawai'i and Israel for inclusion in an anthology project on which I am working. The planned anthology (which I am co-editing with AnnaMarie Christiansen) will collect writing by Māori outside Aotearoa. These later poems by Wineera will provide scope for much further critical discussion.
30. Pere, p. 18
31. I am working on a longer version of this comparison elsewhere.
32. Pere, p. 28.
33. Pere, p. 26.
34. R. Sullivan, 'A Cover Sail', *Star Waka*, Auckland University, Auckland, 1999, back cover.
35. R. Sullivan, *Captain Cook in the Underworld*, Auckland University, Auckland, 2002.
36. Sullivan, p. 99.
37. I gained this insight after talking with Robert about his collection. R. Sullivan, pers comm., 2004.
38. I am more carefully exploring this distinction between 'Indigenous' and 'Migrant' identifications in my forthcoming book, *Once Were Pacific*.
39. Sullivan, p. 3.
40. Sullivan, p. 36.
41. Sullivan, p. 79.
42. Sullivan, pp. 110–1.
43. Sullivan, pp. 3–4.
44. The man remembered by the English as Omai, the first Pacific person to go to London in 1774, was known as Mai at home. Now we have records of two men: 'Mai' is the man as he was known in the Pacific and 'Omai' is the man who has been captured in the European written record. Omai was understood to be the manifestation of the mythical Rousseau-imagined Noble Savage and enjoyed immense popularity in London whilst there and as a figure of the English imaginary for years after he left.
45. Sullivan, *Voice Carried My Family*, p. 26.
46. *Ibid*.
47. Sullivan, 'Queen Charlotte Sound', p. 29.
48. Sullivan, 'Tupaia', p. 27.
49. Sullivan, 'Mai', p. 28.
50. Sullivan, 'Queen Charlotte Sound', p. 29.
51. Sullivan, 'Pearl Harbour', p. 40.
52. *Ibid*.
53. Pere, 'A Taste of Learning', p. 39.

54. *Ibid.*
55. *Ibid.*

Chapter 3: Culture: Compromise or Perish!

1. D. Awatere, *Māori Sovereignty*, Broadsheet Magazine, Auckland, 1984, p. 28.
2. H. Kawharu, *Conflict and Compromise*, Reed, Auckland, 2003, p. 2.
3. A. Beaglehole, 'Languages Other than English, Māori and Pacific Island', *Book & Print in New Zealand: A Guide to Print Culture in Aotearoa*, Victoria University, Wellington, 1997. New Zealand Electronic Text Centre (NZETC). Online. Available: http://www.nzetc.org/tm/scholarly/tei-GriBook-_div2-N13B00-1.html (accessed 9 October 2008).
4. Awatere, p. 26.
5. 'While transformation might be said to describe the kind of change all human cultures experience, compromise appears to carry a negative weight, as if there might be some transformations that are positive or neutral in their cultural effects, while there are others which are not and that the latter can be called compromise' (Reilly, pers comm. with the writer, 2008).
6. H. Williams, *A Dictionary of the Maori Language*, 7th ed., Government Printer, Wellington, 1971, p. 416.
7. Wikipedia, 'Cultural Identity'. Online. Available: http://en.wikipedia.org/wiki/Cultural_identity (accessed 15 May 2008).
8. Ministry of Social Development, 'Social Report 2003: Cultural Identity'. Online. Available: http://www.socialreport.msd.govt.nz/2003/cultural-identity/cultural-identity.shtml (accessed 15 May 2008).
9. 'Mana' equates to self-esteem, pride, high regard and social standing, power, authority and influence.
10. C. Barlow, *Tikanga Whakaaro*, Oxford University, Auckland, 1991, p. 165.
11. Kawharu, p. 5.
12. P. Hohepa, *A Maori Community in Northland*, A.H & A.W Reed, Wellington, 1964, p. 101, describes *marae* in the following: 'In front of each meeting hall, in no way visibly distinct, there is a grassed space. This is the marae, the courtyard of the speakers, the sacred zone whereon only males can deliver speeches and orations of welcome, farewell, pleasure and anger, of fact and fiction'. Also see H.M. Mead, *Tikanga Māori: Living by Māori Values*, Huia, Wellington, 2003, pp. 109–16 for Polynesian comparisons of '*marae*'.
13. K. Mataira, *Pukapuka Pānui* [Course Reader for Te Kura Puaotanga. Kōwae Ako 6: karanga/whaikōrero], Te Ataarangi, Kuratini o Waikato, Kirikiriroa, 1995.
14. R. Ward, *Life Among the Maories of NZ*, G. Lamb, London, 1872, p. 91.
15. R.T. Mahuta, 'Whaikōrero', MA thesis, University of Auckland, 1974, p. 165.
16. R. Walker, Whakatōhea, Ahorangi (Professor)/Kaumātua, Interview with the writer, 1998.
17. A. Salmond, *Hui: A Study of Maori Ceremonial Gatherings*, 2nd ed., Reed, Auckland, 1994, p. 167.
18. T. Reedy, Ngāti Porou, Ahorangi/Kaumātua, Interview with the writer, 1996.
19. H. Yoon, *Maori Mind, Maori Land: Essays on the Cultural Geography of the Maori People from an Outsider's Perspective*, P. Lang, Berne, 1986, p. 45.
20. Salmond, p. 127.
21. Te Patu Hohepa, Ngā Puhi, Ahorangi/Kaumātua, Interview with the writer, 1998.
22. Tauroa, pp. 21, 79.
23. A. Mikaere, 'Maori Women: Caught in the Contradictions of a Colonised Reality'. Online. Available: http://www.waikato.ac.nz/law/wlr/1994/article6-mikaere.html (accessed 28 October 2004).
24. Tauroa, p. 78.
25. John Rangihau, at Te Waimako in 1978, said 'kāre e tika te wahine ki te kōrero i te mea, koia te kōpū tuku mai i ngā rangatira ki waho … Koirā kāre e whakaaetia ki te kōrero.' Cassette recording in the writer's possession, 1978.
26. R. Higgins and J.C. Moorfield, 'Ngā tikanga o te marae: Marae practices', in T.M. Ka'ai et al. (eds.), *Ki te Whaiao: An Introduction to Māori Culture and Society*, Pearson Education, Auckland, 2004, p. 80.
27. S. Karetu, 'Kawa in Crisis', in M. King (ed) *Tihe Mauri Ora: Aspects of Maoritanga*, Methuen Publications, Wellington, 1978, p. 71; T. Pouwhare, Ngāi Tūhoe, Kaumātua. Informal conversation with the writer, 1996; and Te Hue Rangi, Ngāi Tūhoe, Pūkenga, Interview with the writer, 2003.
28. J. Tahuri, Ngāi Tūhoe, Kaumātua, pers comm. with the writer, 1996.
29. E. Best, *Notes on the Art of War*, Reed Books, Auckland, 2001, pp. 68–9.

30. M. Reilly, pers comm. with the writer, 2008.
31. An example of full loss could, for example, be a decision against modifying a cultural practice in its pure form, however minute. This would see the end of that practice.
32. These major tribes are located in the Bay of Plenty, North Island, New Zealand.
33. R. Moran et al., *Managing Cultural Differences: Global Leadership Strategies for the 21st Century*, 7th ed., Elsevier/Butterworth-Heinemann, Amsterdam/Boston, 2007.
34. Salmond, p. 112.
35. Māori-language resource document from 501 file. n.a. Te Pua Wānanga ki te Ao [copy in writer's possession].
36. T. Reedy, 'Evaluation Speech', World Indigenous Peoples' Conference, Turangawaewae Marae, Ngaruawahia, 1990.
37. Te Wharehuia Milroy, Ngāi Tūhoe, Ahorangi/Kaumātua, Interview with the writer, 1997.
38. Salmond, pp. 128–9.
39. *Ibid.*
40. 'Statement of Sir Kingi Ihaka, Maori Language Commissioner …', Report of the Waitangi Tribunal on the Allocation of Radio Frequency Claim, wai 150, doc. A40, GP Publications, Wellington, 1990, p. 3.
41. '… ka kangakanga ia i Te Reo Pākehā ki ngā minita. Ka tū atu te rangatira o te marae ki te whakanoho i a ia – 'kāre e tika ana wērā kōrero, kei te mōhio koe ki tō tāua tikanga ka tū ana tāua, me kōrero Māori tonu. Kua hē katoa i a koe tō tāua kawa o te marae nei [i]tō kōrero Pākehātanga, me ō kōrero hahani i ngā minita. Kāre e pai ana terā,' Kāre tonu [taua kaikōrero] i whakarongo mai ki te rangatira, kāre tonu i noho. Ka haere atu tētahi tangata i runga i te pae, e kōrero tonu ana te tangata, ka mekea atu, kurua atu. Ka hinga ki te papa. Mehemea ka takahia te kawa i roto i ngā whaikōrero, koirā'. (Te Hiko Hohepa, Te Arawa, Kaumātua, Interview with the writer, 1997).
42. In short, the Treaty of Waitangi is 'an agreement in which Māori gave the Crown rights to govern and to develop British settlement, while the Crown guaranteed Māori full protection of their interests and status and full citizenship rights'. Treaty of Waitangi, Online. Available: http://www.waitangi-tribunal.govt.nz/treaty/ (accessed 2008).
43. One of the bastions of cultural conservatism in the alien environment of the city is the *tangi*, the mortuary customs for farewelling the dead. The most appropriate place to conduct the rituals of the *tangi* is the *marae*, the other bastion and focal point of the culture. Although there were tribal *marae* engulfed by urban sprawl in Auckland and Wellington, the first wave of pre-war migrants felt they needed a hall or *marae* of their own. (A. Saunders, *A History of New Zealand*, vol. 2, Whitcombe & Tombs, Christchurch, 1896, p. 255.) In any case as the number of urban Māori increased exponentially, *tangata whenua marae* were unable to cope with the need. In the meantime, the normal life-crisis of birth, death and marriage had to be met with what was at hand, the family dwelling. The head of a *whānau* responded to death by turning the suburban state house into a 'mini-marae'. (R. Walker, *Ka Whawhai Tonu Matou: Struggle Without End*, Penguin, Auckland, 1990, p. 200.)
44. M. Dominy, 'Maori Sovereignty: A Feminist Invention of Tradition', in J. Linnekin and L. Poyer (eds), *Cultural Identity and Ethnicity in the Pacific*, University of Hawai'i, Honolulu, 1996, p. 237.
45. T.J. Keelan, 'E Tipu e Rea: An Indigenous Theoretical Framework for Youth Development', *Development Bulletin*, vol. 56 (October 2001), pp. 62–65.
46. Awatere, pp. 29–32.
47. Beaglehole, n.p.
48. Dominy, p. 238.
49. The term '*riwai*' is a generic Māori word for a potato.
50. J. Linnekin and L. Poyer, *Cultural Identity and Ethnicity in the Pacific*, University of Hawai'i, Honolulu, 1996, p. 13.
51. *Ibid.*

Chapter 4: *piko ka-sôhki-nitohtaman ka-nisitohtaman nêhiyawêwin*/You Must Listen Very Hard to Understand the Cree Language

Thank you to Dr. Isabel Altamirano-Jiménez, Dr. Chris Andersen Dr. Nathalie Kermoal, Shalene Jobin-Vandervelde, Dorothy Thunder,

Daniel Johnson, Val Napoleon and the anonymous external reviewer for comments on earlier drafts of this chapter. Thanks very much to Dr. Ellen Bielawski and Tracy Bear-Coon for our many conversations on the significance of language to how we make meaning of experience. I tip my hat to Nuno Luzio for technical assistance. I acknowledge, as well, Emily Hunter et al. for their very practical texts, *Introductory Cree: Part 1* and *Plains Cree Grammar Guide and Glossary*, published by the School of Native Studies, University of Alberta, 1991 and 2001 respectively. Arok Wolvengrey et al. also deserve my deepest thanks for their work on the Cree language in the province of Saskatchewan and for their very valuable texts, *nêhiyawêwin: itwêwina Cree: Words, Volume 1* and *nêhiyawêwin: itwêwina Cree: Words, Volume 2*, published by the Canadian Plains Research Center and the University of Regina, 2001.

1. K.D. Harrison, *When Languages Die: The Extinction of the World's Languages and the Erosion of Human Knowledge*, Oxford University, Oxford, 2007, p. 11.
2. I use the term 'Indian' with caution, because of its place in the historical literature of the Indian Act, because some Indigenous Canadians prefer it over 'Native' or 'Aboriginal' and because others find it offensive. In this chapter I will use the words 'Indigenous' and 'Aboriginal' synonymously in the sense that they are used in cultural recovery language to connote peoples (and their descendants) who lived (and live) in a place before interlopers or colonisers arrived. 'Native' seems too vague a word and where I can I will use more tribally specific terms such as Cree, Ojibwa, Métis, etc.
3. J. Fishman, 'What Do You Lose When You Lose Your Language', in G. Cantoni (ed.), *Stabilizing Indigenous Languages*, ed. G. Cantoni, Center for Excellence in Education, Northern Arizona University, Flagstaff, 1996, p. 2.
4. Fishman, p. 3.
5. D. Welchman Gegeo and K.A. Watson-Gegeo, 'Adult Education, Language Change and Issues of Identity and Authenticity in Kwara'ae (Solomon Islands)', *Anthropology & Education Quarterly*, vol. 30, no. (1999), p. 25.
6. Fishman, p. 4.
7. S. Ortiz, 'Speaking–Writing: Indigenous Literary Sovereignty', in J. Weaver et al. (eds), *American Indian Literary Nationalism*, University of New Mexico, Albuquerque, 2006, pp. xi–xii.
8. M. Abley, 'All-Night Walker Sonata (Endangered Languages)', *World Literature Today*, vol. 81, no. 5 (Sept./Oct. 2007), p. 18.
9. Department of Canadian Heritage, *Towards a New Beginning: A Foundational Report For A Strategy To Revitalize First Nation, Inuit and Métis Languages and Cultures*, Aboriginal Languages Directorate, Aboriginal Affairs Branch, Ottawa, 2005, p. 3.
10. M.J. Norris, 'Aboriginal Languages in Canada: Trends and Perspectives on Maintenance and Revitalization', in J.P. White et al (eds), *Aboriginal Policy Research: Moving Forward, Making a Difference*, vol. 3, Thompson Educational, Inc., Toronto, 2006, p. 224.
11. Norris, p. 198.
12. Norris, p. 224.
13. J.L. Tobias, 'Protection, Civilization, Assimilation: An Outline History of Canada's Indian Policy', in I.A.L. Getty and A.S. Lussier (eds), *As Long As the Sun Shines and Water Flows: A Reader in Canadian Native Studies*, UBC, Vancouver, 1983, p. 39.
14. J. Fiske and E. George, 'Bill C-31: A Study of Cultural Trauma', in J.P. White et al. (eds), *Aboriginal Policy Research: Moving Forward, Making a Difference*, vol. 5, Thompson Educational, Inc., Toronto, 2007, p. 61.
15. J.R. Miller, *Shingwauk's Vision: A History of Native Residential Schools*, University of Toronto, Toronto, 1996, p. 184.
16. Miller, p. 39.
17. J.S. Milloy, *A National Crime: The Canadian Government and the Residential School System 1879 to 1986*, University of Manitoba, Winnipeg, 1999, p. xv.
18. Milloy, p. 38.
19. Miller, p. 204.
20. *Ibid*.
21. Quoted in J. Fear-Segal, *White Man's Club: Schools, Race and the Struggle of Indian Acculturation*, University of Nebraska, Lincoln, 2007, p. 91.
22. Harrison, p. 5.
23. D. Nettle and S. Romaine, *Vanishing Voices: The Extinction of the World's Languages*, Oxford University, Oxford, 2000, pp. 90–1.

24. S.N. Greymorning, 'The 4th Giving the Gift of Language: A Symposium and Workshop on Second Language Instruction and Acquisition', Native American Studies Department, University of Manitoba, Missoula, Montana, 17 April 2008.
25. Ibid.
26. L. Wong, 'Authenticity and the Revitalization of Hawaiian', *Anthropology and Education Quarterly: Journal of the Council on Anthropology and Education*, vol. 30, no. 1 (1999), p. 95.
27. J. Thorburn, 'Self-perceptions, Generational Differences, Prestige and Language Loss in the Innu Community of Sheshatshiu', *Papers of the Thirty-seventh Algonquian Conference*, University of Manitoba, Winnepeg, 2006, p. 346.

Chapter 5: Resisting Language Death: A Personal Exploration

1. T.P. Kōkiri, *Report on the Health of the Māori Language: Kāi Tahu*, Te Puni Kōkiri, Wellington, 2002, p. 18.
2. K.D. Harrison, *When Languages Die – The Extinction of the World's Languages and the Erosion of Human Knowledge*, Oxford University, New York, 2007, p. 7.
3. Harrison, pp. 3–5.
4. E. Bialystok, *Bilingualism in Development – Language, Literacy, & Cognition*, Cambridge University, New York, 2001, p. 18.
5. Bialystok, p. 16.
6. Ibid.
7. S. Döpke, *One Parent One Language – An Interactional Approach*, John Benjamins Company, Amsterdam/Philadelphia, 1992, p. 1.
8. Bialystok, p. 3.
9. C. Baker, *A Parents' and Teachers' Guide to Bilingualism*, Multilingual Matters, Clevedon, 2004, p. 635.
10. Baker, p. 18.
11. Baker, p. 86.
12. Ibid.
13. Harrison, p. 159.

Chapter 6: Towards a Model for Indigenous Research

1. Most of the examples used will be from Ngāi Tahu, the Indigenous people of the South Island of New Zealand, as that is my area of expertise.
2. G.A. Selwyn, 'Journal', 10 January 1844, Hocken Archives ARC-0411.
3. H.K. Taiaroa, 'Mahika kai lists', 1879 and 1880, Macmillan Brown Ms. 140, Hii/19, various folders.
4. A. Leopold. *A Sand County Almanac*, Oxford University, New York, 1987, p. 174.
5. In this chapter, 'traditional' is used to mean reference to pre-contact events. The chapter began as an oral discourse and retains much of the Māori oral style.
6. The word 'Indigenous' has been given an initial capital, consistent with the convention adopted by many original peoples. It is a statement of identification in the same way that names of races, nationalities, tribes, religions and geographic collectivities generally are afforded capitals.
7. C. Royal, *Te Haurapa*, Bridget Williams Books, Wellington, 1992; E. Stokes, 'Maori Research and Development: A Discussion Paper', New Zealand Research Council, Wellington, 1985; J. Tucker, *Maori Claims: How to Research and Write a Report*, Waitangi Tribunal Division, Department of Justice, Wellington, 1994; R.T.M. Tau, *Ngā Pikitūroa o Nḡai Tahu: The Oral Traditions of Ngāi Tahu*, Otago University, Dunedin, 2003; R. Walker, *Ka Whawhai Tonu Matou: Struggle Without End*, Penguin, Auckland, 1990.
8. Cook Strait, which separates the North and South Islands of New Zealand.
9. S.P. Smith, 'The Lore of the Whare Wananga', *Journal of the Polynesian Society (JPS)*, vol. 22 (1913), p. 127.
10. A.H. Carrington, 'History of Ngai Tahu', 1934, typescript, p. 10, Alexander Turnbull Library, Wellington.
11. Smith, p. 127; Carrington, p. 10.
12. S. Cormack, 'Some Comments on South Island Maori History', *Te Karanga*, vol. 6, no.1 (1990), p. 5.
13. H.C. Evison, 'Kaiapohia, The Story of a Name', *Te Karanga*, vol. 6, no. 2 (1990), pp. 3–9.
14. Evison, p. 3. The early nineteenth-century invasion by Ngāti Toa, though ultimately repelled, remains a sore point with Ngāi Tahu and anything associated with it has negative connotations, much as any reference to Hitler is automatically seen negatively.
15. I. Barber, 'Constructions of Change: A

History of Early Maori Culture Sequences', *JPS*, vol. 104 (1995), p. 357. See also B. Fankhauser, 'Archeometric Studies of Cordyline (*ti*) based on ethnobotanical and archaeological research', PhD thesis, University of Otago, 1986.
16. Barber, p. 384.
17. *Ibid*.
18. B.F. Leach, 'The Ngai-Tahu Migration: The 'Norman Conquest' of the South Island', *New Zealand Archaeological Association Newsletter*, vol. 21 no. 1 (March 1978), p. 13.
19. A. Anderson, *When All the Moa Ovens Grew Cold*, Otago Heritage Books, Dunedin, 1983.
20. Anderson, pp. 41, 52.
21. Anderson, p. 38.
22. For example, Anderson 1996: 'Wakawaka and Mahinga Kai: models of traditional land management in southern New Zealand', in Davidson, J.M., Irwin, G., Leach, B.F., Pawley, A. and Brown, D. (eds) *Oceanic Culture History: Essays in Honour of Roger Green*. NZJA Special Publication: 631–640.
23. J.W. Stack, *Kaiapohia: The Story of a Siege*, Whitcombe & Tombs, Christchurch, 1893.
24. J. Reuben and J. Leech, 'Foreword', in J.W. Stack, *Kaiapohia: The Story of a Siege*, reprint ed., William Bros, Rangiora, 1990. Originally published 1893.
25. G. Leslie Adkin, *Horowhenua: Its Maori Place-names and their Topographic and Historical Background*, Department of Internal Affairs, Wellington, 1948.
26. See *whakapapa* table 1, J.H. Beattie, 'Moriori', *Otago Daily Times*, Dunedin, 1941, p. 64.
27. J.W. Stack, *South Island Maoris: A Sketch of Their History and Legendary Lore*, Whitcombe and Tombs, Christchurch, 1898, p. 108.
28. T. O'Regan, 'A Kai Tahu History', *Te Karanga*, vol. 6, no. 1 (1990), p. 7.
29. J.W. Stack, 'Sketch of the Traditional History of the South Island Maoris', *Transactions and Proceedings of the New Zealand Institute*, vol. 10 (1877), pp. 92–3.
30. J. White, *The Ancient History of the Maori*, vol. III, Government Printer, Wellington, 1887, p. 265.
31. H.C. Jacobson, *Tales of Banks Peninsula*, Akaroa 'Mail' Office, Akaroa, 1917, p. 19, in chapter 1, which we are told is 'Contributed by Rev. J.W. Stack'.
32. K.R. Urry, 'Te Hakari: Feasting in Maori Society and its Archaeological Implications', MA thesis, University of Auckland, 1993, p. 11.
33. E. Shortland, *Southern Districts of New Zealand*, Longman, London, 1851.
34. See, for example, J.H. Beattie, 'Our Southernmost Maoris', *Otago Daily Times*, Dunedin, 1954, pp. 11–12, where he lists a number of misconceptions that he had to revise over the years.
35. Beattie, *Moriori*, p. 7.
36. Beattie, *Our Southernmost Maoris*, p. 82.
37. Beattie, *Our Southernmost Maoris*, p. 83.
38. Shortland, p. 232.
39. T.T. Tikao, *Tikao Talks*, A.H. & A.W. Reed, Wellington, 1939, p. 58.
40. P. Freire, 'Research Methods', *Literary Discussion* (Spring 1974), p. 134.
41. T.L. Buick, *An Old New Zealander*, Whitcombe & Tombs, Wellington, 1911, p. 193.
42. P. Burns, *Te Rauparaha: A New Perspective*, Reed, Wellington, 1980, p. 189.
43. Ever since this event, Ngāti Toa have been 'Kāti-kai-wai-tai' (the tribe that eats sea water) to Ngāi Tahu (*iwi* dialogue over many years). (Stack, *Kaiapohia*, p. 88.).
44. Buick, pp. 191–2.
45. Burns, p. 190.
46. *Whakataukī*.
47. Te Wanikau Tapiha, 'The History of Ngai Tahu (Ngati Kuri Clan)', nd, p. 21, in I.A.D. Macdonald papers, Canterbury Museum Archives.
48. Carrington, p. 1.
49. *Ibid*.
50. Carrington, p. 40.
51. Carrington, p. 60, n. 7.
52. Te Wanikau Tapiha, p. 18.
53. B. Biggs, 'The Translation and Publishing of Maori Material in the Auckland Public Library', *JPS*, vol. 61 (1952), p. 181.
54. Te Wanikau, p. 18.
55. As explained by the recorder, Tame Green, in parenthesis. Te Wanikau, p. 19.
56. Tikao, p. 117.
57. H.W. Williams, *A Dictionary of the Maori Language*, Government Printer, Wellington, 1988, p. 78.
58. Carrington p. 60, n. 6.
59. M. Roberts et al., 'Whakapapa as a Mental Construct', *The Contemporary Pacific*, vol. 16, no. 1 (Spring 2004), p. 1.
60. Royal, pp. 28–30.
61. Royal, p. 30.
62. Royal, p. 78.

63. R. Broughton, *The Origins of Ngaa Rauru Kiitahi*, Dept. of Maori Affairs, Wellington, 1979, p. 31.
64. Tahmatua [sic] and his group went to avenge the deaths of his younger brothers, Tamaraeroa and Huirapa (see A. T. Ngata and P. Te Hurinui, *Nga Moteatea*, vol. 4, Polynesian Society, Wellington, 1988–90, pp. 80–1).
65. Broughton, pp. 30–1.
66. Broughton, p. 31.
67. J. McEwen, 'Migrations to and Settlement of the Wellington Area', Lecture 1 notes, Victoria University Wellington, 1971, p. 10.
68. B. Biggs, 'Oral Literature of Polynesia', *Te Ao Hou*, no. 49 (November 1964), p. 42.
69. McEwen, p. 9.
70. Leopold, p. 127.
71. M. Orbell, 'A South Island Waiata Tangi', *Te Karanga*, vol. 4, no. 1 (1988), p. 6.
72. Orbell, p. 7.
73. Te Mahana Walsh, Taua, Puketeraki, in conversation with the writer, 1994.
74. Orbell, p. 5.
75. B. Dacker, *Te Mamae me te Aroha. The Pain and the Love*, University of Otago Press, Dunedin, 1994.
76. Broughton, p. 2.

Chapter 7: Rediscovering the Hidden Heritage from Ancient Mangaia

1. S.M. Mead, *Landmarks, Bridges and Visions: Aspects of Maori Culture*, Victoria University, Wellington 1997, pp. 26, 34.
2. W.W. Gill, *Life in the Southern Isles; or, Scenes and Incidents in the South Pacific and New Guinea*, The Religious Tract Society, London, 1876, pp. 353–5. I have adopted Mamae's spelling of the brothers' names as Kōtū and Kōā in preference to Gill's spelling. The second name might also be spelt as either Koʻa (as nineteenth-century macrons sometimes indicated glottal stops) or Kōʻā.
3. M.P.J. Reilly, *War and Succession in Mangaia from Mamae's Texts*, Memoir no. 52, The Polynesian Society, Auckland, 2003, pp. 45–53. I should emphasise that the estimated date is a very approximate one based on genealogical and traditional information.
4. W.W. Gill, *From Darkness to Light in Polynesia*, reprint ed., Institute of Pacific Studies, University of the South Pacific, Suva, 1984, p. 309. Originally published London, 1894.
5. Gill, *Life in the Southern Isles*, p. 353 fn. 1.
6. W.W. Gill, *Myths and Songs from the South Pacific*, reprint ed., University Press of the Pacific, Honolulu, 2004, p. 301. Originally published London, 1876.
7. Gill, *Life in the Southern Isles*, p. 353.
8. Gill, *Life in the Southern Isles*, p. 354.
9. *Ibid*.
10. Gill, *Life in the Southern Isles*, p. 355.
11. For example, Gill, *Life in the Southern Isles*, p. vi.
12. Gill, *Life in the Southern Isles*, p. 355.
13. Gill, *Life in the Southern Isles*, p. 356.
14. W.W. Gill, 'Original MSS of Native Songs etc., used in his *Myths and Songs* and *Historical Sketches of Savage Life*', GNZMSS 45, Auckland City Libraries, Special Collections.
15. This last point is based on the quotation which concludes both the brothers' story and *Life in the Southern Isles*: 'The people which sat in darkness saw great light; and to them which sat in the region and shadow of death light is sprung up.'
16. Gill, 'Original MSS of Native Songs ...'.
17. The text has been slightly modified, to aid readability, by including some extra full stops, as well as inserting both macrons and hamzahs.
18. Gill, *Life in the Southern Isles*, p. 355, fn. 1; Gill, 'The brothers', in Gill, 'Original MSS of *Historical Sketches of Savage Life in Polynesia*', GNZMSS 44, Auckland City Libraries, Special Collections.
19. The following line divisions are my own. Mamae wrote his lines across the page.
20. The following is a literal rendering of the song text. 'That is, the section of *peʻe* (chant on historical themes) composed about them: I climbed/Up the long hill-range, Tavaikura/I am Kōā, who almost perished./It rained and rained there,/Kōtū climbed and climbed./Standing, standing in anger, Eve/Standing, standing in anger, Eve/Fighting with malice for ages/Until the light was above'.
21. According to a note by Gill, Tavaikura is a place in Ivirua. In the published version he stated that it was in Karanga. The lengthened 'a' in 'roa' (long) probably reflects a poetical stress to harmonise with Tavaikura.
22. Gill annotated the word 'ʻakarērē' (written 'ākarērē' by Mamae) 'kua ʻakaʻui rava' (truly

ended). After '*Kōā ē*' Gill wrote '*mei mate*' (from death).
23. After both '*ua*', Gill wrote 'rain'. Following the phrase '*tō reirē*', presumably sounded like this for poetical reasons, Gill annotated it as meaning '*i reira*' (then).
24. After the second use of Eve, Gill wrote '*metua*' (father).
25. Gill annotated '*'akaāuriri*' 'malice' and '*kānotau*' as meaning '*tuatau*' (season, period). '*Tē*' here reproduces Mamae's stress, presumably the word was lengthened for poetical considerations.
26. N. Shibata, *Part 2 Mangaian–English Dictionary*, in K. Katayama and N. Shibata (eds), *Prehistoric Cook Islands People, Life and Language*, an Official Report for Kyoto University Cook Islands Scientific Research Programme (KUCIP) in 1989–1998, Cook Islands Library and Museum Society Occasional Publications, Cook Islands Library and Museum Society, Rarotonga, 1999, p. 242.
27. Mamae, ''*E tara amo nō teia 'enua nei*', in W.W. Gill, 'Rarotonga Notes, Songs, Stars, Stories, [and] Letters', Polynesian Society MS Papers 1187, folder 59 (microfilm 131, 132), Alexander Turnbull Library, National Library of New Zealand.
28. The story of Te Manava-roa is related in Gill, *Myths and Songs*, pp. 128–30 and T.R. Hiroa (P.H. Buck), *Mangaian Society*, Bernice P. Bishop Museum Bulletin 122, reprint ed., Kraus Reprint, New York, 1971, p. 126. Originally published Honolulu, 1934. Gill was adamant that the *atua* buried there was not the spirit ancestor of Vari-mā-te-takere. Hiroa regarded it as 'another example of the inconsistency of the Mangaian myth-makers'. I assume that the two *atua* of this name are actually one and the same being.
29. Gill, *Myths and Songs*, pp. 1–22, Hiroa, pp. 9–25.
30. Gill, *Myths and Songs*, p. 128.
31. Gill, *Life in the Southern Isles*, pp. 103–4.
32. Gill, *Myths and Songs*, pp. 128–9.
33. P. Aratangi, 'The Entry of Christianity into Mangaian Society in the 1820s', BD Project, Suva, Pacific Theological College, 1986, pp. 67–70; Shibata, p. 224.
34. See, for example, the assassination of the Ngāti Vara *mangaia*, Te Uanuku, and the subsequent attack against Ngāti Vara's leaders (originating from Veitātei) by a party comprising 'most of the men of the northern half of the island', as told in Gill, *From Darkness to Light*, p. 210.
35. Gill, *From Darkness to Light*, p. 210; Gill, *Myths and Songs*, p. 36.
36. Hiroa, p. 107.
37. Reilly, pp. 44–5.
38. Mamae, ''*E Pe'e nō 'Iro*', in Gill, 'Original MSS of Native Songs …'.
39. Gill, *From Darkness to Light*, pp. 45–8; Reilly, p. 44.
40. For example, Gill, *Jottings from the Pacific*, London, The Religious Tract Society, 1885, pp. 105–7, 226–9; Hiroa, p. 96.
41. Gill, *Life in the Southern Isles*, p. 353.
42. Gill, *Life in the Southern Isles*, p. 355.
43. An excellent example is the relationship between Te Uanuku and his *teina*, Raumea, especially as retold by the modern '*are kōrero* (traditional expert), Tere'ēvangeria Aratangi, 'Te Tua i te mate'anga o Te Uanuku', Cultural Development Division, Ministry of Social Services, Mangaian *Kōrero* series, National Archives of the Cook Islands, Rarotonga.
44. S. Savage, *A Dictionary of the Maori Language of Rarotonga*, reprint ed., Institute of Pacific Studies, University of the South Pacific in association with the Ministry of Education, Government of the Cook Islands, Suva and Rarotonga, 1980, p. 54. Originally published Wellington, 1962.
45. Hiroa, p. 156.
46. *Ibid*.

Chapter 8: Indigenous Political Representation and Comparative Research

1. See, for example, A. Armitage, *Comparing the Policy of Aboriginal Assimilation: Australia, Canada and New Zealand*, UBC, Vancouver, 1995; A. Fleras and R. Maaka, *Politics of Indigeneity: Challenging the State in Canada and Aotearoa New Zealand*, Otago University, Dunedin, 2005; A. Fleras and J.L. Elliot, *The Nations Within: Aboriginal – State Relations in Canada, the United States and New Zealand*, Oxford University, Toronto, 1992; P. Havemann (ed), *Indigenous Peoples' Rights in Australia, Canada and New Zealand*, Oxford University, Auckland, 1999.
2. Māori are the Indigenous people of New Zealand. In Canada, 'Indigenous' refers to three distinct social, cultural and legal

groups of people: 'Indians' (referred to in this chapter as First Nations), Métis and Inuit (previously known as Eskimo). This discussion focuses on a comparison of the experiences of Māori and First Nations peoples because, arguably, First Nations and Māori exhibit the greatest similarity in terms of their colonial history and contemporary circumstances, which makes the differences between them more interesting and challenging to explain.

3. C.J. Irons Magallanes, 'Indigenous Political Representation: Identified Parliamentary Seats as a Form of Indigenous Self-Determination', in B.A. Hocking (ed), *Unfinished Constitutional Business? Rethinking Indigenous Self-determination*, Aboriginal Studies, Canberra, 2005, p. 109.

4. Communal property was a major obstacle to citizenship for First Nations. Through the Gradual Civilization Act (1857) individual property was seen as essential to civilised society. See F. Abele, 'Belonging in the New World: Imperialism, Property and Citizenship', in G. Kernerman and P. Resnick (eds), *Insiders and Outsiders: Alan Cairns and the Reshaping of Canadian Citizenship*, UBC, Vancouver, 2005, pp. 213–26.

5. Magallanes, p. 110.

6. For example, see J.H. Hylton (ed), *Aboriginal Self-Government in Canada: Current Issues and Trends*, Purich, Saskatchewan, 1994.

7. Four First Nations, Vunut Gwitchin, Nacho Nyak Dun, Champagne and Aishihik and Teslin Tlingit, also signed individual land claim and self-government agreements in 1993, which came into effect in 1995. See Parliamentary Information and Research Service, 'Aboriginal Self-Government', 19 June 1999. Online. Available: http://www.parl.gc.ca/information/library/PRBpubs/962-e.htm (accessed 17 June 2008).

8. C. Orange, *The Treaty of Waitangi*, Port Nicholson, Wellington, 1987, pp. 42–3.

9. L. Cox, *Kotahitanga: The Search for Maori Political Unity*, Oxford University, Auckland, 1993.

10. For some discussion of reserve making in Canada and New Zealand, see, for example, A. Ward, *An Unsettled History: Treaty Claims in New Zealand Today*, Bridget Williams Books, Wellington, 1999; J.R. Miller, *Skyscrapers Hide the Heavens: A History of Indian–White Relations in Canada*, 3rd ed., University of Toronto, Toronto, 2000.

11. M. Durie, *Launching Maori Futures: Nga Kahui Pou*, Huia, Wellington, 2003, p. 169.

12. For example, see Miller, pp. 139–43.

13. Cited in M.S. Williams, 'Sharing the River: Aboriginal Representation in Canadian Political Institutions', in D. Laycock (ed), *Representation and Democratic Theory*, UBC, Vancouver, 2004, p. 103.

14. K.L. Ladner, 'The Alienation of Nation: Understanding Aboriginal Electoral Participation', *Electoral Insight*, vol. 5, no. 3 (2003), p. 24.

15. Durie, p. 169.

16. W. Kymlicka, *Multicultural Citizenship*, Oxford University, Oxford, 1995, p. 143. But Kymlicka does qualify this by saying it is important that self-governing groups have representation on the larger government that 'created' the self-government and has the capacity to make decisions effecting it. But this would still be a reduced form of representation.

17. Kymlicka, p. 143.

18. *Ibid*. Note that Alan Cairns argues the opposite position with regard to guaranteed representation giving government the 'sense' that it governs aboriginal affairs. Cairns argues that the Royal Commission on Aboriginal Peoples for Indigenous representation is seriously flawed and would 'isolate First Nations from mainstream Canadian politics and reduce their input to a largely watchdog role ... [I]t might distance Aboriginals from the conventional parties ... and it might decrease the sensitivity of non-Aboriginals to Aboriginal concerns, as arguably occurred in New Zealand under the ... system of guaranteed Maori seats.' (A.C. Cairns, *First Nations and the Canadian State: In Search of Co-existence*, Institute of Inter-governmental Studies, Queens University, Kingston, 2005, citing Roger Gibbins, 'Electoral Reform and Canada's Aboriginal Population: An Assessment of Aboriginal Electoral Districts', in R.A. Milen (ed), *Aboriginal Peoples and Electoral Reform in Canada*, Dundurn, Toronto and Oxford, 1991, p. 172.

19. Williams in Laycock, p. 95.

20. Williams in Laycock, pp. 101–02.

21. Williams in Laycock, p. 104.

22. Cairns, *First Nations*, p. 51, in reference to his work published on this in A.C. Cairns,

'Aboriginal People's Electoral Participation in the Canadian Community' *Electoral Insight*, vol. 5, no. 3 (2003), p. 8.
23. J. Burrows, 'Landed Citizenship', in Cairns et al., *Citizenship, Diversity and Pluralism: Canadian and Comparative Perspectives*, McGill-Queens University, Montreal/Kingston, 1999, pp. 74–80.
24. Cited in J. Schmidt, 'Aboriginal Representation in Government: A Comparative Examination', Law Commission of Canada, Ottawa, unpublished paper, 2003, p. 1.
25. Williams in Laylock, p. 110.
26. *Ibid*.
27. Durie, p. 169.

Chapter 9: Urban Indigenous Governance Practices

My deepest appreciation to the community-based advisory committee: Shauna Seneca, Cheryl Whiskeyjack, Donna Leask and Brad Seneca. Thank you to Dr. Nathalie Kermoal, Naomi McIlwraith, Dr. Chris Andersen, Dr. Isabel Altamirano-Jiménez, Lewis Cardinal and the external reviewers for reading earlier drafts of this chapter.

1. The Canadian constitution recognises three groups of Aboriginal peoples termed Indian, Métis and Inuit. Today 'First Nation(s)' is preferred to 'Indian' in Canada. 'Aboriginal', 'Indigenous' and 'Native' will be used interchangeably in this chapter. There are additional usages that reflect the complexities surrounding appropriate terminologies past and present and the diverse contexts in which these terms applied.
2. Edmonton, Alberta (table), Aboriginal Population Profile, 2006 Census. *Statistics Canada Catalogue no. 92-594-XWE*, Ottawa, released 15 January, 2008.
3. J. Graham and J. Wilson, 'Aboriginal Governance in the Decade Ahead: *92-594-XWE* Towards a New Agenda for Change', *Institute on Governance*, 2004, p. 2. Online. Available: http://www.iog.ca/publications/tanaga_framework.pdf (accessed 2 May 2008).
4. D. Newhouse, 'Invisible Infrastructure: Urban Aboriginal Institutions and Organizations', in D. Newhouse and E. Peters (eds), *Not Strangers in These Parts: Urban Aboriginal Peoples*, Policy Research Initiative, Ottawa, 2003, pp. 247–8.
5. C. Clatworthy et al., 'Urban Aboriginal Organizations: Edmonton, Toronto and Winnipeg', in E.J. Peters (ed), *Aboriginal Self-Government in Urban Areas*, Institute of Intergovernmental Relations, Queen's University, Ontario, 1995, p. 37.
6. *Ibid*.
7. Unless specifically stated, all Indigenous words in this chapter are from the Cree language. When referring to specific organisational names and programmes, I use their spelling. Unless specifically stated, all other Cree words are spelt using the *Alberta Elders Cree Dictionary*.
8. E. Waugh et al., *Alberta Elders' Cree Dictionary*, Duval House and University of Alberta, Edmonton, 1998, p. 295.
9. L. Goyette, *Edmonton in our Own Words*, University of Alberta, Edmonton, 2004, p. 11.
10. Goyette, pp. 22–4.
11. Edmonton Urban Aboriginal Accord Initiative (E.U.A.A.I.), 'Aboriginal Edmonton: A Statistical Profile of the Aboriginal Population of the City of Edmonton', 2005.
12. Report of the Royal Commission on Aboriginal Peoples, vol. IV, ch. VII, table 7.4, 1996. Online. Available: http://www.ainc-inac.gc.ca/ch/rcap/sg/cj7_e.pdf (accessed 5 June 2008).
13. E.U.A.A.I., p. 1.
14. M.J. Norris and L. Jantzen, 'Aboriginal Languages in Canada's Urban Areas: Characteristics, Considerations and Implications', in Newhouse and Peters, p. 109.
15. Alberta Aboriginal Relations, 'A Guide to Aboriginal Organizations in Alberta', Province of Alberta, 2008, pp. 1–32. Online. Available: http://www.aboriginal.alberta.ca/documents/First_Nations_and_Metis_Relations/Aboriginal OrganizationsGuide (accessed Jan 2009).
16. R. Groves, *Re-fashioning the Dialogue: Urban Aboriginal Governance in Canada*, National Association of Friendship Centers, Ottawa, 1999, p. 54.
17. Groves, p. 50.
18. Report of the Royal Commission on Aboriginal Peoples (R.C.A.P.), vol. II, ch. III, p. 168–169. Online. Available: http://www.ainc-inac.gc.ca/ch/rcap/sg/ch3a_e.pdf (accessed 8 June 2008).

19. *Ibid.*
20. E. Peters (ed), *Aboriginal Self-Government in Urban Areas*, Institute of Intergovernmental Relations, Kingston, Queen's University, 1995, p. vii; R. Walker, 'Searching for Aboriginal/Indigenous Self-determination: Urban Citizenship in the Winnipeg Low-Cost-Housing Sector, Canada', *Environment and Planning A*, vol. 38, no. 12 (2006), p. 2347.
21. B. Lawrence, *'Real' Indians and Others: Mixed-Blood Urban Native Peoples and Indigenous Nationhood*, University of Nebraska, Lincoln, 2004, p. 204.
22. See n. 2.
23. Aboriginal e-notice (Edmonton) 6 June 2008, p. 2.
24. First Nations, Métis and Inuit Elders have been invited to participate in the IECRCS. The Elders will practise the cultural traditions and ceremonies that are specific to them. Indigenous Elders Cultural Resource Circle Society (IECRCS), e-mail, 1 March 2007.
25. Graham et al., p. 2.
26. In this chapter I use the term 'traditional' to refer to those practices that Bent Arrow and the Elders involved in their programming have said are traditional. Taiaiake Alfred provides a helpful commentary on this: 'Working within a traditional framework, we must acknowledge the fact that cultures change and that any particular notion of what constitutes 'tradition' will be contested. Nevertheless, we can identify certain common beliefs, values and principles that form the persistent core of a community's culture. It is this traditional framework that we must use to build a better society. I am advocating a self-conscious traditionalism, an intellectual, social and political movement that will reinvigorate those values, principles and other cultural elements that are best suited to the larger contemporary political and economic reality' (G.A. Taiaiake, *Peace, Power and Righteousness: An Indigenous Manifesto*, Don Mills, Oxford University, 1999, p. xviii.).
27. Bent Arrow Traditional Healing Society homepage. Online. Available: http://www.bentarrow.ca (accessed 17 November 2008).
28. Shauna Seneca passed away in December 2006. She was a mentor to many in Edmonton and is greatly missed. Shauna hoped to one day write a book about Bent Arrow's philosophy and unique model. This chapter is dedicated to her.
29. B. Seneca, Interview with the writer, 4 April 2005.
30. C. Bridges, Interview with the writer, 14 July 2005.
31. R. Woodman, Interview with the writer, 10 July 2005.
32. B. Mussel et al., 'The Mental Health and Well-Being of Aboriginal Children and Youth: Guidance for New Approaches and Services', vol. 1, Report 9, UBC, Vancouver, 2004, p. 23.
33. Lawrence, p. 169
34. B. Seneca, Interview with the writer, 21 July 2005.
35. This chapter is based on research and writing completed during my Masters of Arts in Indigenous Governance, University of Victoria, Canada.
36. L.T. Smith, *Decolonising Methodologies: Research and Indigenous Peoples*, University of Otago, Dunedin, 2002, p. 127.
37. G. Dickson and K.L. Green, 'Participatory Action Research: Lessons Learned with Aboriginal Grandmothers', *Health Care for Women International*, vol. 22 (2001), p. 472.
38. P. Freire, *Pedagogy of the Oppressed*, Seabury, New York, 1970, p. 3.
39. L. Makokis, 'Teachings from Cree Elders: A Grounded Study of Indigenous Elders', PhD thesis, University of San Diego, 2001, p. 90.
40. J. Bopp et al., *The Sacred Tree: Reflections on Native American Spirituality*, Lotus Light Publications, Twin Lakes, 1989, p. 9.
41. Bopp et al., p. 26; M. Hart, 'An Aboriginal Approach to Social Work Practice', in T. Heinonen and L. Spearman (eds), *Social Work Practice – Problem Solving and Beyond*, Irwin, Toronto, 2001, p. 237.
42. Four Arrows Programme, Staff Questionnaire, 15 June 2005.
43. S. Seneca, 'Relationship-based Practice Model', Edmonton, 2001.
44. Bopp et al., p. 18.
45. S. Seneca, Interview with the writer, 2005.
46. *Ibid.*
47. *Ibid.*
48. Bridges, Interview with the writer, 2005.
49. *Healthy Families Programme*, Questionnaire, 1 June 2005.
50. S. Seneca, Interview with the writer, 2005.
51. *Ibid.*

52. Sacred Circle Programme, Questionnaire, 14 July 2005.
53. S. Seneca, Interview with the writer, 2005.
54. Bopp et al., p. 50.
55. Circle of Hope Programme, Questionnaire, 9 June 2005.
56. Ibid.
57. Bopp et al., p. 51.
58. S. Seneca, Interview with the writer, 2005.
59. Bopp et al., p. 35.
60. Circle of Hope, Questionnaire, 2005.
61. Mary, Interview with the writer, 16 July 2005. Mary preferred to use only her first name for this interview.
62. Ibid.
63. Ibid.
64. S. Ghostkeeper, Interview with the writer, 11 July 2005.
65. E. Peters, 'Three Myths about Aboriginals in Cities', Breakfast on the Hill Presentation, Canadian Federation for the Humanities and Social Sciences, Ottawa: Ontario, 2004, p. 9.
66. Ibid. D. Newhouse, 'From the Tribal to the Modern: The Development of Modern Aboriginal Societies', in R.F. Laliberte et al. (eds), *Expressions in Canadian Native Studies*, University of Saskatchewan, Saskatoon, 2000, pp. 395–409; J. Silver et al., *In Their Own Voices: Building Urban Aboriginal Communities*, Fernwood, Halifax, 2006.
67. Bent Arrow has used the findings of this research to give to new employees and external people organisations interested in their model.
68. Clatworthy et al., p. 64.
69. Silver, pp.169–70.
70. Silver, p. 169; J. Wherrett and D. Brown, 'Models for Aboriginal Government in Urban Areas', in Peters, p. 105.

Chapter 10: The Nationalist Gaze of an Aboriginal Artist

I would like to thank Dr Ellen Bielawski, Dr Chris Andersen and Dr Isabel Altamirano-Jiménez for their very constructive feedback as well as the anonymous reviewers of this chapter. Thank you to Eve-Marie Forcier, Dr Bielawski and Dr Andersen for working with me to improve my written English.

1. D. Nemiroff et al., *Land Spirit Power: First Nations at the National Gallery of Canada*, National Gallery of Canada, Ottawa, 1992.
2. J. Webb, 'Negotiating Alterity: Indigenous and "Outsider" Art', *Third Text*, vol. 16, no. 2 (2002), p. 144.
3. A. Young Man, 'Towards a Political History of Native Art', in A. Suzuki (ed), *Visions of Power: Contemporary Art by First Nations, Inuit and Japanese Canadians*, The Earth Spirit Festival, Toronto, 1991, p. 27.
4. R.L. Irwin and R. Farrell, 'The Framing of Aboriginal Art', in D.A. Long and Olive Patricia Dickason (eds), *Visions of the Heart: Canadian Aboriginal Issues*, Harcourt Brace and Company, Toronto, 1996, p. 69.
5. Since the 1980s, a number of Aboriginal artists like Carl Beam, Joanne Cardinal-Schubert, Jane Ash Poitras, Faye HeavyShield, Robert Houle, Gerald McMaster, Shelley Niro, Teresa Marshall, Rebecca Belmore and many others have 'share[d] a common desire to challenge one mode of thought and, to change what and who history is, thereby enabling revision for the past and inclusion for the future'. (C. Podedworny, *Rethinking History: Group Exhibition: John Abrams, Stephen Andrews, Robert Houle, Sara Leydon, Edward Poitras, Jane Ash Poitras*, 1992. Online. Available: http://mercerunion.org/archive95/317.html (accessed 5 September 2008).
6. It should be noted here that the author recognises that historical thinking has gone through controversies and debates from the 1960s onward, in Canada, as well as other countries around the world including New Zealand and that 'the old organizing frameworks that presupposed the privileging of various centres (things that are, for example, Anglo-centric, Euro-centric, ethno-centric, gender-centric, logo-centric) are no longer regarded as legitimate ….' (K. Jenkins, *Rethinking History*, Routledge, London, 1991, p. 71). According to historian Sarah Carter, 'The great majority of [Canadian] scholars have attempted to dramatically shift and expand the focus of historical inquiry from Europeans to Aboriginal people. They are reacting against earlier approaches that saw a weak and subordinate people quickly disappearing from sight. Most of the scholars … have stressed the power of human agency, drawing upon developments in other areas of social history, including women's, working-class and ethnic history. Within this framework Aboriginal people are no longer cast as 'passive victims' but

as 'active agents', genuine actors with strategies and interests of their own that they rigorously pursued. They had some control over their own fate, despite the uneven power relationship that eventually favoured Europeans. As active agents they did not allow themselves to be victimized. The history of contact, then, is no longer seen as one dominant group imposing will and authority on an oppressed group; rather, it is seen as a process of reciprocity and exchange among all participants' (S. Carter, *Aboriginal People and Colonizers of Western Canada to 1900*, University of Toronto, Toronto, 1999, pp. 9–10). Aboriginal artists are questioning the earlier approach of history or meta-narrative and the generalisations that came with it.
7. b. hooks, 'Altars of Sacrifice: Re-membering Basquiat', in *Outlaw Culture: Resisting Representations*, Routledge, London, pp. 25–37. b. hooks's pseudonym, her great-grandmother's name, celebrates female legacies and is in lower case because 'it is the substance of my books, not who is writing them, that is, important' (http://www.answers.com/topic/bell-hocks accessed 8 September 2008).
8. O. Dickason, *Canada's First Nations: A History of Founding Peoples from Earliest Times*, McClelland & Stewart, Toronto, 1992, p. 420.
9. The work of Teresa Marshall is diverse and complex. I have chosen *Elitekey* because this art piece was created at a time of political unrest in Canada. Despite repeated attempts to contact Ms. Marshall, I have been unsuccessful. I, therefore, provide a link to its picture rather than an illustration to respect the artist's copyright. Go to http://home.eol.ca/~dord/ngc_bc01.html, scroll towards the end of the page and you will see the installation.
10. E. Said, *Orientalism*, Vintage Books, New York, 1979, p. 207.
11. M. Foucault, *Surveiller et Punir: Naissance de la Prison*, Gallimard, Paris, 1975.
12. L.T. Smith, *Decolonising Methodologies: Research and Indigenous Peoples*, Otago University, Dunedin, 2001, p. 2.
13. K. Absolon and C. Willett, 'Putting Ourselves Forward: Location in Aboriginal Research', in L. Brown and S. Strega (eds), *Research as Resistance: Cultural, Indigenous, & Anti-oppressive Approaches*, Canadian Scholars', Toronto, 2005, p. 98.
14. Smith, p. 28.
15. D. Delâge, 'L'histoire des Premières Nations, Approches et Orientations', *Revue d'Histoire de l'Amérique Française*, vol. 53, no. 4 (2000), p. 521.
16. C. West, 'The New Cultural Politics of Difference', in R. Ferguson et al. (eds), *Out There: Marginalization and Contemporary Cultures*, MIT, Cambridge, 1990, p. 36.
17. Ibid.
18. E. Said, *Culture and Imperialism*, First Vintage Books, New York, 1994, p. xii.
19. Smith, p. 34.
20. Said, *Culture and Imperialism*, pp. 66–7.
21. E. Larocque, 'Native Writers Resisting Colonizing Practices in Canadian Historiography and Literature', PhD thesis, University of Manitoba, 1999, p. 137.
22. J. Acland, *First Nations Art: An Introduction to Contemporary Native Artists in Canada*, 19 February 1999, p.1. Online. Available: http://collections.ic.gc.ca/artists/marshall_teresa.html (accessed 24 August 2006).
23. W. Kymlicka, 'Le Fédéralisme Multinational au Canada: Un Partenariat à Repenser', in Guy Laforest and Roger Gibbins (eds), *Sortir de l'Impasse: Les Voies de la Réconciliation*, IRPP, Montréal, 1998, p. 15.
24. D. Francis, *The Imaginary Indian: The Image of the Indian in Canadian Culture*, Arsenal Pulp, Vancouver, 1992, p. 221.
25. Royal Commission on Aboriginal People, Volume 1: Looking Forward Looking Back, 1996. Online. Last updated 02 August 2006. Available: http://www.ainc-inac.gc.ca/ch/rcap/sg/sgmm_e.html (accessed 24 August 2006).
26. Nemiroff et al., p. 197.
27. Dickason, p. 409.
28. 'Oka, which its First Nations inhabitants know as Kanesatake, is located on the north shore of the Lake of Two Mountains, just at the confluence of the Ottawa and St. Lawrence rivers in South-western Quebec' (J.R. Miller, *Lethal Legacy: Current Native Controversies in Canada*, McClelland & Stewart Ltd, Toronto, 2004, p. 165). While the recent dispute started over a golf course, the conflict in Oka has deep historical roots. The French colonisation in the area of Montreal brought settlers and missionaries in the 1600s. Over time, the Sulpicians developed a settled community in the La Montagne area, later moving the mission to *Lac des deux montagnes*. The

Native community wanted to settle the title of their land quickly and continued to protest the Sulpicians' claim until after the mid-nineteenth century. The Mohawks argued that they 'used and occupied that territory and exercised sovereignty over it long before the land grants by the King of France' (J. Frideres, *Aboriginal Peoples in Canada: Contemporary Conflicts*, Prentice Hall Allyn and Bacon Canada, Scarborough, 1998, p. 340). Over the years, the seminary sold part of the land, creating deeper tensions with the Aboriginal people. Later, 'both the community of Kanesatake and the Municipality of Oka are faced with the dual problems of making decisions regarding land use and management that may affect the other community and dealing with decisions made by the other community affecting them' (Frideres, p. 338). The dispute in 1990 over 39 hectares of land for a golf course expansion involved land sold by the Sulpicians. This piece of land is very important to the Mohawks. It was part of their common lands used for community activities and they also had a cemetery in the pine forest. Several blockades were erected and in response, the government of Quebec sent the provincial police. The tensions escalated and in August 1990, the Federal government sent 2500 soldiers to dismantle the barricades and control the area. Blockades and protests erupted in many parts of the country in solidarity with the Mohawk people of Kanesatake while at the same time anti-aboriginal sentiments developed, supported by the media's portrayal of the Mohawks as terrorists.

29. Nemiroff et al., p. 199.
30. Nemiroff et al., p. 201.
31. A. Hornborg, 'Différentes Perceptions du Paysage: Changement et Continuité chez les Micmacs', *Recherches Amérindiennes au Québec*, vol. XXXIV, no. 3 (2004), p. 45.
32. L. Spence, *North American Indians: Myths and Legends*, Bracken Books, London, 1985, pp. 146–7.
33. Hornborg, p. 48.
34. Nemiroff et al., p. 200.
35. J. Acland, 'Elitekey: The Artistic Production of Mi'kmaq Women', *Revue d'art canadienne/Canadian Art Review*, vol. XXV, nos 1–2 (1998), pp. 6–7.
36. Acland, 'Elitekey', p. 7.
37. Acland, 'Elitekey', p. 3.
38. *Ibid*.
39. G. Van Woudenberg, 'Des Femmes et de la Territorialité': Début d'un Dialogue sur la Nature Sexuée des Droits des Autochtones', *Recherches amérindiennes au Québec*, vol. XXXIV, no. 3 (2004), pp. 74–86.
40. Van Woudenberg, p. 80.
41. These discriminatory measures were enacted in the *Enfranchisement Act* of 1869 and re-affirmed in the Indian Act of 1876. Aboriginal women would have to wait until 1985 with *Bill C-31* to see any changes to the discriminatory measures.
42. Van Woudenberg, p. 76.
43. Nemiroff et al., p. 196.
44. S. Spears, 'Reconstructing the Colonizer: Self-representation by First Nations Artists', *Atlantis*, vol. 29, no. 2 (Spring/Summer 2005), p. 127.
45. H. Cixous, 'Castration or Decapitation?', in R. Ferguson et al., p. 353.
46. Fanon in Smith, p. 29.
47. Webb, p. 150.
48. J. Rickard, 'After Essay – Indigenous is the Local', in L. Jessup and S. Bagg (eds), *On Aboriginal Representation in the Gallery*, Canadian Museum of Civilization, Ottawa, 2002, p. 121.
49. Podedworny, 1992.

Chapter 11: The Fiction of Post-Colonial Pacific Writers

1. T. Teaiwa, 'Lomani Viti: Reflections on Patriotic Literature from Post-Coups Fiji', *SPAN*, no. 53 (April 2004), p. 85.
2. Archdiocese of Sāmoa, *Faith and Patriotism – Cardinal Pio Taofinu'u*. Tautai, Sāmoa, 2006, p. 42.
3. *Ibid*.
4. A. Wendt, 'Towards a New Oceania', *Mana Review*, vol. 1, no. 1 (January 1976), pp. 49–60.
5. Wendt, p. 54.
6. Wendt, p. 53.
7. Wendt, p. 52.
8. *Ibid*.
9. S. Nandan, 'The Indian–Fijian: A Complex Fate', in S. Nandan, *Fiji: Paradise in Pieces*, Centre for Research in the New Literatures in English and Pacific Indian Publications, ANU, Canberra, 2000, pp. 34–48.
10. Nandan, p. 48.
11. E. Hau'ofa, 'Our Sea of Islands', in E. Waddall et al. (eds), *A New Oceania:*

Rediscovering Our Sea of Islands, USP in assoc. with Beake House, Suva, 1993, pp. 2–16.
12. E. Hau'ofa, 'Epilogue: Pasts to Remember', in R. Borofsky (ed), *Remembrance of Pacific Pasts*, University of Hawai'i, Honolulu, 2000, p. 454.
13. Wendt, p. 54.
14. Hau'ofa, 'Our Sea of Islands', p. 16.
15. N. Thiong'o, *Decolonising the Mind – The Politics of Language in African Literature*, James Currey in assoc. with Heinemann, London, 1986, p. 3.
16. *Ibid*.
17. *Ibid*.
18. P. Manoa, 'Singing in their Genealogical Trees', *Mana Review*, vol. 1, no. 1 (January 1976), p. 69.
19. S. Vaai, *Literary Representations in Western Polynesia: Colonialism and Indigeneity*, National University of Sāmoa, Apia, 1999, p. 30.
20. S. Mishra, 'Ferringhi – A Play in Seven Lilas', in I Gaskell (ed), *Beyond Ceremony: An Anthology of Drama From Fiji*, Institute of Pacific Studies and Pacific Writing Forum, USP, Suva, 2000, pp. 332–91.
21. Teaiwa, p. 85.
22. P. Craddock, 'Play looks at life from the grog bowl', *The Fiji Times*, 1 December 1993, p. 13.
23. I. Gaskell, 'Theatrical Representation and National Identity in Fiji', in H. Trivedi et al (eds), *The Nation Across the World: Postcolonial Literary Representations*, Oxford University, New Delhi, 2007, p. 240.
24. M. Field, 'The Indian Factor', *Islands Business*, vol. 32, no. 4 (April 2006), p. 23.
25. S. Mishra, interview with the writer, Canberra, November 1995.
26. *Ibid*.
27. Mishra, 'Ferringhi', p. 333.
28. Mishra, p. 336.
29. Mishra, p. 338.
30. *Ibid*.
31. Mishra, p. 340.
32. Mishra, p. 343.
33. *Ibid*.
34. Mishra, p. 345.
35. *Ibid*.
36. Mishra, p. 346.
37. Mishra, p. 347.
38. Mishra, p. 382.
39. Mishra, p. 385.
40. Mishra, p. 386.
41. Mishra, p. 387.
42. *Ibid*.
43. Mishra, p. 389.
44. *Ibid*.
45. *Ibid*.
46. Mishra, p. 390.
47. Craddock, p. 13.
48. R. Keith-Reid, 'Fiji's Simmering Election Pot', *Island's Business*, vol. 32, no. 4 (April 2006), pp. 16–20.
49. B. Ashcroft, 'The Emperor's New Clothes', in C. Vijayasree et al. (eds), *Nation in Imagination: Essays on Nationalism, Sub-Nationalisms and Narration*, Orient Longman, Hyderabad, India, 2007, p. 137.
50. S. Figiel, *Where We Once Belonged*, Pasifika, Auckland, 1996. See also S. Figiel, *The Girl in the Moon Circle*, Mana Publications, Suva, Fiji, 1996 and S. Figiel, 'The Dancers', in S. Tusitala Marsh (ed), *Niu Voices; Contemporary Pacific Fiction 1*, Huia, Wellington, 2006, pp. 195–201.
51. S. Figiel, pers comm. with the writer, Apia, 2007.
52. *Ibid*.
53. *Ibid*.
54. S. Figiel, 'O le Solo ia Lupe ma le I'a/Poem of Lupe and the Fish', *Rongorongo Studies: A Forum for Polynesian Philology*, vol. 4, no. 2 (1994) p. 40.
55. *Ibid*.
56. *Ibid*.
57. Figiel, p. 41.
58. Figiel, p. 42.
59. Figiel, p. 43.
60. S. Figiel, 'The Centre', *The UTS Review: Cultural Studies and New Writing*, vol. 1, no. 1 (August 1995), p. 93.
61. *Ibid*.
62. M. Meleisea, *O Tama Uli: Melanesians in Samoa*, Institute of Pacific Studies, USP, Suva, 1980.
63. Figiel, 'The Centre', p. 107.
64. Figiel, p. 108.
65. Figiel, p. 112.
66. Figiel, p. 132.
67. Figiel, p. 137.
68. Figiel, p. 119.
69. Figiel, pers comm. with the writer, 2007.
70. Ashcroft, p. 133.
71. K. Helu Thaman, *Kakala*, Mana Publications, Suva, 1993, p. 28.
72. R. Crocombe, pers comm. with the writer, 1993.
73. Thaman, p. 28.
74. *Ibid*.

Chapter 12: Neoliberalism, Racialised Gender and Indigeneity

1. T.D. Hall and J.V. Fenelon, 'Indigenous Movements and Globalization: What is Different? What is the Same?', *Globalizations*, vol. 5, no. 1 (2008), pp. 1–11.
2. T. Hall and S. Bobones, 'Introduction', in C.K. Chase-Dunn and Salvatore J. Babones (eds), *Global Social Change: Historical and Comparative Perspectives*, John Hopkins University, Baltimore, 2006, p. 4.
3. R. Niezen, 'Recognizing Indigenism: Canadian Unity and the International Movement of Indigenous Peoples', *Comparative Studies in History and Society*, vol. 42, no. 1 (2000), p. 121.
4. D. Harvey, *Neoliberalism: A Brief History*, Oxford University, Oxford, 2005.
5. P. O'Connell, 'On Reconciling Irreconcilables: Neo-liberal Globalisation and Human Rights', *Human Rights Law Review*, vol. 7, no. 3 (2007), p. 15.
6. C.R. Hale, *NACLA Report on the Americas*, vol. 38, issue 2 (Sept./Oct. 2004), pp. 16–21; C.R. Hale, 'Neoliberal Multiculturalism: The Remaking of Cultural Rights and Racial Dominance in Central America', *PoLAR: Political and Legal Anthropology Review*, vol. 28, no. 1 (2005), p. 13.
7. N. Castree, 'Differential Geographies: Place, Indigenous Rights and "Local" Resources', *Political Geography*, vol. 23 (2004), p. 137.
8. E. Boris, 'From Gender to Racialized Gender: Laboring Bodies That Matter', *International Labor and Working-Class History*, vol. 63 (2003), p. 10.
9. V. Newdick, 'The Indigenous Woman as Victim of Her own Culture in Neoliberal Mexico', *Cultural Dynamics*, vol. 17, no. 1 (2005), pp. 73–92.
10. Royal Commission on Aboriginal Peoples Report, Volume 4, Perspectives and Realities, Ottawa, 1996, chapter 2. Health Canada, Women's Health Bureau, 'The Health of Aboriginal Women'. Online. Available: http://www.hc-sc.gc.ca/english/women/facts_issues/facts_aborig.htm, p.1.
11. S. Clarkson, 'The Multi Level State: Canada in the Semi-Periphery of both Continentalism and Globalization', 2000. Online. Available: http://www.envireform.utoronto.ca/publications/stephe.clarkson/multi-level-state.pdf (accessed January 2007).
12. B.J. Barton, in R. McPherson, *New Owners in Their Own Land. Minerals and Inuit Land Claims*, University of Calgary, Calgary, 2003, p. xix.
13. McPherson, p. xx.
14. B.S. d'Anglure and F. Morin, 'The Inuit People, Between Particularism and Internationalism: An Overview of their Rights and Powers in 1992', *Inuit Studies*, vol. 16, nos 1–2 (1992), pp. 14.
15. D. Raunet, *Without Surrender Without Consent. A History of the Nishga Land Claims*, Douglas and McIntyre, Vancouver, 1984, p. 161.
16. F. Abele et al., 'Negotiating Canada: Changes in Aboriginal Policy over the Last Thirty Years', in L. Pal (ed), *How Ottawa Spends 1999–2000*, Oxford University, Toronto, 1999, p. 259.
17. McPherson, pp. xviii–xix.
18. *Ibid.*, p. xxi.
19. D.B. Rose, 'Land Rights and Deep Colonising: The Erasure of Women', *Aboriginal Law Bulletin*, vol. 3, no. 85 (1996), pp. 6–14.
20. McPherson, p. xviii.
21. R.S. Ratner et al., 'Wealth of Nations: Aboriginal Treaty Making in the Era of Globalization', in John Torpey (ed), *Politics and the Past: On Repairing Historical Injustices*, Rowan and Littlefield Publishers, Lanham, 2003, p. 218.
22. G.A. Slowey, 'Globalization and Self-Government: Impacts and Implications for First Nations in Canada', *The American Review of Canadian Studies*, (Spring/Summer 2001) pp. 265–81.
23. T. Wotherspoon and V. Satzewich, *First Nations: Race, Class and Gender Relations*, Canadian Plains Research Centre, Regina, 2000, p. xxv.
24. N. Fontaine, 'Aboriginal Women's Perspective on Self-Government', *Canadian Dimension* 2002. Online. Available: http://www.canadiandimension.mb.ca/v36_6nf.htm (accessed 5 January 2006).
25. First Ministers and National Aboriginal Leaders, 'Strengthening Relations and Closing the Gap', 24–25 November 2005, Kelowna B.C. Online. Available: http://www.parl.gc.ca/information/library.prbpubs/prb0604-e.html (accessed May 2007).

26. D. Perkins, L. Nelms and P. Nelms, 'Beyond Neo-liberalism: the Social Investment State?', *Social Policy Working Paper*, no. 3 (2004), p. 2. Online. Available: http://www.bsl.org.au/pdfs/beyond_ neoliberalism_social_investment_state.pdf (accessed 20 January 2008).
27. R. Lister, 'Investing in the Citizen-Workers of the Future: Transformations in Citizenship and the State under New Labour', *Social Policy & Administration*, vol. 37, no. 5 (2003), p. 437.
28. A. Porter, 'The Harper Government: Towards A New Social Order?', *Socialist Project E-Bulletin* 21 (2006). Online. Available: http://www.socialistproject. ca/bullet/bullet021.html (accessed January 2007).
29. S. Harper, Speech on the Government Achievements for Aboriginal Peoples, Halifax, 2 November, 2007. Online. Available: http:www.pm.gc.ca/
30. Native Women Association of Canada (N.W.A.C.) Report: *Reclaiming our Way of Being: Matrimonial Real Property Solutions*. What We Heard, Ottawa, 2007.
31. National Council of Welfare Report, *First Nations, Métis and Inuit Children and Youth Time to Act*, 2007. Online. Available: http://www.ncwcnbes.net/en/research/ TimeToAct-AgissonsMaintenant.html
32. A. Côté, 'The Broken Promises of Prime Minister Harper', *Jurisfemme*, vol. 25, no. 1 (2007). Online. Available: http://www. nawl.ca/ns/en/jf_spring2007.html (accessed January 2008).
33. See n. 29.
34. Conservative Party of Canada, *Stand Up for Canada*, Federal Election Platform, 2006. Online. Available: http://www. cbc.ca/canadavotes2006/leadersparties/ pdf/conservative_platform20060113.pdf (accessed May 2007).
35. *Government's Response to the Seventh Report of the Standing Committee on Aboriginal Housing*. Online. Available: http://www2. parl.gc.ca/HousePublications/Publication. aspx?DocId=3077327&Language=E&M ode=1&Parl=39&Ses=1 (accessed August 2008).
36. J. Fiske and A.J. Browne, 'Aboriginal Citizen, Discredited Medical Subject: Paradoxical Constructions of Aboriginal Women's Subjectivity in Canadian Health Care Policies', *Policy Sciences*, vol. 39 (2006), p. 94.
37. Report of the Royal Commission on Aboriginal Peoples, vol. 1, Minister of Supply and Services, Ottawa, 1996; Amnesty International, 'Stolen Sisters: A Human Rights Response to Discrimination and Violence Against Indigenous Women In Canada', 2004. Online. Available: http://www.amnesty.ca/campaigns/sisters_ overview.php (accessed January 2007).
38. First Nations and Inuit Health Branch, 2002 quoted in Fiske and Browne, p. 94.

Chapter 13: A Genealogy of Indigenous Resistance

1. Cited R.J. Walker, *Ka Whawhai Tonu Matou: Struggle Without End*, Penguin, Auckland, 1990, pp. 227–8.
2. Cited L.T. Smith, *Decolonising Methodologies: Research and Indigenous Peoples*, University of Otago, Dunedin, 1999, p. 110.
3. Walker, p. 214.
4. Cited J. Williams, *Politics of the New Zealand Maori: Protest and Cooperation 1891–1909*, Auckland University, Auckland, 1969, p. 134.
5. Cited Williams, p. 135.
6. B. Anderson, *Imagined Communities*, Verso, London, 1983, p. 5.
7. Cited I. Stuart, 'The Construction of a National Maori Identity by Maori Media', *Pacific Journalism Review*, vol. 9 (2003), p. 48.
8. Walker, p. 111.
9. Williams, p. 137.
10. Williams, pp. 136–7.
11. Walker, p. 214.
12. Walker, p. 235.
13. E. Poata-Smith, 'Ka tika a muri, ka tika a mua?: Maori Protest Politics and the Treaty of Waitangi Settlement Process', in P. Spoonley, C. Macpherson and D. Pearson (eds), *Tangata Tangata: The Changing Ethnic Contours of New Zealand*, Thomson/ Dunmore, Victoria, 2004, p. 69.
14. Poata-Smith, p. 68.
15. F. Nietzsche, *The Genealogy of Morals: A Polemic; Peoples and Countries* (fragment), translated by H.B. Samuel, T.N. Foulis, Edinburgh, 1910.
16. Smith, p. 110.
17. C. Te Kawehau Hoskins, 'In the Interests of Maori Women: Discourses of Reclamation', *Women's Studies Journal*, vol. 13, no. 2 (1997), p. 26.

18. Smith, p. 34.
19. Hoskins, p. 27.
20. C. West, 'The New Cultural Politics of Difference', in S. During (ed), *The Cultural Studies Reader*, Routledge, London, 1993, p. 212.
21. Cited Williams, p. 3.
22. L. Paterson, 'Mana Māori Motuhake: Challenges to "Kāwanatanga", 1840–1940', in T. Ka'ai, J. Moorfield, M. Reilly and S. Mosley (eds), *Ki te Whaiao: An Introduction to Māori Society*, Pearson, Auckland, 2004, p. 163.
23. A. Harris, *Hīkoi. Forty Years of Māori Protest*, Huia, Wellington, 2004, p. 13.
24. Walker, p. 220.
25. Harris, p. 26.
26. Harris, pp. 24–5.
27. D.T. Goldberg, 'Modernity, Race and Morality', in D.T. Goldberg, *Racist Culture: Philosophy and the Politics of Meaning*, Blackwell, Oxford, p. 19.
28. K. Nash, 'The "Cultural Turn" in Social Theory: Towards a Theory of Cultural Politics', *Sociology*, vol. 35, no. 1 (2001), p. 86.
29. Goldberg, p. 37.
30. Goldberg, p. 20.
31. M. Foucault, *The Archaeology of Knowledge*, Routledge, London, 1972.
32. A. Camus, *The Plague*, London, The Folio Society, 1987, pp. 59–60.
33. R. Consedine and J. Consedine, *Healing Our History: The Challenge of the Treaty of Waitangi*, Penguin, Auckland, 2001, pp. 104–5.
34. P. Temm, *The Waitangi Tribunal: The Conscience of a Nation*, Random Century, Auckland, 1990, p. 64.
35. Smith, p. 112.
36. Walker, p. 112.
37. G. Hegel, *Phenomenology of Spirit*, translated by A. Miller, Clarendon, Oxford, 1977.
38. M. Peters, 'Cultural Studies and the Future of "Culture"', *New Zealand Sociology*, vol. 16, no. 2 (2001), p. 33.
39. Cited Peters, p. 33.
40. Cited Peters, p. 34.
41. A. Memmi, *The Colonizer and the Colonized*, Oxford University, London, 1967, p. 89.
42. A. Simpson, 'Commentary: The "Problem" of Mental Health in Native North America: Liberalism, Multiculturalism and the (Non)Efficacy of Tears', *Ethos*, vol. 36, no. 3 (2008), p. 376.
43. Cited T. Flynn, *Existentialism: A Very Short Introduction*, Oxford University, Oxford, p. 102.
44. Smith, p. 107.
45. D. Brown, 'Pierre Bourdieu's "Masculine Domination" Thesis and the Gendered Body in Sport and Physical Culture', *Sociology of Sport Journal*, vol. 23 (2006), p. 180.
46. S. Lash, 'Power after Hegemony', *Theory, Culture & Society*, vol. 24, no. 3 (2007), p. 56.
47. F. Nietzsche, *Human, All Too Human: A Book for Free Spirits*, Cambridge University, Cambridge, 1999, p. 100.

Glossary of Māori Words

Ahi	fire
Ahi kā	concept of cooking fires on land to maintain possession through continuous physical habitation
Aotearoa	New Zealand, literally 'land of the long white cloud'
Ahorangi	professor
Atua	god(s), spirit power(s), ancestor(s) of ongoing influence
Hāngi	earth oven to cook food
Hapū	sub-group(s) of *iwi*
Hawaiki	ancient homeland from where Māori migrated
Hīkoi	walk, political protest march
Hui	gathering(s)
Iwi	people, nation
Kanakanaia	inferred abuse
Kanga	verbal abuse
Karakia	prayer(s), chant(s)
Kaumātua	elder(s) of either sex, old man
Kaupapa Māori	Māori topics, strategies and practices (of research) carried out according to appropriate Māori cultural protocols
Kāuru	edible stem of cabbage tree (*Cordyline*)
Kīngitanga	Māori King Movement
Kirehu	idiom with obscured meaning
Kīwaha	idiom, colloquialism
Kōhanga reo	early childhood immersion language nest(s)
Kotahitanga	one people, unity
Kura kaupapa	immersion language primary school(s)
Mahika kai	site where work is undertaken on food resources (hunting, harvesting etc)
Mākutu	cursing, sorcery
Mana	prestige, power
Mana whenua	right of occupation, concept that groups with ancestral connection to land may have additional responsibilities
Manuhiri	visitor(s)
Māori	the Indigenous people of Aotearoa New Zealand
Māoritanga	Māori identity, Māori culture, essence of being Māori (including all aspects of Māori life)

Marae	courtyard
Marae ātea	courtyard or grass space immediately in front of a meeting house
Mātāmua	first born
Mātauranga Māori	Māori or Indigenous knowledge inherited from ancestors
Mauri	personality, life principle
Mihi whakatau	rituals of welcome between visitor and host, less formal than *pōhiri*
Mihimihi	personal introduction, form of greeting
Pā	fortified village
Pākehā	a New Zealander of European descent
Pōhiri	formal rituals of welcome between visitor and host
Rangatira	chief, leader
Reo	language
Rīwai	potato
Taero	to obstruct
Taero waka	traffic jam
Taiaha	Long staff-shaped close-quarters fighting weapon
Tapu	sacred, restricted, under influence of *atua*
Takiwā	district, space
Tāmi	press down, pressure
Tangihanga	rites for the dead, funeral
Te Reo	the language
Te Reo Māori	the Māori language
Tekoteko	carved human-like figure on the gable of meeting house or figurehead on canoe
Te Waipounamu	the South Island of New Zealand, literally 'the place of greenstone'
Tī	cabbage tree(s)
Tiamu	jam
Tikanga	culture, customary and correct cultural practice(s)
Tino rangatiratanga	the sovereignty of chiefs, used now to describe autonomy or self-government for Māori in Aotearoa
Tohunga	priest, spirit medium, expert
Tuakana	eldest sibling or cousin of same sex
Tuatua	a bivalve shellfish
Tūpuna	ancestor(s)
Tūpuna wahine	female ancestor(s)

Tūrangawaewae	a place to stand
Tūturu	true, permanent, fixed
Ūpoko ariki	paramount chief
Waiata	song(s)
Wero	formal challenge as part of *pōhiri*
Whaikōrero	art of Māori oratory
Whaiwhaiā	cursing
Waka	ocean- or river-going vessel(s)
Whakairo	carving(s)
Whakapapa	genealogy(ies)
Whakapōhatutia	turned to stone
Whakataukī	proverb(s)
Whānau	extended family(ies), part of *hapū*
Whānui	wider group
Whakatau	ritual(s) of welcome between visitor and host, less formal than *pōhiri*
Wharenui	large meeting house(s)

List of Contributors

CHRIS ANDERSEN is Metis from Saskatchewan, Canada. He is an Associate Professor at the Faculty of Native Studies, University of Alberta. His research is focused on the role of racial discourses in Canadian administrative constructions (specifically with respect to the courts and the census). His most significant publication is 'From Nation to Population: The Racialization of 'Métis', in the Canadian census's *Nations and Nationalism*, vol. 14, no. 2, pp. 347–68.

ISABEL ALTAMIRANO-JIMÉNEZ is an Indigenous Zapotec from southern Mexico. She holds a joint appointment as Assistant Professor in the Department of Political Science and the Faculty of Native Studies at the University of Alberta. Her research interests are the politics of indigeneity, nationalism and gender, mapping and development, among others.

JANINE HAYWARD is an Associate Professor in the Department of Politics at the University of Otago. She has a particular interest in constitutional politics and how Indigenous peoples and minorities can achieve constitutional recognition and protection. She has previously worked at the Waitangi Tribunal, New Zealand's Indigenous claims commission.

BRENDAN HOKOWHITU is Ngāti Pukenga. Hokowhitu is an Associate Professor at Te Tumu School of Māori, Pacific and Indigenous Studies, University of Otago, where he is Programme Coordinator for the Masters of Indigenous Studies. Brendan's research focuses on indigeneity, popular culture (e.g. sport, film, masculinity) and theory.

SHALENE JOBIN VANDERVELDE is Cree and Métis and belongs to Red Pheasant Cree First Nation in Saskatchewan. She is pursuing a PhD in Political Science and Native Studies at the University of Alberta. Shalene taught for the Faculty of Native Studies and was the founding Coordinator for the Certificate in Aboriginal Governance and Partnership program, University of Alberta. Her research interests lie in Indigenous perspectives on self-determination, economies and societies and how these interests interact with the state.

NATHALIE KERMOAL is of Breton descent and is an Associate Professor at the University of Alberta, holding a joint appointment between the Faculty of Native Studies and the Campus Saint-Jean. She is a bilingual specialist in Canadian history and more specifically in Métis history. Recently she published two books: *Alberta's Francophones* and *Un Passé Métis au Féminin* with the Éditions GID in Québec. Her areas of interest are Métis issues (historical and contemporary), Aboriginal constitutional issues, contemporary Aboriginal art and Aboriginal women's issues.

NAOMI MᶜILWRAITH teaches English Literature and advises Aboriginal students at MacEwan University, a mile from where she was born and raised in Edmonton, Alberta, Canada. Naomi has a Bachelor of Physical Education in Outdoor Education (University of Alberta, 1989), Bachelor of Arts in English Literature with Great Distinction (Augustana University College, 2000), and Master of Arts in English Literature (University of Alberta, 2007).

HANA O'REGAN is Kāi Tahu, Kāti Māmoe and Waitaha. She holds the position of Dean, Te Puna Wānaka Faculty of Māori Studies, Christchurch Polytechnic Institute of Technology, Christchurch, New Zealand. Hana is an educationalist who has committed her professional life to working in the areas of Māori language revitalisation and Māori education. She is a member of the Māori Language Commission and is passionate about restoring the language of her own peoples, the Kāi Tahu of the South Island of New Zealand.

MICHAEL REILLY is currently Professor of Māori, Pacific and Indigenous Studies at Te Tumu School of Māori, Pacific and Indigenous Studies, University of Otago. He descends from Irish, Scottish, Cornish and English ancestors. He researches Māori and Pacific histories, especially those of parts of Eastern Polynesia. He first wrote about Mangaia in the Cook Islands for his PhD and has continued to produce a series of books and articles about the island's traditional history.

POIA REWI is Ngāi Tūhoe, Ngāti Manawa, Te Arawa, Tūwharetoa and an Associate Professor at Te Tumu, University of Otago. He completed his PhD at Otago, researching 'Te Ao O Te Whaikōrero', the diverse 'World of Oratory'. Māori culture is a particular research interest, especially the oral arts and the vast amount of knowledge contained within these forms. He has also researched the participation of Māori in sports and recreation.

ALICE TE PUNGA SOMERVILLE is Te Āti Awa and a Senior Lecturer at Victoria University of Wellington specialising in Māori, Pacific and Indigenous writing in English. Born and raised in Aotearoa New Zealand, she received her PhD in English and American Indian Studies at Cornell University and spent time at the University of Hawai'i at Mānoa during her doctoral studies. She is putting the finishing touches on her first book *Once Were Pacific*, which explores Māori articulation of connection with the Pacific and is working on her second book *Kanohi ki te Kanohi: Indigenous–Indigenous Encounters*. She also writes the occasional poem.

SINA VAAI is currently an Associate Professor of English at the National University of Sāmoa (NUS) in Apia. Born in Fiji of a Sāmoan-German mother and a Fijian-British father, she has taught at the University of the South Pacific in Fiji and for the last twenty-five years at NUS in Sāmoa while pursuing research interests in post-colonial Pacific identities, literacy and the development of an 'oceanic imaginary' in fiction and poetry. Her PhD thesis, published in 1999, examined literary representations in Western Polynesia from Tonga, Fiji and Sāmoa by Indigenous and migrant writers.

JIM WILLIAMS of Kāi Tahu is a Senior Lecturer in Te Tumu School of Māori, Pacific and Indigenous Studies, University of Otago, where he teaches a stream of Kāi Tahu and environmental management papers. His area of research includes traditional Māori ways and Māori environmental management, with particular emphasis on his own *iwi*.